MISSION TO CHINA

MEMOIRS OF A SOVIET MILITARY ADVISER TO CHIANG KAISHEK

VASILII I. CHUIKOV

*(Vasilii Ivanovich Chuikov,
Marshal of the Soviet Union, 1900–1982)*

MISSION TO CHINA

*MEMOIRS OF A SOVIET MILITARY
ADVISER TO CHIANG KAISHEK*

*(Missiya v Kitae: Zapiski Voennogo Sovetnika,
Moscow Nauka, 1981)*

TRANSLATED WITH AN INTRODUCTION BY
DAVID P. BARRETT

Foreword by Alexander Chuikov

Eastbridge
BOOKS

Published by Eastbridge Books, an imprint of Camphor Press Ltd
83 Ducie Street, Manchester, M1 2JQ
United Kingdom

www.eastbridgebooks.com

First published in 1981 as Миссия в Китае (*Missïya v Kitaė*)

ISBN   978-1-910736-73-9 (pbk)
            978-1-910736-74-6 (cloth)

CONTENTS

FOREWORD

Moscow, July 2004

Dear Readers:

Vasilii Ivanovich Chuikov, born February 12, 1900, often called himself a "son of the century." I would say that he was truly a son of his time—one of the most difficult and tragic eras in Russia's history. Those who came from the ranks of the people, as he did, created the new Russia—the USSR—with their will, talents and energy. They forged its power and made its history.

Vasilii Chuikov served as an intelligence officer, warrior and diplomat. He worked and fought when our country was allied with the West against the common enemy in the Second World War. And he did so again when the logic of history made the East and West rivals and enemies.

Now we are building a new world, that of the 21st century. So that it may be humane, just and durable, we must know each other better. I am truly happy to learn of the interest shown abroad in the career of Vasilii Chuikov, and in the events about which he writes.

With best wishes for your happiness and prosperity,

Alexander Chuikov

Son of Marshal and Twice Decorated Hero of the Soviet Union,
V. I. Chuikov
Sculptor and Member of the International Art Foundation

PREFACE

General Chuikov composed this memoir late in life. It first appeared in the November and December 1979 issues (numbers 11 and 12) of the journal *Novyi Mir* under the title "Missiya v Kitae" (Mission in China). In 1981 Nauka Press published it as a book, under the title *Missiya v Kitae: Zapiski Voennogo Sovetnika* (Mission in China: Notes of a military adviser), in an enlarged version incorporating further reminiscences of General Chuikov, as well as additional background information. This is the text used in the present translation, which has been entitled *Mission to China: Memoirs of a Soviet Military Adviser to Chiang Kaishek*. In 1983 the Soviet Ministry of Defense reprinted the 1981 edition in its "War Memoirs" series under the shorter title *Missiya v Kitae*. Respective press runs for the two editions were fifty thousand and one hundred thousand copies. In 1989 extracts from the memoir were published by Nauka Press in *Po Dorogam Kitaya, 1937–1945: Vospominaniya* (Along Chinese roads, 1937–1945: Reminiscences), pp. 256-280.

Mission to China is not in the first instance a chronicle of General Chuikov's fifteen months as military adviser in China; it is rather a series of reminiscences of personalities and events of that time, complemented by reflections on the political and military condition of the Nationalist Chinese state. The memoir gives the appearance of having been partly written and partly dictated. Judging by the sharpness of detail, especially in regard to military events, and the high level of accuracy in regard to Chinese politics, it is evident that Chuikov or his assistants had access to files and reports from his time in Chungking. In his preface, Chuikov thanks his editors for helping assemble the materials of the text.

From his earlier books on the battle of Stalingrad and the advance to Berlin one can readily recognize the voice of the author in the present China memoir. However, Chuikov did not receive the best service from his editors. Considerable rearrangement of materials within each chapter has been necessary to create a fluent text. Some gaps or abrupt transitions have unavoidably survived into the present English version.

Chuikov wrote in a direct and vivid manner, and he remained remarkably free of the Soviet jargon of the time. A few adjustments have been made to his vocabulary, however. In the Russian original the Japanese are commonly referred to as aggressors, the Germans as Hitlerites, and both as fascists. Some use of this terminology is retained for flavor, but what was conventional shorthand in the Soviet Union of Chuikov's time is burdensome to the Western reader if translated in every instance. In sum, apart from the deletion of repetitive expressions of this sort, and the insertion of the occasional explanatory word or date, the language of the memoir is Chuikov's own.

This translation represents about two-thirds of the Russian version. The original contains a great amount of material added by the editors on events in Europe and East Asia, both during the 1930s and during the time of Chuikov's posting to China. Some of this is of minimal relevance; some is of a general nature and can be found elsewhere. In my introduction I have outlined the international setting against which Chuikov went to China, as well as the domestic political situation he encountered once he arrived there. Some observations about Chinese politics and history that appear to be the work of the editors rather than the author have also been deleted. The intent of this translation is to convey everything Chuikov himself experienced in Chiang Kaishek's China, and about which he wrote so forcefully and perceptively.

About half of General Chuikov's memoir was published in Chinese by Xinhua Shudian in 1980 under the title *Zai Hua shiming: Yige junshi guwen di biji* (translated by Wan Chengcai). This volume was of help in clarifying some of the place names referred to in the Russian text.

I have added the subtitles to each chapter, and the maps.

David P. Barrett

ACKNOWLEDGEMENTS

My thanks, first of all, go to Mr Doug Merwin, for his generous and patient support. For assistance in identifying some of the more elusive figures in the narrative, I wish to acknowledge Dr Marianne Bastid-Bruguière, Centre National de la Recherche Scientifique, Paris; Professor Patrick Fuliang Shan, Grand Valley State University, Michigan; and Dr Jiu-jung Lo, Academia Sinica, Taiwan. My colleague Professor John Campbell carefully read the manuscript and provided valuable guidance on military terminology. The maps were done by Mr Ric Hamilton, cartographer of the School of Geography and Geology, McMaster University. In the technical preparation of the manuscript Graham Barrett provided indispensable help.

The map, China 1941, is based on the map, China 1937-1945, in John W. Garver, *Chinese-Soviet Relations, 1937-1945: The Diplomacy of Chinese Nationalism*, (Oxford: Oxford University Press, 1988).

I wish to single out Professor Vitaly Kozyrev, Moscow State University, for his steadfast assistance, and I give my thanks to Mr Alexander Chuikov and family for their welcome support of this rendering of their father's earlier career.

Throughout this work I have been inspired by the memory of my first Russian teacher, Dr Maurice Kalinowski, great friend and humanist.

NOTE ON ROMANIZATION

Except in a few instances, the pinyin system is used for romanization of Chinese. The exceptions are certain names well known in the West in earlier idiosyncratic versions. These are as follows, with the pinyin given in parentheses: Chiang Kaishek (Jiang Jieshi), Mao Tsetung (Mao Zedong), Soong Meiling (Song Meiling: Mme Chiang Kaishek), Sun Yatsen (Sun Yixian/Sun Zhongshan). H. H. Kung (Kong Xiangxi) and T. V. Soong (Song Ziwen) rendered their names in western style. Prior to the adoption of pinyin as the standard system of transliteration, the Wade-Giles system was commonly used. Wade-Giles equivalents are given in the Glossary following the pinyin entry for the person in question.

Chinese and Japanese surnames are placed first.

Two pinyin letters give English speakers difficulty: "q" and "x." These are read as "ch" and "sh." Less problematic is "zh," which is read as "j." Thus the name of Chuikov's contact in the Nationalist government, Zhang Qun, sounds like Jang Chun.

The province in China's northwest, Xinjiang, sounds close to Shin-jiang. Two other letters to note are "c," which is read as "ts," and "z," which is read as "dz" (as in the English words "its" and "adze"). Otherwise, pinyin letters are read as they are in English. Those unfamiliar with the pinyin system should take care to distinguish between the adjacent northern provinces of Shaanxi and Shanxi. Formerly these were written as Shensi and Shansi.

Place names are given in pinyin, with the following four exceptions: Yangtze River (Yangzijiang), Canton (Guangzhou), Yenan (Yan'an), and because the old version is so evocative of wartime China of the 1940s, Chungking (Chongqing).

MAPS

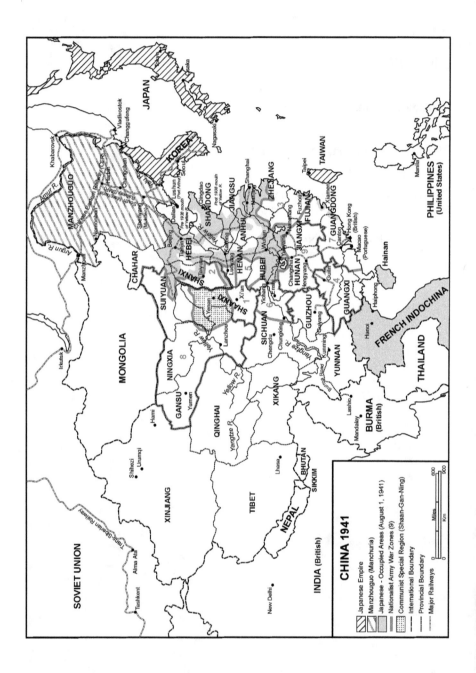

CHINA 1941

Japanese Empire

Manzhouguo (Manchuria)

Japanese - Occupied Areas (August 1, 1941)

Nationalist Army War Zones (9)

Communist Special Region (Shaan-Gan-Ning)

International Boundary

Provincial Boundary

Major Railways

Miles 600

Km 900

SOVIET UNION

Trans-Siberian Railway

Tashkent

Alma Ata

Irkutsk

Shihezi

Urumqi

Hami

XINJIANG

MONGOLIA

CHAHAR

SUIYUAN

NINGXIA

GANSU

Yumen

Lanzhou

Yellow R.

QINGHAI

XIKANG

TIBET

Lhasa

NEPAL

New Delhi

INDIA (British)

BHUTAN

SIKKIM

Yangtze R.

SICHUAN

Chengdu

Chungking

Yalong R.

YUNNAN

Kunming

Mekong R.

Salween R.

BURMA
(British)

Lashio

Mandalay

THAILAND

FRENCH INDOCHINA

Hanoi

Haiphong

Hainan

GUANGXI

Guilin

Nanning

Suiyang

GUIZHOU

Hengyang

Changsha

HUNAN

GUANGDONG

Canton

Hong Kong (British)

Macao (Portuguese)

FUJIAN

Fuzhou

Xiamen

JIANGXI

Nanchang

ZHEJIANG

Ningbo

Wenzhou

JIANGSU

Nanjing

Shanghai

ANHUI

HUBEI

Wuhan

Yichang

Enshi

Xiangyang

HENAN

Luoyang

Kaifeng

SHANXI

Taiyuan

SHAANXI

Xi'an

Yan'an

Yellow R.

HEBEI

Beijing

Tianjin

SHANDONG

Qingdao

Jinan

Pre-1938 mouth of Yellow R.

Post 1938 mouth of Yellow R.

Weihai

Dalian (Dairen)

Lushun (Port Arthur)

MANZHOUGUO

Shenyang (Mukden)

Changchun

Harbin

Qiqihar

Manzhouli

Hailar

Amur R.

Argun R.

Khabarovsk

Vladivostok

Chinese Eastern Railway

CER

Nomonhan

KOREA

Seoul

JAPAN

Nagasaki

Changchunfeng

Osaka

TAIWAN

Taipei

PHILIPPINES
(United States)

Manila

1

2

3

4

5

6

7

8

9

xvi

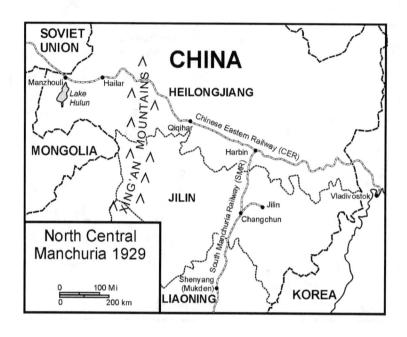

North Central
Manchuria 1929

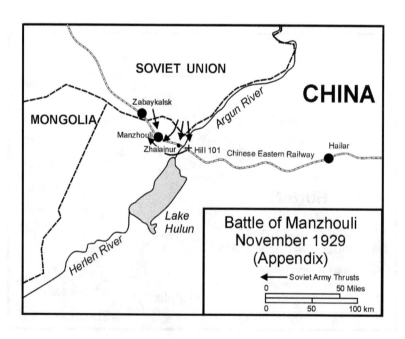

Battle of Manzhouli
November 1929
(Appendix)

INTRODUCTION

For members of the Soviet wartime generation, and for students of the Second World War, the author of *Mission to China*, General Vasilii Chuikov, holds a position of high prominence, for he was the commander of the epic defense of Stalingrad, the turning point of the war on the eastern front and arguably of the war in Europe as a whole. Chuikov went on from Stalingrad to the gates of Berlin, where, fittingly enough, he took the surrender of the city at the war's end. Subsequently he served in a succession of high-level posts in military administration. Named a marshal of the Soviet Union, and much honored in his country, he had traveled far from his peasant origins at the time of his death in 1982.

Chuikov wrote extensively on his command experience in the Second World War, and he also wrote on his early life and career before the war. It is to this second genre that *Mission to China* belongs. In it Chuikov first recalls his posting to China in 1926 as a diplomatic courier, and his assignment to the staff of the Soviet Far Eastern Command at the time of the Manchurian border conflict with China in 1929. The bulk of the memoir is devoted to the year 1941, during which Chuikov served simultaneously as Soviet military attaché in Chungking (Chongqing), the wartime capital of Nationalist China, and as chief military adviser to the head of the Nationalist state, Chiang Kaishek. It was in this second capacity that Chuikov had regular access to Chiang and the top level of the Nationalist Chinese political and military structure. The interest of this memoir lies partly in the portrait drawn at close quarters by Chuikov of the Nationalist leadership. But it is also of considerable to students of the Sino-Japanese War, because Chuikov, as a seasoned commander and skilled tactician, treats in detail the strengths and weaknesses of the Nationalist forces in their desperate struggle against the powerful Japanese enemy. And, finally, for all readers, Chuikov's descriptions of people, events and everyday life in wartime Nationalist China vividly bring to life once more that long-gone, distant world.

The comments of two leading British military historians may be noted in regard to Chuikov as a writer. His two major works on the war, *The Battle for Stalingrad* and *The Fall of Berlin,* appeared in translation in the West in the mid-1960s, soon after their publication in the Soviet Union.[1] Alistair Horne described *The Battle for Stalingrad* as "one of the most significant accounts on the Second World War to emerge from any country" and went on to say that *The Fall of Berlin* was "no less noteworthy" a contribution to military history.[2] John Keegan, in an extended historiographical essay on the Second World War, singled out Chuikov's account of Stalingrad as "an exception to the dreary obfuscation of Soviet war memoirs." Both Horne and Keegan were impressed by the personality of the author. Chuikov, in Keegan's words, "writes with passion and frankness, and also with great compassion for the sufferings of the surviving citizens . . . as the desperate struggle raged over their heads."[3] For Horne, "there are times when a strong sense of humanity breaks through, and at others Chuikov expresses himself with a descriptive power not always associated with generalship."[4]

These observations about Chuikov's writings on the European war are equally applicable to *Mission to China.* In similar language Soviet reviewer A. G. Yakovlev summed up the strengths of the book: "*Mission to China* is the work of a man who was not only an outstanding military commander . . . but a writer of considerable talent as well. It is this combination which gives the book interest both to the historian of Far Eastern events and to the educated reading public."[5] But before further consideration is given to General Chuikov's China memoir, the remarkable career of the author will be outlined.

CAREER

Vasilii Ivanovich Chuikov was born into a large peasant family in Tula province, south of Moscow, on February 12, 1900. At the age of twelve he had to leave school to earn his living in a factory in St Petersburg, where he worked at a bench turning out spurs for cavalry officers. In a memoir of his civil war years, he wrote that "departure from my father's home meant for me the end of childhood."[6] In 1917 he found himself unemployed because of the turmoil of the revolution, but an older brother serving in the marines at the

Kronstadt Fortress arranged his recruitment into the Red Guards there. He joined the Bolsheviks, inspired by their vision of a new Russia of proletarians and peasants and by their determination to redeem Russia from the foreign interventionists and local strongmen who had beset the nation since the collapse of the tsarist empire. In 1918 he entered the First Military Instruction Course of the Red Army for several months of training.[7] As he recounts in the introductory chapter of *Mission to China*, he was soon serving at the front in the civil war, first in the Ukraine against the Cossacks, then in Siberia against the White armies under Kolchak. It was in the Siberian campaign that he rose to command a rifle regiment (5th Rifle Division, 43rd Regiment) at the age of nineteen. The brutal civil war opened such possibilities for rapid promotion of young men of determination, courage and toughness.

In the tormented history of the Soviet Union, Chuikov's generation was to be unusually favored. The revolution not only gave them a future, but also promised them a glorious future for the nation and its people. Those born in the succeeding Soviet generations, who came of age under Stalinist tyranny and deprivation or post-Stalinist stagnation and corruption, would never share the conviction in the "radiant future" that drove Chuikov's generation. Speaking of Stalin's successor, Nikita Khrushchev, with whom Chuikov's career was closely linked, Martin Malia wrote, "For Khrushchev's generation the mystique of the Revolution was always very real." Khrushchev and Chuikov were contemporaries, only six years apart, and rose from the most humble of backgrounds to the highest military and political offices in the land.[8]

At the end of the first chapter in *Mission to China* Chuikov alludes briefly to his second posting to China, which fell between 1927 and 1929. He mentions that upon graduating from the Far Eastern Institute in the fall of 1927, his class was assigned to work in China. A number of military advisers were sent to Chinese Communist Party (CCP) military units. At this time communist forces were in full retreat following the purge launched by Chiang Kaishek in April of that year. Presumably the political sensitivity of Chuikov's mission to the CCP prevented him from discussing this in his memoir. He mentions that he traveled through much of northern and southern China, and refers specifically to time spent in Beijing, Tianjin and in the southwestern province of Sichuan. He also states that he learned to speak "quite fluent Chinese." Chuikov does recount one episode from this time that is of considerable interest to the military historian. In November 1929 he witnessed the punitive action taken by the Soviet army on the border of Manchuria in retaliation for Chinese seizure of Soviet property on the Chinese Eastern Railway. Chuikov not only provides a detailed account of military operations, but also memorably depicts the turbulent conditions of the far-off Soviet-Chinese frontier. Because of its intrinsic interest, this chapter appears as an appendix to this translation.

Chuikov's subsequent military career in the Soviet Union is compactly narrated and assessed by Richard Woff in his contribution to *Stalin's Generals,* a biographical compendium of Soviet Second World War commanders.[9] After two years' further service in the Far Eastern command, Chuikov returned to Moscow to direct a senior officers' course. He then held a succession of staff and field positions, becoming a corps commander by 1938 and an army commander the next year. In November 1939, as Stalin prepared to unleash war on Finland, Chuikov received an appointment that fortuitously for him did not bring this career to an early end: he was given command of the 9th Army, which was to attack across the Karelian isthmus on the central part of the long Soviet-Finnish front. Fighting in winter conditions on terrain favorable to the Finns, the Soviet army was cut to pieces. Soviet forces to the south eventually prevailed over the Finns through sheer superiority of numbers, but the 9th Army had no part in the victory. Despite this setback, Chuikov was promoted to lieutenant-general in June 1940, but Woff speculates that he appeared unlikely to hold a major command again.[10] It is against this immediate background that Chuikov was sent to China at the end of 1940.

Chuikov's experience in China and the circumstances of his return home are recounted elsewhere in this introduction; here it need only be noted that from the moment of the Nazi invasion of the Soviet Union Chuikov repeatedly requested to be recalled to serve at the front. In the spring of 1942, soon after his return, Chuikov was appointed deputy commander of a reserve army, then promoted to full command when it was sent to the southern front, where the German 6th Army under Paulus was advancing toward the Volga River. On September 8, as the Germans closed in upon Stalingrad, which Stalin ordered held at all cost, Chuikov was given command of the 62nd Army, based in the city. This was the challenge that displayed to the full Chuikov's tactical skills, as well as his qualities of personal courage and unswerving determination. From September until November, Chuikov's army fought the 6th Army to a standstill in a vicious battle of attrition amidst the rubble of Stalingrad. This masterful defensive operation served to boost Soviet morale, and more significantly gave the Soviet high command the time to prepare a massive counterstroke, launched in mid-November, that cut off the 6th Army and constricted it relentlessly into the Stalingrad pocket. The end for the 6th Army, the greatest defeat yet suffered by Hitler, came on February 2, 1943. Even at the time, the battle was seen by the Soviets and their Western allies as a turning point in the war.

In *Russia's War*, his masterful synthesis of the war on the eastern front, Richard Overy calls Chuikov's appointment to the command of the 62nd Army an "inspired choice." Chuikov was able "to gather together scattered, leaderless soldiers and weld them into a more effective fighting force." He was a "tough, burly man . . . [who] endured what his men endured and faced death without flinching."[11] Antony Beevor, in his compelling account of the battle of Stalingrad, is less attracted by Chuikov, whom he calls "one of the most ruthless" of the new generation of Soviet commanders.[12] Beevor holds Chuikov's military talents in high regard. His reservations center upon the harsh discipline imposed on the men fighting at Stalingrad, for which he holds Chuikov responsible. In contrasting the postwar fates of Paulus, the German commander at Stalingrad, and Chuikov, Beevor remarks in the closing lines of his book: "General Chuikov . . . became a marshal of the Soviet Union . . . [the] thousands of Soviet soldiers executed at Stalingrad on his orders never received a marked grave."[13] This censure appears unduly harsh. Beevor himself emphasizes the draconian nature of discipline in the Soviet army, best exemplified in Stalin's Order No. 227 of August 1942, which decreed that "panic-mongers and cowards must be destroyed on the spot." Chuikov, it is true, said that "in the blazing city we did not suffer cowards, we had no room for them." But, as Beevor notes, Soviet discipline applied just as ferociously to commanders.[14] They were no less answerable than the common soldier to Stalin and the secret police battalions standing to the rear of every frontline formation.

Following Stalingrad, the 62nd Army was redesignated the 8th Guards Army in recognition of its achievement. It was first assigned to the Ukrainian front, and then in 1944 to the Belorussian front, whose commander in chief was K.K. Rokossovski, alongside whom Chuikov had served in the Far East. By April 1945 Chuikov's army was at the outskirts of Berlin. As Richard Woff observes, the house-to-house fighting amidst the rubble of Berlin almost replicated the conditions of Stalingrad.[15] On May 2, Chuikov took the surrender of the Berlin garrison on behalf of the Soviet high command. The battle of Berlin was finished; six days later war in Europe was over. Chuikov remained in Germany for eight years, serving first as deputy commander in chief of Soviet occupation forces in the Soviet eastern zone, and then as commander in chief and head of the Soviet Control Commission following the establishment of East Germany as a separate state in 1949.

After Stalin's death in March 1953, Chuikov returned to the Soviet Union, where his career continued to prosper under Khrushchev, who soon established himself as Stalin's successor. The connection between Chuikov and Khrushchev went back to Stalingrad, where Khrushchev served as party commissar for the Stalingrad Front. Each supported the other—though Khrushchev remarked in an aside in his memoirs that Chuikov "is not the pleasantest of men, but he was a brilliant soldier and the supreme hero of Stalingrad."[16] In 1955 Chuikov was named a marshal of the Soviet Union. From 1960 to 1964 he served jointly as commander in chief of Soviet Ground Forces and deputy minister of defense. He retained responsibility for civil defense until 1972, when he fully retired. During his last years he continued to write, *Mission to China* belonging to this period. General Chuikov died on March 18, 1982. He was buried five days later at a wartime memorial site on the Mamaev Kurgan hill in Stalingrad—now renamed Volgograd—where his command post had been located in the early days of the fateful battle.

CHINA IN 1941

When General Chuikov arrived in Chungking in December 1940, Nationalist China had been at war with Japan for more than three years. The origins of the war lay in the relentless territorial aggrandizement by the Japanese army, carried out with the concurrence of the home government in Tokyo, of large areas of northeastern and northern China. Following the seizure of Manchuria in 1931, Japan steadily extended its control south of the Great Wall, either through outright seizure of territory or through forced Nationalist government "neutralization" of designated areas. On July 7, 1937, a minor incident at the Marco Polo Bridge (Lugouqiao) outside the former capital of Beijing resulted in the decision of Chiang Kaishek and the Nationalist government to resist Japan by armed force. By August the two nations were fully engaged in an undeclared war, called the "war of resistance" by the Chinese and, more euphemistically, the "China incident" by the Japanese.

On August 21, 1937, before the war was two months old, the Soviet Union and China signed a treaty of nonaggression, which, in the words of diplomatic historian John Garver, meant "active political, economic, diplomatic, and military cooperation short of a commitment to actual belligerency."[17] The Soviet Union was driven by fears of growing Japanese militancy, which might be directed toward its Pacific maritime region. Beyond this lay the gnawing worry that Japan would link itself to Nazi Germany in a combined offensive upon the Soviet Union, which would find itself in the most feared of all its possible worlds, a war on two fronts. Soviet aid was intended to sustain Chinese military resistance to Japan. Between 1937 and 1941 the Soviets supplied Nationalist forces with some 900 aircraft, 2,100 motor vehicles, 1,100 artillery pieces with 2 million shells, 9,700 machine guns with 180 million rounds, and 3,100 aerial bombs, as well as 82 tanks. Much of this aid was of the latest Soviet model, the SB-2 bomber and the T-26 tank being cases in point. Approximately 1,500 Soviet advisers served in China; the number is twice as high if ancillary personnel and "volunteer pilots" are included.[18] Two hundred Soviet pilots lost their lives over Chinese skies. Aid provided by the Soviet Union was not inconsiderable and in Garver's estimation stands up very well to assistance provided by the United States to China after Pearl Harbor, all the more so in view of the great disparity in national wealth between the two nations.[19]

Despite Soviet assistance, Nationalist China was unable to turn the tide of the war, but it did succeed in fighting a retreat that took a much greater toll on the invaders than the Japanese high command had expected. By 1940 the heaviest fighting was over and the front had stabilized. The Japanese occupied the major towns and cities of coastal China and controlled the communications lines between them. Along the Yangtze, Japanese control reached beyond Wuhan, five hundred miles in the interior. The Nationalist government had retreated into the fastnesses of the southwest, building a resistance base in the provinces of Sichuan and Yunnan, which were guarded from ready land attack by mountainous terrain and the Yangtze gorges. In the areas under Japanese control, some political power had been handed to Chinese collaborative regimes, the principal one located in the former capital of Nanjing, under Wang Jingwei. In the northwest, the Chinese Communist Party had its base area in Shaanxi province, and by 1940 it had established many guerrilla bases behind Japanese lines in northern China. They were to be of increasing concern to Chiang Kaishek, who saw the steady growth of base areas controlled by the Chinese Communist Party as a direct threat to the Nationalist government, regardless of the United Front into which the two had entered to prosecute the war against Japan. It was into this array of contending forces that General Chuikov stepped when he took up his post of head of the Soviet military advisorate on January 28, 1941.

CHUIKOV AND CHIANG KAISHEK

Of particular interest is General Chuikov's portrayal of Chiang Kaishek. Once he was named chief adviser, Chuikov met Chiang on numerous occasions and was called on by Chiang to participate directly in emergency military planning such as the defense of Changsha in September 1941. In chapter 3, Chuikov describes his first meeting with Chiang at a New Year's Eve reception on December 31, 1940, immediately after his arrival in Chungking. Chuikov saw Chiang as a complex figure, not to be underestimated. He describes Chiang as a "man predatory by nature, expert in marching over the bodies of the dead towards his goals, willing to use blackmail and deceit." But he notes that the Chinese leader is "clever" and "talented," even though his talents "serve evil as well as good." And contrary to what some of his detractors charged, Chiang was "not a puppet in the hands of some unknown power." Reading the memoir as a whole, one is struck by Chuikov's depiction of the straightforwardness of the working relationship between the two men. Yet, as a true believer in the promise and inevitability of communism, Chuikov could write that Chiang would be destroyed, "not by plots or schemes or coups, but only by the tide of the people's wrath." As a realist, though, Chuikov saw that Soviet national interest made it essential to establish cooperative state-to-state relations. Fear of a two-front war was an obsession of the Soviet political and military leadership. China must continue to resist Japan, and the Soviet Union would provide as much military aid and advice as it could afford.

The question, then, was how committed Chiang was to the war of resistance. On this score, Chuikov presents, at least from the distance of his memoir, a not always unsympathetic picture of the many pressures that bore down upon Chiang. Chuikov points out the limits to Chiang's power as national leader and war leader. He emphasizes not so much the material backwardness of China as the traditionalism of its political culture in setting limits on Chiang's maneuverability. On one side, Chiang faced various cliques of militarists, who offered him only a tenuous loyalty; on the other side, he faced the communists, who were only temporarily in alliance with the man they sought to destroy. And even within the ranks of the Nationalist Party (Guomindang), factional infighting routinely weakened the effectiveness of the chain of command. Although Chuikov does not put this in so many words, his portrayal of Chiang is of a man simultaneously struggling to fend off the deadly Japanese threat from the outside while just managing to keep the many disruptive domestic pressures in check on the inside.

Chuikov comments on the growing unwillingness of the Nationalist armies in 1940–41 to prosecute the war vigorously. War weariness partly explained this, but so did the decision of the Nationalist high command to conserve precious resources of men and especially of war matériel (such as that provided by the Soviets) in order to safeguard their position from warlord or communist challenge. This decision was taken by Chiang for compelling domestic political reasons, which Chuikov recognizes. Nevertheless, Chuikov remains critical of Chiang's unwillingness to take the initiative against Japan. With proper preparation and sufficient equipment, Chinese forces in Chuikov's view were capable of successfully mounting small- and medium-scale offensives. These not only would have regained territory from the enemy but also would have resulted in a marked strengthening of national unity and morale. For Chuikov, the gamble appeared highly likely to be successful. For Chiang Kaishek, any gamble that was not unconditionally guaranteed of success put him at risk and could never be taken. The divide between the two men in this respect was unbridgeable.

It is more difficult to gauge Chiang's opinion of Chuikov. Chinese traditions of formal politeness interfere in determining the real opinions of political leaders. Nevertheless, it would appear that Chiang regarded Chuikov with respect. Soviet military advisers made their name in Nationalist circles in the 1920s, when the advisory mission under General Blyukher offered valuable guidance to Chiang's armies in mounting the Northern Expedition to unify China. (Chiang held Blyukher in such high esteem that in 1938 he asked that Blyukher be sent back to China, remarking that Blyukher's presence was worth 100,000 men, to which he was given an evasive answer by Moscow, covering up the fact that Blyukher had just been liquidated in the Stalinist terror.)[20] Ambassador Aleksandr Panyushkin received a high-level inquiry from the Chinese in May 1942 as to when General Chuikov should be expected back from the Soviet Union. He replied that Chuikov would not be returning, since the ferocious battles now unfolding on the Soviet-German front made "bold commanders" like General Chuikov vital to the Red Army. Panyushkin also recounts a conversation with Chiang Kaishek in January 1943, shortly after returning from leave in Moscow. Chiang asked Panyushkin if he had seen his former chief military advisers, Kachanov and Chuikov. Panyushkin answered that he had seen neither, as both were at the front, but that Stalin personally had told him that General Chuikov had "done very well in his command of the 62nd Army in the defense of Stalingrad."[21] In sum, it seems fair to say that whatever his suspicions about Stalin and ultimate Soviet intentions may have been, Chiang valued the Soviet military advisers for their dedicated professionalism.

A last word should be said about Chiang Kaishek's "English voice," his wife, Soong Meiling, whom Chuikov regarded with some disfavor. Like her sisters, Ailing and Qingling, the former married to H. H. Kung, the latter the widow of Dr. Sun Yatsen, and her brother T. V. Soong, she aspired to a political role in her own right. As secretary-general of the Aeronautical Affairs Committee of the Central Military Commission, she was in effect civilian head of the air force. Chuikov regarded her as a "provocationist," striving by any means to bring the Soviet Union into war against Japan. He saw her as a leading intriguer on the Chungking scene, an estimate not necessarily wrong insofar as he was affected. Owen Lattimore, Chiang Kaishek's personal political adviser, later recalled Mme. Chiang saying to him: "Of course, our Soviet advisers are no good, because now that the Soviets are being attacked by the Germans, they need every competent officer they've got. So anybody we've got must be third or fourth rate." Reflecting upon this later, Lattimore remarked that when the head of the mission, "the famous General Vasilii Chuikov," returned to the Soviet Union, "he became one of the heroes of the defense of Stalingrad, showing how fourth rate he was."[22]

CRITICAL EVENTS IN SINO-SOVIET RELATIONS IN 1941

During 1941 three events complicated relations between the Nationalist government and the Soviet Union, and Chuikov was an observer or participant, if peripherally, in all three. These were the New 4th Army Incident, the Soviet-Japanese Neutrality Pact, and the outbreak of the Pacific War. Of these, the New 4th Army Incident threatened most to undermine relations between Moscow and Chungking.

The New 4th Army Incident, January 1941

Chapter 5 of Chuikov's memoir is devoted primarily to the New 4th Army Incident, also known as the South Anhui Incident. The events in question occurred during the second week of January 1941, when Nationalist forces under Gu Zhutong inflicted several thousand casualties (the number remains undetermined) on the staff column of the communist New 4th Army, the last unit of that army moving north for redeployment across the Yangtze River. The incident had its origins in the growth of communist military power in east-central China after the Japanese invasion. The Nationalists sought to keep communist operations north of the Yellow River; failing that, the communists must at all costs be kept north of the Yangtze. During late 1940 Chiang issued a number of commands to the CCP to remove all units of the New 4th Army operating in Jiangsu and Anhui provinces south of the Yangtze. Ironically, in terms of the later incident, the CCP leadership in Yenan wanted these units to regroup north of the Yangtze, both for greater military effectiveness and for tighter control by the party center. However, autonomous tendencies on the part of New 4th Army commander Xiang Ying caused him to delay. Chiang Kaishek, unaware of the differences within the CCP on this question, ordered his forces in southern Anhui to take action. When Gu Zhutong attacked on January 9, all but the New 4th Army staff column bringing up the rear had been evacuated north of the Yangtze. Xiang Ying was killed, several thousand men killed or wounded, and several hundred taken prisoner.[23]

The action taken by the Nationalist army in southern Anhui was immediately publicized by the communists as an act of treachery on the part of Chiang Kaishek. It put the Soviet embassy and the military advisorate in an awkward position, since, as Chuikov observes, "We had treaty obligations to Chiang's government, but our spiritual sympathies lay with the Chinese communists." Chuikov refers in several places to the deep concern on the part of the Soviets in both Moscow and Chungking that the United Front was about to collapse into civil war between the Nationalists and the communists. Such a development would work to Japan's favor, and in fact raised the possibility, however remote, of Chiang making peace with Japan in order to concentrate on the destruction of the communists. For the Soviet position in the Far East to be secure, it was essential that the United Front be kept alive and active in its resistance to Japan.

On January 15, Chuikov and Panyushkin met the CCP representatives in Chungking, Zhou Enlai and Ye Jianying. Zhou stated that Chiang's chief of staff, He Yingqin, and his deputy, Bai Chongxi, had organized the plot to destroy the New 4th Army. In Zhou's view, Chiang did not know that his subordinates were planning to do so, but when the attack took place he readily countenanced it.[24] The next day Chuikov took the occasion of a business meeting with Chiang to ask for further information about the incident. Chiang refused the request, stating that what was at stake was the preservation of military discipline by the government. Chuikov did not press Chiang on the issue.[25] Subsequently Chuikov met He Yingqin and Bai Chongxi and, as he indicates, spoke more forwardly to them. He presented the Chinese communist case that the attack was not only unjustified but was also a dangerous diversion from the war with Japan. Chuikov further suggested that when he reported to his superiors in Moscow he would have to present the Nationalist actions in an unfavorable light, which might result in the termination of Soviet military aid, since the Nationalist government was using it against fellow Chinese.

On Moscow's instruction, Panyushkin requested a meeting with Chiang on January 25, at which he indicated Soviet fears that a civil war was in the offing. Chiang replied that it was the communists who had attacked first in Anhui, but that in any case he would do everything possible to peacefully resolve differences with the CCP and prevent the outbreak of a civil conflict. His overriding goal remained prosecution of the war against Japan to a victorious conclusion.[26] So the matter of the New 4th Army Incident rested. Three days later Panyushkin and Chuikov, accompanied by K. M. Kachanov, the outgoing chief military adviser, called upon Chiang to introduce Chuikov in his new role. As Chuikov describes, the occasion went agreeably, with no mention made of recent events. In the following months Chiang eased up pressure on the communists, and Soviet aid continued to arrive. The United Front survived in name until the end of the war, but in reality it had ceased to exist in January 1941.

The Soviet-Japanese Neutrality Pact, April 1941

The signing of a five-year neutrality pact between the Soviet Union and Japan on April 13, 1941, came as a rude jolt to the Nationalist government, even though the progress of Japanese Foreign Minister Matsuoka Yosuke through the Soviet Union to Berlin raised suspicion that something was afoot. Soviet fears of being caught between Germany and Japan in a two-front war drove its negotiation, along with continuing Soviet suspicions that the Western powers were plotting a sellout to Japan through a so-called Far Eastern Munich, whereby they would safeguard their colonial interests in exchange for giving Japan free rein against the Soviet Union.[27] Chuikov recalls the atmosphere in Chungking as quite frosty over the next few days, until it was determined by Chiang just how much damage had been done. The Nationalist leaders took exception in the first place to the mutual recognition by the Soviet Union and Japan of the "territorial integrity" of each other's client states in Manchuria (Manzhouguo) and Outer Mongolia. Chiang steadfastly refused to recognize the Japanese seizure of Manchuria, and neither his government nor its predecessors had acknowledged the separation of Outer Mongolia from China in 1912. However, Chiang was prepared to live with these realities. What was of much more pressing concern was whether the pact meant the termination of Soviet aid to China. The Soviets sought at once to put Chiang's fears to rest. In Moscow Foreign Minister V. I. Molotov assured the Chinese ambassador that "with respect to Soviet support for China's war of resistance, there was absolutely no change."[28]

Chuikov was present when Panyushkin met H. H. Kung, the deputy premier and minister of finance, as well as brother-in-law to Chiang Kaishek, immediately after the announcement of the pact. Panyushkin assured Kung that nothing had changed in regard to Soviet support for China. Military aid would continue unabated, and the Soviet Union would maintain, or even increase, its forces along the Manchurian border. Chuikov nodded his assent to Panyushkin's remarks. On April 19 Panyushkin met Chiang to reassure him of Soviet support and to present the Soviet position that the pact was intended to limit the spread of hostilities in the Far East.[29] As Chuikov's memoir indicates, his activities as chief military adviser were not affected in any way by the pact. As for the supply of Soviet war matériel, its flow was determined by Soviet domestic priorities and by the state at any given moment of the precarious Moscow-Chungking-Yenan relationship. The Neutrality Pact had no impact upon this. For Chiang the crucial implication of the pact was geopolitical, as it abruptly ended any hopes he had of drawing the Soviet Union directly into the war against Japan.

The Outbreak of the Pacific War, December 1941

Eight months later, within hours of the Japanese attack on Pearl Harbor and the beginning of the Pacific War, Chiang resumed his efforts to bring about Soviet entry into the war. On the morning of December 8, Chiang asked the Soviet, British and American ambassadors to his residence. The argument was put that since Japan had now seized the initiative on behalf of the Axis bloc, the three leading opponents of the Axis should concentrate their forces and knock Japan out of the war. This they could do by spring, at which point they would turn to the elimination of Nazi Germany. Chiang said that he was proposing that China, Britain, the United States and the Soviet Union form a united front to prosecute the war against Japan. Since three of the powers were now at war with Japan, the message was directed obviously at the Soviet Union. Stalin replied on December 12 and expressed sympathy for the anti-Axis struggle in the Pacific. However, he emphasized that the great battles the Soviet Union was fighting with the Germans were a vital part of the world anti-Axis struggle, and that the Soviet Union must prosecute this to its conclusion and not become engaged in a war on two fronts.[30]

Stalin adhered to his decision until August 8, 1945, when the Soviet Union, three months after the surrender of Germany and two days after the bombing of Hiroshima, entered the war against a Japan on the brink of defeat. But in the first months after Pearl Harbor there were a number of further attempts, both official and unofficial, by the Chinese to bring about Soviet entry into the war, some of which Chuikov mentions in his closing chapter. In his capacity as Soviet military attaché Chuikov was present at a meeting in December 1941 where Chiang called for the creation of a four-power military council. This too failed to evoke a Soviet response. In the government-monitored Chinese press, many stories appeared of Japanese plans to launch an attack on the Soviet Union. It was against this background that Chuikov himself was quoted, though not by name, as allegedly having declared that the Soviet Union would turn against Japan once Germany was defeated.[31] This episode is treated below in regard to Chuikov's recall home. But regardless of the "disinformation" and "provocations" that Chuikov mentions, Soviet commitment to neutrality in the Pacific War remained unshakable until Stalin deemed the time right to act otherwise.

HISTORICAL PROBLEMS IN THE TEXT

There are two places in the text where the version given by General Chuikov requires emendation or further comment. The first is the analysis he provides in chapter 11 of the battle of Changsha in September 1941; the second is the account he gives in chapter 12 of his return to the Soviet Union in February 1942.

The Battle of Changsha

Chuikov's narrative of the battle of Changsha must be read with care. While Chuikov had a role to play in offering strategic advice to Chiang Kaishek, he did so at a distance far removed from the actual events taking place. Chuikov thus bases his account of a great Chinese victory on reports received in Chungking from Chinese commanders in the field. The version of the battle that Chuikov presents is the official, public version, which was relayed thereafter in Nationalist Chinese historiography and was accepted by Western military historians.[32] Yet the in camera postmortem of the battle conducted by Chiang Kaishek reveals a much different picture of events. Chiang initially was taken in by the evasive and self-serving dispatches of his generals at Changsha. Soon he learned from a number of confidential reports that the battle, while not a major setback, was far from the glorious victory declared by the local commanders. At the third Nanyue military conference, convened in October 1941, he severely criticized his generals for failing to grasp the opportunity they had within their reach at Changsha.

Apart from his chronology being slightly off in places, Chuikov accurately summarizes the first stage of the battle. This began on September 18 when four divisions of the Japanese 11th Army crossed the Xinqiang River, sixty miles north of Changsha, where the major strength of the Chinese 9th War Zone was concentrated. Chinese forces were steadily driven back toward Changsha and into the hills to the east. On September 22, the Japanese forced the crossing of the Miluo River, halfway to Changsha, and inflicted heavy casualties on the 10th Army, which had been sent in to shore up the rapidly deteriorating Chinese position. By September 26, the 10th Army was in full retreat. The last defensive line for Changsha was prepared along the Laodao River, ten miles to the east of the city, where the highly reputed 74th Army dug in on both sides of the river.

It is at this point that Chuikov's narrative—and the official Nationalist record—diverge from the actual course of events. The 74th Army was forced south after heavy fighting, thus leaving the road to Changsha open. At 6 P.M. on September 27, a Japanese advance unit entered the city through the north gate as Chinese defenders hurriedly made their escape. On September 29 the Japanese 4th Division marched into the city, while the 3rd Division continued southward to invest Zhuzhou, in order to knock out the whole Chinese defensive position south of Lake Dongting. After destroying the local military fortifications, the 3rd Division withdrew from Zhuzhou. In the view of Japanese 11th Army headquarters in Wuhan, the goal of smashing the principal Chinese force in the 9th War Zone had been attained. On September 30 the whole Japanese strike force was ordered to begin withdrawing to the original pre–September 18 position on the north bank of the Xinqiang River.

When it was learned in Chungking that the Japanese had begun to withdraw, the high command ordered Chinese units in the vicinity of Changsha to divide up and cut off the Japanese "retreat." Because of the extended Japanese lines, Chinese troops were able to mount harassing attacks. Local commanders now reported to Chungking that they were engaged in "fierce battles with the retreating enemy," on whom they were inflicting "heavy casualties." There was some truth in these claims: for example, the Japanese 4th Division, after evacuating Changsha, was ambushed as it crossed the Laodao River, and took serious losses. By October 9 the withdrawal to the Xinqiang River was complete. In the course of the battle the Chinese had lost up to 70,000 dead and wounded, while the Japanese suffered as many as 10,000 fatalities.[33]

It is clear that the Japanese did not suffer a "debacle" at Changsha. Neither did the Chinese, though their forces were badly mauled. From almost the beginning of the war the Chinese took, and expected to take, far higher casualty figures than the much better trained and equipped Japanese. What is at error in Chuikov's account of the battle is the assertion that Chinese forces at Changsha took the initiative and in a bold counterstroke inflicted abnormally high losses on the Japanese. On this assumption, Chuikov argues that if the Chinese commanders had prosecuted a more aggressive and better coordinated attack on the "retreating" Japanese, they could have used their knowledge of the terrain and their advantage of numbers to put out of action much of Japan's vaunted 11th Army. Had Chuikov been advising at such a high level at home, he would have expected the tightly controlled and integrated Soviet chain of command to translate his recommendations into policy. But Chiang Kaishek was dealing with semi-independent commanders determined to hold on to as much of their military strength as possible, and who were long practiced in tactics of delay, evasion or halfhearted compliance with orders from the center.

At the Nanyue conference in October 1941 Chiang excoriated his commanders for failing to coordinate their forces effectively during the whole course of the battle. The Japanese were always the ones to take the initiative, he declared. Nevertheless, the Chinese had the opportunity to strike when the Japanese began to withdraw from their advanced positions. His commanders had missed the chance to score a major victory. Chiang was used to verbally assaulting his commanders from time to time and, as in the case of this battle, shooting one or two for dereliction of duty.[34] Given the limitations of his political and military power base, he could not go further in inspiring his commanders to take a more aggressive stance.

As for the final verdict on the battle of Changsha, Chuikov's positive assessment, though based on faulty premises, is not completely without merit. Limited reserves of manpower meant that Japan could not readily afford to take 10,000 casualties in an engagement on only one small part of the long China front. Japan already had occupied southern Indochina in the summer of 1941, and was now preparing to move against the European-American colonial empires in Southeast Asia. Japanese military strength would be strung out even further. The Nationalist Chinese capacity to harass Japanese forces once they moved out of their fixed positions and to inflict upon them a significant casualty toll meant that the Japanese were increasingly bound to these positions, and that the likelihood of their moving out to force the "final battle" with Chiang Kaishek was ever more remote. In this sense the battle of Changsha indicated to the Japanese that while they could still force the attack, they would have to weigh very carefully their purported goals and likely casualties before taking the offensive.

Return to Soviet Union, 1942
In February 1942 General Chuikov was recalled to the Soviet Union. He was assigned command of the First Reserve Army, then undergoing training. Chuikov had indicated on numerous occasions since the outbreak of the war with Germany his desire to return home and serve at the front. There is, however, some mystery surrounding the timing and precise circumstances of his departure from China.

In chapter 12 of his memoir Chuikov cites an occasion when he was the object of Nationalist government disinformation. Sometime after the German invasion (a precise date is not given) he was quoted as referring in a press interview to "increased Soviet aid to China." This, he said, was a complete fabrication—even the interview was an invention of "political schemers," whose goal was to trigger a war between Japan and the Soviet Union. If Chuikov's memory is correct, then this is the first of two such incidents involving the Chinese press. The second occurred in late December and is mentioned in some detail in an article by A. M. Ledovskii, who as a young man served in the Soviet diplomatic service in China from 1942 to 1952. Ledovskii states that Chuikov spoke to Chinese newsmen at a Soviet reception, where he apparently said that as soon as the Soviet Union had finished off Germany, it would "take care" of Japan. This news item immediately appeared as a major story in the Chungking daily, *Xin Shu Bao* (New Sichuan News), under the caption, "Discussion with leading Soviet military figure in China regarding strategic plans of the USSR." According to Ledovskii, the report, in which Chuikov was not mentioned by name, stirred great interest not only in China, and likewise Japan, but in the United States and Great Britain as well. The Soviet embassy in Chungking responded on January 2 with a denial of the story, and Panyushkin presented the Nationalist government's Foreign Ministry with a demand that it issue a denial of the "provocationist remarks" published in the press. However, the Foreign Ministry held its ground, confirming the veracity of the story, and both sides decided it was best to let the matter rest and eventually drop from sight. Soon afterward Chuikov was recalled to Moscow.[35]

Whether Chuikov's comments were such a cause célèbre and whether Moscow reacted in so peremptory a manner are open to some question: Ledovskii did not arrive in Chungking in 1942 until after the events described, and his retelling of events suggests a touch of professional disdain for the amateur military diplomat. Furthermore, as Chuikov rightly notes, the entry of the United States into the war with Japan meant that China now looked first to the Americans for aid. The remaining Soviet advisers were recalled for service on the home front. Chuikov was the last Soviet chief military adviser; his replacement was General Joseph Stilwell, who was to have such a rancorous relationship with Chiang.

Chuikov took a graceful departure from his post, much feted and honored by the Chinese. Nevertheless, he had been fortunate. In 1937 or 1938 rumor alone would have been enough to result in personal tragedy. Ledovskii recounts a conversation with Ambassador Panyushkin following the latter's return to Chungking from his leave in Moscow in December 1942. Panyushkin had met Stalin to brief him on the China situation—Stalin was most eager to learn everything possible about Chiang Kaishek, including details of his daily life and personal habits—and in the course of the discussion Chuikov's name came up. Stalin recounted that when Chuikov reported to him upon his return he had said to Chuikov: "We haven't made a diplomat of you, but perhaps we can make you into a good soldier."[36] With this Chuikov was sent to take command of the First Reserve Army, soon to be transferred to the Stalingrad front. Once again Chuikov's apparent lucky star held good for him, and from this time onward it was to be unerringly in the ascendant.

NATIONALIST CHINA'S WAR CAPABILITY

Chuikov's assessment of the Nationalist armies is similar in many respects to that of his successor as chief military adviser, Joseph Stilwell. Like General Stilwell, Chuikov was a field commander who looked at the army as much from the bottom up as from the top down. Both noted the defeatism and corruption that sapped the higher levels of the command, and the reluctance of so many generals to commit their forces to battle. Both were impressed by the endurance and courage of the common soldiers. That both Chuikov and Stilwell, products of ideologically opposed societies, identified basically the same problems and were equally stymied by them serves as testimony to the intractable nature of the Chinese wartime reality.

At first reading, Chuikov's comments on the state of the Nationalist soldiery appear highly negative. He noted the malnourishment of so many soldiers and the nearly complete lack of medical services. He commented on the harsh treatment officers meted out to their men. He noted the demoralizing effect of the long separation of men from families. He spoke of a "general war weariness" that was setting in, and he remarked on increased cases of desertion and pilfering of military supplies. Nevertheless, he came to conclusion that the "overall fighting capacity of the Chinese army was not undermined."

Why the seeming paradox? The best explanation may be that Western observers of the Nationalist Chinese army were assessing it according to conditions under which Western armies would be effective. Whether the men came from the city or the farm, these armies were drawn from a modern society. Chuikov was looking at the Chinese army from a Russian perspective. The Soviet armies in the civil war and in World War II were not far beyond the peasant stage, for the Soviet Union, despite its recent forced industrialization, remained overwhelmingly peasant, or peasant but one generation removed. The society out of which the Soviet and Chinese armies came, and for that matter the Japanese, had inured their men to a degree of hardship, misery, suffering, and brutalization that Westerners found difficult to imagine. Chuikov's criteria for assessing the effectiveness of the Chinese army were different from those used by Western observers. He pointed to the absence of widespread desertion and mutinies, which was telling for one who had witnessed the disintegration of the Russian imperial army in 1917. He noted the commitment of the middle-ranking and junior officers to an active war of resistance. What China's military needed was better leadership at the top and a readiness to take the initiative in limited campaigns where the chances of success were high. But these were first of all political, not military, questions, over which neither Chuikov nor his successor Stilwell could exert any influence.

Chuikov's analysis of the tactical weaknesses of the Nationalist army is of particular interest. Chuikov was at his best in tactical matters, so his observations on the shortcomings of the Chinese army at the platoon and company level are particularly of note. In chapter 4 Chuikov analyzes in detail military exercises he attended near Chungking in June 1941, and in chapter 10 he describes an inspection he made at the Yichang front downriver from Chungking. Further comments are scattered through the book. His account of the 1929 Soviet operation on the Manchurian border should also be read in regard to Chinese battle tactics.

The weakness of the Nationalist army at the tactical level Chuikov ascribed to inadequacies in officer training. He comments a number of times on the "textbook application" of tactical exercises he observed when present at military reviews. Officers had been drilled to recite instructions but could not apply what they had learned in battle. There was a smattering of modernization in the Nationalist army in 1941—some up-to-date weapons, some Western-style tactical exercises, and some recent instruction manuals from abroad—but nothing had been absorbed systematically. In actual battle conditions this resulted in many lost opportunities. The failure to exploit numerical superiority and familiarity with the terrain was not only a result of a lack of will on the part of the high command, but also the result of ineffective tactical leadership when the will to do battle was present.

Despite the various problems noted above, Chuikov concluded that the Nationalist armies were capable of waging vigorous defensive operations (so-called offensive defense) and that they were capable of scoring victories in limited-scale offensive operations against Japanese formations of up to divisional strength. The Nationalist armies, he stated, were not capable of broad, large-scale offensives because of problems of supply and coordination, as well as the lack of airpower. Such operations would run up against the overwhelming technological superiority of the Japanese. But limited offensive operations would eliminate many isolated Japanese outposts and give the Chinese forces combat experience they much needed. Perhaps of greatest import, battlefield success would immeasurably boost morale and commitment to the war effort. Chuikov, therefore, did not see the military picture in 1941 as uniformly bleak for the Nationalist government. There were excellent senior commanders to be found, the commander of the 6th War Zone, Chen Cheng, being singled out by him for high praise. The lower-ranking field officers were patriotic and shared many of the hardships of the common soldiers. The latter may have been ill fed and harshly treated but were courageous and tough.

Finally, looking at the larger picture, Chuikov concluded that Nationalist China could not be defeated militarily by Japan. Despite severe setbacks such as Zhongtiaoshan (in southern Shanxi), the Nationalist armies had not broken. Chiang Kaishek held on to key points in the north, such as Xi'an and Luoyang, as well as large parts of central and eastern China. Chuikov himself had traveled to the central China front at Yichang. Most important, however, was the fact that the Sichuan base of the Nationalist government was close to impregnable. Direct attack by the Japanese from their midriver staging point in Wuhan would have entailed unsustainable casualties. Chuikov returned by boat from Yichang, stopping along the way to inspect Chinese artillery emplacements. He was highly commendatory of the fortifications along the gorges, one of the great natural defense lines in China.[37] The only alternative for the Japanese was to mount a flanking attack on Sichuan by land either from the northeast through Shaanxi province or from the southeast through Guizhou province. Such an operation would be highly risky because of the long distances to be covered by vehicle and by foot over difficult terrain. Gone would be the railway lines that served the Japanese so effectively in extending and maintaining their power in northern and eastern China. But whether by land or river, an attack on Sichuan would require an outlay of men and matériel that Japan would be hard pressed to meet, all the more so after the expansion of the war into Southeast Asia and the Pacific in December 1941.

To sum up, what does General Chuikov's memoir tell us about Nationalist China at war at the halfway point in the eight-year struggle with Japan? Some things we already know, though often they are minimized and so we need to be reminded of them. First, for more than four years China had been fighting a powerful, modern military machine, with only the Soviet Union providing military aid of significance, and that until the godsend of the Pacific War, China had been doing so alone. Despite the many setbacks suffered, Nationalist China not only had not surrendered, but, together with its communist allies, had forced the Japanese to commit over a million troops to the China war. Second, Nationalist China's land forces deserve more credit than usually given. Once the front had stabilized in late 1938, the Japanese were not to mount another major offensive until Operation Ichigo in 1944. While capable of launching limited offensive forays, such as that directed at Changsha in September

1941, none brought Japan any closer to forcing China to the peace table. And while Japan might successfully attain short-term objectives, the casualties taken, while far less than those of the Chinese, could not be so easily absorbed by the Japanese. Third, if the Pacific War of 1941–45 is to be grasped in its totality, and not only as a U.S.-Japan conflict in the Pacific or a British-Japanese struggle in Burma, the role played by Nationalist China must be incorporated, and not only for the events following Pearl Harbor. The years from 1937 to 1941 are vital to the story, since China's sustained resistance set major limitations on Japan's exercise of military might in regard to the Western powers. Japan did not launch the Pacific War with a *tabula rasa*. It is therefore necessary to attempt an accurate assessment of not only the weaknesses and limitations of the Nationalist Chinese war effort, but also its strengths and potentialities. To this end the highly astute and remarkably dispassionate observations of General Chuikov make a most valuable contribution.

NOTES

[1] Vasilii I. Chuikov, *The Beginning of the Road: The Battle for Stalingrad*, trans. Harold Silver (London: Macgibbon and Kee, 1963); and *The Fall of Berlin*, trans. Ruth Kisch, foreword by Alistair Horne (New York: Holt, Rinehart and Winston, 1967). The British editions were entitled *The Beginning of the Road* and *The End of the Third Reich*.

[2] Horne in Chuikov, *Fall of Berlin*, 9.

[3] John Keegan, *The Battle for History: Re-Fighting World War Two* (Toronto: Vintage Books, 1995), 56.

[4] Horne in Chuikov, *Fall of Berlin*, 12.

[5] A. G. Yakovlev, "Nezabyvaemoe v Istorii" [Unforgettable in History], in *Problemy Dal'nego Vostoka*, 1984:1, 182.

[6] V. I. Chuikov, *Zakalyalas' Molodost' v Boyakh* [A Youth Tempered in Battle] (Moscow: Izdatel'stvo TsK VLKSM, 1968), 5.

[7] Ibid., 10–12, 17–20.

[8] Martin Malia, *The Soviet Tragedy: A History of Socialism in Russia, 1917–1991* (New York: The Free Press, 1994), 320. Walter Laqueur captures the mood of Chuikov's generation especially well in *The Dream That Failed: Reflections on the Soviet Union*

(Oxford: Oxford University Press, 1994), chapter 1, "The Age of Enthusiasm," 3–18.

[9] Ricard Woff, "Vasily Ivanovich Chuikov," in Harold Shukman, ed., *Stalin's Generals* (London: DIANE Publishing Co., 1993), 67–74.

[10] Ibid., 69.

[11] Richard Overy, *Russia's War* (Harmondsworth, U.K.: Penguin, 1997), 172.

[12] Antony Beevor, *Stalingrad: The Fateful Siege: 1942–1943* (Harmondsworth, U.K.: Penguin Books, 1998), 89.

[13] Ibid., 431.

[14] Ibid., 85; for the quote from Chuikov, 166.

[15] Woff, 72.

[16] Nikita Khrushchev, *Khrushchev Remembers,* trans. and ed. Strobe Talbott (Boston: Little, Brown and Company, 1970), 193, n. 1.

[17] John W. Garver, *Chinese-Soviet Relations, 1937–1945: The Diplomacy of Chinese Nationalism* (Oxford: Oxford University Press, 1988), 20–21.

[18] Ibid., 38–40. Figures for Soviet supplies are somewhat approximate, as Soviet and Chinese sources do not tally precisely.

[19] Ibid., 49–50.

[20] Andrei Mefod'evich Ledovskii, "Zapiski Diplomata" [Notes of a Diplomat], in *Problemy Dal'nego Vostoka*, 1991:1, 108–18: 115.

[21] Aleksandr Semyonovich Panyushkin, *Zapiski Posla: Kitai, 1939–44* [Notes of an Ambassador: China, 1939–44], ed. P. I. Smirnov (Moscow: Institute of the Far East, Academy of Sciences of the USSR, 1981; privately printed and circulated), 222, 235. I am indebted to Professor Vitaly Kozyrev of Moscow State University for obtaining a copy for me.

[22] Owen Lattimore, *China Memoirs: Chiang Kai-shek and the War Against Japan*, comp. Fujiko Isono (Tokyo: University of Tokyo Press, 1990), 140.

[23] Gregor Benton, "The South Anhui Incident," *Journal of Asian Studies*, XLV:4 (1986): 681–720, in particular 705–13.

[24] S. L. Tikhvinskii, gen. ed., *Russko-Kitaiskie Otnosheniya v XX veke. Tom IV: Sovetsko-Kitaiskie Otnosheniya, 1937–1945 gg. Kn. 1: 1937–1944 gg.* [Russo-Chinese Relations in the Twentieth Century; Volume IV: Soviet-Chinese Relations, 1937–1945; Book I: 1937–1944] (Moscow: Pamyatniki Istoricheskoi Mysli, 2000), Document 469, January 15, 1941 (Minutes), 627–28; Ray Huang, "Chiang Kai-shek and His Diary as a Historical Source" [Part 1], *Chinese Studies in History*, fall-winter 1995–96, 116.

[25] Garver, *Chinese-Soviet Relations,* 146; Huang, "Chiang Kai-shek," 116, for Chiang's notation in his diary of Chuikov's visit.

[26] Panyushkin, *Zapiski Posla*, 126–28.

27 Garver, *Chinese-Soviet Relations*, 109–10. The term "Far Eastern Munich" was a commonplace of Soviet historiography; Chuikov uses it in a number of places in the text.

28 Zhang Xianwen, gen. ed., *Zhongguo KangRi Zhanzheng Shi (1931–1945)* [A History of China's War of Resistance Against Japan, 1931–1945] (Nanjing: Nanjing Daxue Chubanshe, 2001), 813–14.

29 Panyushkin, *Zapiski Posla*, 139–41; Garver, *Chinese-Soviet Relations*, 115–17.

30 Raisa Mirovitskaya, *Kitaiskaya Gosudarstvennost' i Sovetskaya Politika v Kitae: Gody Tikhookeanskoi Voiny, 1941–1945* [Chinese Statehood and Soviet Policy in China: The Period of Pacific War, 1941–1945] (Moscow: Pamyatniki Istoricheskoy Mysli, 1999), 75–77.

31 Ibid., 84.

32 Hsu Long-hsuen and Chang Ming-kai, eds., *History of The Sino-Japanese War (1937–1945)*, trans. Wen Ha-hsiung (Taipei: Chung Wu Publishing Co., 1971), 357–62; Frank Dorn, *The Sino-Japanese War, 1937–41: From Marco Polo Bridge to Pearl Harbor* (New York: Macmillan, 1974), 368–71; Roy M. Stanley, *Prelude to Pearl Harbor* (New York: Charles Scribner's Sons, 1982), 128. In contrast to the battle of Changsha, Chuikov's treatment in chapter 8 of the battle of Zhongtiaoshan is very accurate. This may be due to the fact that Zhongtiaoshan was such a severe defeat that, unlike Changsha, it could not be sanitized. Chuikov's summary also indicates familiarity with high-level official sources.

33 Zhang Xianwen, *Zhongguo KangRi Zhanzheng Shi (1931–1945)*, 825–30 for the summary of military operations of the battle. The chapter on the battle of Changsha, including the section in the following note, was written by Professor Chen Hongmin.

34 Ibid., 830–35 for the Nanyue conference.

35 Ledovskii, "Zapiski Diplomata," 116; Mirovitskaya, *Kitaiskaya Gosudarstvennost', 1941–1945*, 84. After his retirement from the diplomatic service, Ledovskii took up a senior research post at the Far Eastern Institute of the Soviet (later Russian) Academy of Sciences.

36 Ledovskii, "Zapiski Diplomata," 117.

37 Any traveler, the present writer being a case in point, going upstream cannot fail to be impressed by the defensive potential of the gorges.

BIBLIOGRAPHY

Beevor, Antony. *Stalingrad: The Fateful Siege, 1942–1943.*
Harmondsworth, U.K.: Penguin Books, 1998.

Benton, Gregor. "The South Anhui Incident." *Journal of Asian Studies,*
XLV:4 (1986): 681–720.

Chuikov, Vasilii I. *The Beginning of the Road: The Battle for Stalingrad.*
Trans. Harold Silver. London: Macgibbon and Kee, 1963.

Chuikov, Vasilii I. *The Fall of Berlin.* Trans. Ruth Kisch, foreword by
Alistair Horne. New York: Holt, Rinehart and Winston, 1967.

Chuikov, V. I. *Zakalyalas' Molodost' v Boyakh* [A Youth Tempered in
Battle]. Moscow: Izdatel'stvo TsK VLKSM, 1968.

Dorn, Frank. The Sino-Japanese War, 1937–41: From Marco Polo
Bridge to Pearl Harbor. New York: Macmillan, 1974.

Garver, John W. Chinese-Soviet Relations, 1937–1945: The
Diplomacy of Chinese Nationalism. Oxford: Oxford
University Press, 1988.

Hsu Long-hsuen and Chang Ming-kai, eds. *History of The Sino-Japanese
War (1937–1945).* Trans. Wen Ha-hsiung. Taipei: Chung Wu
Publishing Co., 1971.

Huang, Ray. "Chiang Kai-shek and His Diary as a Historical Source"
[Part 1]. *Chinese Studies in History,* fall-winter 1995–96.

Keegan, John. The Battle for History: Re-Fighting World War Two.
Toronto: Vintage Books, 1995.

Khrushchev, Nikita. *Khrushchev Remembers.* Trans. and ed. Strobe
Talbott. Boston: Little, Brown and Company, 1970.

Laqueur, Walter. *The Dream That Failed: Reflections on the Soviet Union.*
Oxford: Oxford University Press, 1994.

Lattimore, Owen. *China Memoirs: Chiang Kai-shek and the War Against
Japan.* Comp. Fujiko Isono. Tokyo: University of Tokyo
Press, 1990.

Ledovskii, Andrei Mefod'evich. "Zapiski Diplomata" [Notes of a
Diplomat]. *Problemy Dal'nego Vostoka,* 1991:1, 108–18.

Malia, Martin. The Soviet Tragedy: A History of Socialism in Russia, 1917–1991. New York: The Free Press, 1994.

Mirovitskaya, Raisa. *Kitaiskaya Gosudarstvennost' i Sovetskaya Politika v Kitae: Gody Tixookeanskoi Voiny, 1941–1945* [Chinese Statehood and Soviet Policy in China: The Period of Pacific War, 1941–1945]. Moscow: Pamyatniki Istoricheskoi Mysli, 1999.

Overy, Richard. *Russia's War.* Harmondsworth, UK: Penguin, 1997.

Panyushkin, Aleksandr Semyonovich. *Zapiski Posla: Kitai, 1939–44* [Notes of an Ambassador: China, 1939–44]. Ed. P. I. Smirnov. Moscow: Institute of the Far East, Academy of Sciences of the USSR, 1981 (privately printed and circulated).

Stanley, Roy M. *Prelude to Pearl Harbor.* New York: Charles Scribner's Sons, 1982.

Tikhvinskii, S. L., gen. ed. *Russko-Kitaiskie Otnosheniya v XX veke. Tom IV: Sovetsko-Kitaiskie Otnosheniya, 1937–1945 gg. Kn. 1: 1937–1944 gg.* [Russo-Chinese Relations in the Twentieth Century; Volume IV: Soviet-Chinese Relations, 1937–1945; Book I: 1937–1944]. Moscow: Pamyatniki Istoricheskoi Mysli, 2000.

Woff, Richard. "Vasily Ivanovich Chuikov." In Harold Shukman, ed., *Stalin's Generals.* London: DIANE Publishing Co., 1993, 67–74.

Yakovlev, A. G. "Nezabyvaemoe v Istorii" [Unforgettable in History]. *Problemy Dal'nego Vostoka,* 1984:1, 180–83.

Zhang Xianwen, gen. ed. *Zhongguo KangRi Zhanzheng Shi. 1931–1945)* [A History of China's War of Resistance Against Japan, 1931–1945]. Nanjing: Nanjing Daxue Chubanshe, 2001.

MISSION TO CHINA

*MEMOIRS OF A SOVIET MILITARY
ADVISER TO CHIANG KAISHEK*

Chapter 1

Prologue 1926: First Mission to China

It was not by chance that I was first sent to China in 1926. Now in my twenty-seventh year, I already had much experience of life. I had served on three fronts during the Civil War, commanding a regiment at the age of nineteen, and had been wounded in battle. In 1922, with the war over, I enrolled in the M. V. Frunze Military Academy in Moscow, as did many other veterans. When I graduated in 1925, it was recommended to me that I enter the academy's Far Eastern School to begin the study of Chinese. This was the very time the revolutionary movement of millions of peasants, workers and merchants was surging through China. As Soviet officers who had been inspired by our great leader Lenin to destroy the White armies and repel the foreign interventionists, we considered it an honor to take part in the national liberation movement of the Chinese people. We wished to help them in their struggle against the imperialist predators and completely took to heart the famous slogan of the time, "Hands off China."

We studied with great fervor and determination. Day and night we crammed Chinese characters into our heads and struggled to master their correct pronunciation. We painstakingly studied the history of China and the customs and traditions of its people. Our school was frequently visited by comrades who had been to China. They told us a great deal about what was going on there. We often went to the Narimanov Institute of Eastern Studies to attend meetings of the Chinese students, who discussed and argued over the problems of the Chinese revolution. I must admit that at the time we were still badly informed about the situation in China. It was not easy to understand the sudden changes in the revolutionary storm brewing there or to imagine what the future might bring.

In 1926 several of us were given the opportunity to make a trip to China. My duty was to act as a diplomatic courier. I was to proceed to Beijing via Harbin, Shenyang, Dalian, and Tianjin. Let the reader think back to that distant time and imagine the length of such a journey, first across Siberia and then through northeastern China. One has to remember that after the devastation of the Civil War the railway system was just coming back into regular use.

Siberia was familiar to me from my youthful military service. I had received my baptism of fire there as a regimental commander. The campaign against Kolchak and the other tsarist generals had been a bitter one. Now, from the windows of the train, peaceful railway stations flashed by. Villages and countryside had recovered from fire and devastation. The trains were often delayed, but no longer were they on the timetable of the Civil War. In 1919 our regiment had taken more than a month to get to Moscow from Kurgan in western Siberia by rail. Now the express (not the kind we have today, of course) brought us to the border of Manchuria in seven days. From there we were to continue our journey on the Chinese Eastern Railway (CER).

We crossed the border. We did not immediately sense that Russian soil was no longer under our carriage wheels; nor did we note any sharp change in the landscape. But soon, when glancing out the window during a train stop, we realized that we were in a different world. It was as if life had come to a stop here. In an instant we had been transported several years into the past.

On the platform Russian officers in uniform and shoulder boards were walking about. They had served under Kolchak or one of the Cossack chieftains and had been driven, along with their men, out of the motherland. The Chinese authorities now engaged them to protect the railroad. They continued to wear their old uniforms, waiting to be hired by the atamans Semyonov or Merkulov for some new bandit raid on Bolshevik Russia. We encountered not only army officers. Now and then a light blue gendarme's uniform would momentarily appear. For us this seemed to come out of an unbelievably ancient world.

We peered at the officers' faces with curiosity. Their uniforms were unclean, shabby and rumpled. There was none of that luster that always distinguished the officer corps of the tsarist army. These men exuded a guarded, hostile look. They at once recognized which of the passengers were Russians, in particular those who were diplomats and envoys from the land of the Soviets, which they detested. But that country was their homeland, and they appeared to long for it deeply. The sun did not shine on them in a foreign land, and with each passing year their hopes faded of returning as victors to the motherland that had banished them. Not all of them had hatred in their faces, though. In some a melancholy despair was to be seen. If these people could return, they would fall on their knees before their native land, but they feared the requital: they had sinned against the motherland—against the Russian people—and many bloody deeds lay behind them.

We saw these former officers and soldiers not only at stations near the border but deep inside Manchuria and other parts of China. They looked far from imposing in their old field shirts and tunics with the shoulder boards ripped off. At some small Chinese station we might catch sight of powerful, broad-shouldered Russian peasants with thick boyars' beards—Cossacks from the Urals, the Amur, and the Transbaikal. A strange fate had taken them from their fertile, fruitful lands, from their scythes and threshers, and had doomed them to an incomprehensible life as exiles. And here were officers—not just junior ones, but colonels and generals as well—who were in the service of one Chinese warlord or another, or who now worked for some big capitalist or were involved in dealings with Japanese intelligence. At a restaurant in a station I heard a White Guard song. It would have been a happy one, only the eyes of the singers were filled with a bewildered sadness:

> *Moscow the golden-domed, the bells that peal,*
> *The mighty tsar-cannon, the scent of your pies.*

Melancholy? Nostalgia? No, not only. The scene carried danger with it. These men who had been defeated and driven from our native soil thought of only one thing: to return to Russia and with bullet, bayonet, knout and gallows return the people to their former enslavement. There remained no other goal in life for them. Whenever possible they repeated one and the same thing, whether to the person sitting beside them on the train or to the individual sitting next to them at some banquet given by a Chinese warlord or Japanese commander: "Bolshevik Russia cannot not last. It's a giant with feet of clay—just touch it and it will collapse. Come join us and divide up the spoils! We'll give you our Baku oil, our Central Asian oases, our Siberian mines and virgin forests, and you can get us back our factories in Petersburg, Tula and the Urals, and our estates in Smolensk and Ryazan." With a generous hand these renegades scattered unrealizable promises, and wherever possible sowed hatred of our Soviet land.

It was interesting to observe former officers who had become railway personnel. Even in civilian clothes or railway uniform, the military bearing of these men made them unmistakably recognizable. From childhood they had been used to deference and respect; the orderly had always been there to clean their boots. And now they were sweeping the car, emptying out ashtrays for the passengers and receiving a few cents' tip from someone who needed his boots cleaned. Oh, how humiliating and difficult it was for a young master to have to work for a piece of bread! I thought back to my boyhood days at the Savelyev harness works and how the shop masters would teach us with a belt and keep us subject to their every whim. Was it really possible that these outcasts could nurse the hope that the millions of us who had given ourselves to the revolution would allow our country to return to its former state?

And so, in our capacity as diplomatic couriers, the old Bolshevik Rozhkov and I made our way to Beijing. In the coach we were often met with sidelong glances from our fellow countrymen. They recognized us as Russians and realized that we were Bolsheviks. Some guessed at the purpose of our trip. Rozhkov advised me to keep a pistol at the ready: the White Guards were nothing but common bandits, for whom a diplomatic courier was tempting prey. International law was an empty phrase to them. One of our couriers already had been the victim of an incident.

At last we were in Harbin. . . . The dangerous part of the journey was behind us. At the station we were met by our consular personnel. We could now breathe more freely and become acquainted with the city, which was the political and commercial heart of Manchuria. It was the provincial capital and the center for smuggling and espionage. The whole city was a black market, where currency, narcotics, guns and people were traded openly. Here everything was considered a commodity. If it was not immediately available, it could be supplied from any corner of the earth. The law did not permit the free import of goods, but there was not an official who was not prepared to ignore this for a bribe. I was never again to encounter moral debasement such as I saw in 1920s Harbin.

There were large numbers of Russians in the city, and not all of them exiles. Many had settled in Harbin during the building of the CER, and some had been born there. Their speech was markedly different from standard Russian, in both accent and vocabulary. Russian words often alternated with English, French and even Chinese expressions. Some of the local Russians were petitioning to return to the homeland. They had submitted requests for citizenship to our consulate. They were sympathetic to the Soviet Union and Bolshevism, despite the constant White Russian attempts to frighten them with "Bolshevik atrocities." When these people submitted their applications the consulate issued them a special receipt. The Whites dismissively called those who were awaiting their Soviet citizenship "receiptmen."

On the main street of Harbin, with its rows of stalls, all-night shops, booths and basement opium dens, I recall a memorable encounter. I was walking with some comrades from the consulate. We could be taken only for Soviet Russians, either diplomats or embassy workers. A man of about thirty-five, wearing a shabby, dusty officer's tunic, blocked our path. It was easy to tell from the traces of the small stars on his uniform that this man at one time had been a captain. He breathed Chinese vodka into my face. The man did not wordlessly extend his hand for alms—he still sought to preserve some nobility in his begging.

"Sirs, give to a former officer!"

We tried to get away from him, but he followed us.

"Sirs, sirs! You are Russians, and I am Russian. Do not let me die!"

Not every act is dictated by logic. This is even more the case when logic collides with feeling. I realized that this man, only a few years ago, had fought against us with weapon in hand, perhaps even against us on the eastern front. And we would have been shooting at each other. . . .

I handed him a dollar, which for a beggar was a huge amount. "Take this, sir," I said to him. "But we are not sirs [gospoda]! We call ourselves comrades now. And the person who has given you this dollar is a Bolshevik, a Soviet commissar."

The "captain" saluted, showing that he had not forgotten his military background even in such miserable circumstances. Uttering each word distinctly, he said: "I am grateful, sirs. I am ready to serve and obey your every command."

We thanked him for his readiness to "serve" and went on our way.

Harbin was a city of contrasts. On one side were the wealthy, making vast amounts of money in the wildest speculation. Once they had made their fortune, they moved away to a more tranquil locale. On the other side were the masses of the poor. The workers dragged out a half-wretched existence as well. A Chinese laborer considered it a stroke of good fortune to find a job in the CER under the Soviets. Here trade unions were organized, and the workers received better-than-average wages. We looked at the picture closely. Did a revolutionary situation exist in Harbin? Were the workers in Harbin ready for organized forms of protest? Alas, there were no indications of any such likelihood. The city was controlled by the black market and police terror, while the Whites stirred up trouble.

I spent five days in Harbin. Then we left for Shenyang, Dalian and Beijing. In Changchun we made the change from the CER to the South Manchurian Railway (SMR). Prior to the 1904–05 war between Russia and Japan, there was one unified railway, built by the tsarist government. Under the Treaty of Portsmouth the part of the SMR that ran from Changchun to Lushun was transferred to Japan. The Japanese became its sole masters, and something of a state within a state emerged. Chinese were employed only as common laborers.

The Japanese imposed a military discipline on the railway. The trains ran exactly on schedule. Dining cars were provided. Gone from the stations were the idlers, prostitutes and drunks, and the White soldiers with their missing shoulder boards. It was, however, a railway for the rich. The price of tickets was very high. In the dining cars trained chefs turned out excellent dinners, but such blessings were for the well-to-do. The portions were so small that a Russian would have to eat two or three meals in order not to leave the table hungry.

The port of Dalian (Dalny), like the adjacent naval fortress at Lushun (Port Arthur), was located at the southern end of the Liaodong Peninsula. Both had been acquired in 1898 on lease by the tsarist government. As a result of the 1904–05 war, they were transferred to Japan and, in effect, became Japanese cities on Chinese soil. The difference between them and their Chinese counterparts was vast. Dalian appeared as a well-built town, with modern architecture—an ice-free ocean port equipped with the most recent technology. The Japanese had built new factories and expanded others. The administration ran smoothly. There were also beggars in the city, but they were not allowed to appear on the main streets. We met many Europeans. Some were travelers, while others were in the shipping business. Rarely did one encounter a Russian. The Whites were not welcome here; rather, they were kept close to the Soviet border as cannon fodder for raids on our territory or as espionage agents in reserve. The Japanese made do with Chinese workers—they were cheaper and more docile. Everything was squeezed out of them. There was no one for them to turn to: there was no way they could assert their rights, and the Japanese authorities banned all trade union activity. We heard nothing of local communists during this time.

It was in Dalian that I first came into contact with the workings of Japanese counterintelligence. This service employed its own distinctive methods, which were quite different from Western practice. For example, Japanese agents shadowing us did not try to camouflage themselves in any way. They would follow on our heels, a couple of steps behind, making it clear that they were trailing us. The situation that developed was both comical and irksome. We would make a trip to one of the heavily frequented beaches, where we would divide up and enter the water, and there alongside each of us would be a determined Japanese. I would swim out from the shore, and my agent would swim after me.

The Japanese agents were most polite. If, when out on a walk, we needed a match to light a cigarette, there they were. One of our companions once went into a store, bought some trinket and purposely dropped it when he left. A Japanese detective obligingly picked it up and returned it to its owner with a charming smile, showing all his teeth. They did not try to stop us from doing anything, but they never fell a step behind us, and would accompany us right to the doors of the consulate. There, with a smile, they would make their bows and go off to their observation posts, where they would wait until we left to go into the city again. Unbelievable!

From Dalian our route was by sea. We boarded a Japanese passenger ship with our cases full of diplomatic correspondence. After rounding the Liaodong Peninsula we disembarked at the port of Tanggu, not far from Tianjin. From the sea I was able to catch sight of Lushun. I very much wanted to stop there, to pay my respects to the ashes of the Russian heroes who had died in its defense in 1904–05, but entry into Lushun was closed to Soviet citizens. It was now a Japanese base. Before docking at Tanggu a severe storm set upon us, which I weathered well, but not my comrades, who were violently ill. From Tianjin we went on by rail to our final destination.

To call Beijing the capital of China in 1926 was no more than an empty formality. There was a revolution in full storm throughout the nation. In July of that year the National Revolutionary Government in Canton launched the Northern Expedition, which cleared much of China as far as the Yangtze River of warlords. By time of our arrival in Beijing the position of the local power holders was badly shaken. Two generals, Zhang Zuolin and Wu Peifu, controlled the city. They were supported by the American, British, French and Japanese imperialists, who used the warlords to protect and strengthen their spheres of influence in China. Zhang Zuolin, warlord of Manchuria, leaned toward the Japanese, his "close neighbors." It should be noted that in 1928, when Zhang's political influence began to wane and differences emerged between him and his patrons, he was at once eliminated—Japanese agents killed him by placing a bomb under his railway car.

By the fall of 1926 the revolutionary armies advancing from the South had inflicted major defeats on Wu Peifu's forces. An atmosphere of uncertainty, something approaching a state of unreality, prevailed in Beijing, though this was not apparent to us immediately upon arrival. Officials of the Beijing government did their best to appear obliging and confident. But commercial life was in a feverish state. Banks were collapsing, new ones were springing up, and the whole financial world was rife with fraud and deception. Factory owners were hurrying to squeeze their last profits out of the workers' backbreaking toil. And, while this was going on, there remained, superficially, the quiet, measured life of the Legation Quarter. This was a state within a state, foreign territory on Chinese soil. Foreign troops were billeted there, together with a special police force that reported directly to the legation administration. Chinese were allowed into the quarter only on rare occasions and required a special permit to do so.

When I was in China I could never look at rickshaw pullers without feeling bitter about this affront to simple human dignity. Nor could I accept the idea that we, as communists, should avail ourselves of the labor of these human beasts of burden. Our embassy in Beijing once tried to stop using their services. When the rickshaw men learned of this, they came to the embassy with a plaintive appeal to lift the ban so that they would not lose the extra money. We had to acquiesce, but we never felt comfortable with this decision.

Beijing, Tianjin and the other Chinese cities I saw on this first trip made me think of a powder keg. But only through revolution could the people of China put an end to their terrible lack of rights. On their northern border the land of the Soviets offered them an example of how this might be done.

Chapter 2

A Discussion in the Kremlin

An Unexpected Assignment

On a fall day in 1940 I received a call to report at once to the people's defense commissar, Semyon Timoshenko. I at first saw nothing unusual in this, as commanders from the military districts were often summoned by the minister to give him firsthand briefings. But almost as soon as his office door closed behind me, I realized our meeting was going to be about something different.

Timoshenko informed me that the Party Central Committee's opinion, which he shared, was that I should go to China. Many of the details of the meeting have not remained in my memory, but the main points I recall. The minister told me straight away that the Soviet government had no faith in the nonaggression pact signed the preceding year with Germany and that, by every account, Hitler was preparing for war against us. Both the government and the defense ministry were of the opinion that Germany would not move alone. Timoshenko correctly identified Germany, Italy, Rumania and Finland as the leading members of the Axis war bloc that would attack us the following year.

Timoshenko continued: "We have no doubt about those four. We are concerned about Turkey, but what worries us more is what Japan will do. The Far Eastern situation, however, is a tough nut to crack. Whatever develops, we must keep a huge covering force out there against a possible Japanese move. . . . If we should we find ourselves in a two-front war, our long line of communications will give us many problems. . . . Japan is the big question so far as the German threat is concerned."

The minister summarized the current state of the Sino-Japanese war. When the Japanese attacked China they were counting on a quick victory. Their forces, however, had become bogged down in the Chinese interior. It was not evident how the Japanese might turn the situation around. Figures I was given on Japanese military strength were of interest. By the end of 1937 some twenty-six divisions totaling 832,000 men were in China. As of fall 1940 Japanese strength stood at thirty-five divisions and 1,120,000 men. But this increase of military capacity had not brought the Japanese any tangible results. This was well known from the news reports of the time.

"We can assume," Timoshenko said, "that in 1941 Japan will do everything it can to gain a military victory over Chiang Kaishek, or, if not, to negotiate a [favorable] settlement of the war. . . . The Japanese want to have their hands free when Hitler turns on us. They must have the way clear to attack us if they are to gain their objectives in the Far East. Our task is to help China hold off Japanese aggression. . . . I do not think Chiang Kaishek's army is capable of winning a decisive victory at present, but if the war goes on, the Chinese people ultimately will prevail over the Japanese militarists. . . . Next year will be the critical year of the war. Either the Chinese will hold their ground and repel every Japanese effort to gain the mastery, or else, if faced with major setbacks, Chiang Kaishek will be tempted to accept a one-sided peace settlement, foisted upon him by the Japanese. . . . Your task is to look into the situation in the Nationalist camp, take the measure of China's strength, and, as Chiang's chief military adviser, see to an increase in Chinese army activity." The minister added, "We have been providing Chiang Kaishek with military aid and will continue to do so, but this aid must be put to actual use against the Japanese."

I realized that my new assignment had not come about by accident. As the reader knows, the "China problem" was not unfamiliar to me. True, more than a decade had passed since I was last in that country, and much would have changed, but the underlying processes would still be the same as when I was there before. The minister outlined the nature of my appointment. Initially I was to be posted to the embassy in Chungking as military attaché to the Chinese Nationalist government. Then, once I had become familiar with the situation, my appointment as head of the Soviet military mission would follow. This would make me chief military adviser to the supreme commander of the Chinese army, Chiang Kaishek.

During our talk I learned of the considerable extent of Soviet military aid to China. This assistance was not always being used with the required skill. Supplies sent by us were often kept in reserve in the rear area. Battles that went badly for the Chinese often saw Japanese troops carrying off our weapons as trophies of war. My task was not only to assist the Chinese high command in their military operations; it was also to train the Chinese forces in the use of modern weaponry under the most advanced tactical conditions.

To the above responsibilities was added a further task. As military attaché and chief adviser, I was to restrain Chiang Kaishek's belligerent intentions toward the Chinese communist armies and the communist-controlled guerrilla areas. In other words, Chiang was to be kept out of a civil war and instead was to mobilize all China's strength against the common enemy. Timoshenko observed that the Chinese Red Army was eager to direct its military forces against Chiang Kaishek and to ignore the danger from Japan, which threatened the whole Chinese nation. The chief military adviser was to bring the Nationalist and Red Army forces into battle against the Japanese, regardless of the differences between them. Being familiar with the character of the Chinese military, I knew that coordinating operations between Chiang and the Chinese communists would be a complicated and delicate undertaking.

MY MEETING WITH STALIN

After I agreed to this new China mission, Timoshenko invited me to go with him in his car to the Kremlin. It was my understanding that I was to have an important discussion with the Party Central Committee. I certainly did not expect that I was to have a meeting with Stalin himself.

A series of long corridors brought us to a reception office, where Stalin's personal secretary, A. I. Poskrebyshev, reported our arrival. This was my first meeting with Stalin. I had only seen Stalin before on a public platform. Now we stood just a few feet apart.

After introducing ourselves, Stalin, without losing a moment, asked me: "What has been decided? Are you willing to go to this country you know so well?"

"I am willing to go wherever I am sent."

"Not so fast! You have to think carefully about where you are being sent."

Stalin returned to his desk and asked us to be seated. "We have to give this some thought and preparation. You were in China in the 1920s. . . . That was one era; now it is the 1940s, a different era. At that time the Nationalist Party was led by Dr. Sun Yatsen. He was a man of the highest moral probity, devoted wholeheartedly to the interests of his people. We had just begun to establish close ties with him. Despite our own problems at home, we helped the Chinese revolution in every way possible, without thought of recompense. Today's rulers of China are not of his kind. And neither is the Guomindang what it was then. Chiang Kaishek is a mere pup compared to the tiger Sun Yatsen.

"There is a new force that has arisen in China—the Communist Party. Chiang Kaishek can count on the petty bourgeoisie and feudal military chieftains, the peasant masses [sic] and on those big capitalists not tied to Japanese capital. The working class follows the communists first and foremost. . . . You were in China and must know that China is a peasant country, not a proletarian one. In China the working class is significantly inferior to the peasantry, not just in numbers but also in its capacity for organization. For centuries the Chinese peasantry has been subject to inhuman oppression. The Chinese peasant is a beaten and exhausted man. Compared to the worker, he is timid, but the peasantry in its mass is capable of great exploits, as history has shown. The Chinese Communist Party draws its support from the most downtrodden, illiterate and poverty-stricken peasants. It underestimates the growing working class, and this cannot but affect the party's ideology, slogans and grasp of the political tasks of the revolution. Nationalistic tendencies are quite pronounced in the Chinese party, and feelings of international solidarity are inadequately developed. Instead of joining in a united front against the Japanese aggressor, Mao Tsetung and Chiang

Kaishek cannot forget their old differences. The struggle goes on between them for influence and power. Mao fears Chiang and Chiang fears Mao."

Stalin spoke slowly, carefully pondering each sentence. He pronounced every word distinctly, and at the end of each phrase he paused, as if to invite Timoshenko or me to express any doubts we might have. Questions came to mind, of course. The main one was why I was being sent to Chiang Kaishek and not to the Chinese Red Army. But the time was not appropriate for questions. Stalin, though, guessed at many of the ones I wanted to ask, and addressed them. He lit his pipe and continued: "It would seem that the Chinese communists are closer to us than Chiang Kaishek and that our aid should be given mostly to them. But such aid would make it look as if we were exporting revolution to a country with which we have diplomatic relations. The CCP [Chinese Communist Party] and the working class are still too weak to lead the struggle against the aggressor. It will require time—how much is difficult to say—for them to win over the masses. Apart from that, the imperialist powers will scarcely allow Chiang Kaishek to be replaced by the Communist Party. We have concluded formal agreements with Chiang's government. You will familiarize yourself with all the documents and act in the strictest accord with them. The task at hand is to unite all forces in China in order to repel the enemy.

"The communist position in China is still precarious. Chiang Kaishek can easily ally himself with the Japanese against the communists, but the communists cannot ally themselves with the Japanese against Chiang. America and Britain are providing Chiang with aid. Mao Tsetung will never receive any support from those powers unless he betrays the communist movement. Hitler's victories in Europe will likely lead America and Britain to increase their aid to Chiang. When theirs is added to what we have provided, it gives us hope that Chiang will be able to tie down the Japanese aggressors for a long time, even if he cannot overcome them."

In the course of our discussion, Stalin got up several times and walked toward us while further working out his ideas. "We must not think," he said, "that the compromisers in the West have departed the scene now that France has fallen. At the moment, in these difficult days for the British people, appeasers are going back and forth between London and Berlin, ready at any moment to make new concessions if only Germany will turn its guns against the Soviet Union. As for the Chinese communists, some of them have had their heads sent spinning by Hitler's easy victories in Europe and Japan's easy victories over Chiang. They seem to think that if the Japanese smash Chiang, the situation in China will turn in their favor and they will then be able to drive out the Japanese. They are very much mistaken. As soon as Chiang feels he is in danger of losing power, or if the West should stop giving him aid, he will at once find a way to work with the Japanese militarists, following the example of Wang Jingwei. Chiang Kaishek and the Japanese will then turn their combined forces upon the Chinese communists, leaving the Red Army no escape.

"Your task, Comrade Chuikov, is not only to help Chiang Kaishek and his commanders make the best use of the equipment we are sending them, but also to fill them with confidence that victory over the Japanese invader will be theirs. If he is assured of victory, Chiang will not come to an understanding with the enemy—and he fears the loss of aid from America and Britain, as well as the loss of Chinese capital held in their banks. . . . Your task, Comrade Chuikov, and the task of all our people in China, is to tightly bind the hands of the Japanese. Only when the enemy's hands are bound can we be free of a war on two fronts if the Germans attack our country."

THE PROSPECT AHEAD

My mission had been formulated clearly and precisely. Stalin asked me not to divulge the contents of our talk. This, of course, was an unnecessary reminder. As a professional soldier, commander of a regiment at nineteen, I understood the meaning of military and state secrets. Stalin's cautionary words were, for me, only an indication of the high confidence with which he assigned me a task whose success would not come easily.

I was given a limited amount of time to prepare myself. In order to understand the current situation in China, I had to do some intensive work in the appropriate government ministries and institutes. The Ministry of Foreign Affairs was especially helpful in providing materials for me to familiarize myself with official policy. As I looked through all these documents and sources, and as I recalled everything I had experienced earlier in China, I had to admit that I knew little, very little, about that country. However, I did understand from my time there what an enormous role centuries-old tradition played in the life of its people. The old order weighed heavily upon all ranks of the populace. The Chinese people were only just awakening from their sleep of centuries.

I was aware of the highly contradictory and complicated political situation in China. The ruling Nationalist Party—the Guomindang (GMD)—was an agglomeration of antagonistic but coexisting political and military factions. Alongside it stood the Chinese Communist Party, which had its own armed forces for the struggle against reaction. Chiang Kaishek had been compelled to enter into a united front with the CCP to fight the external enemy. What interested me, of course, was the specific question of how effective this alliance might be in repelling Japanese aggression. In the course of its arduous struggle, the CCP had worked out its own strategy, tactics and political program. It is not surprising that this might have given rise to a large number of errors and that opportunists might have attached themselves to the party and led it onto a path away from Marxism. These concerns were not at the time linked in my mind to any particular names, but I already knew that the history of the Chinese communist movement was rife with struggles between groups and factions.

I thought repeatedly of the challenge ahead of me. I was going to a man—Chiang Kaishek—who could not be trusted in any way. I was going with the task of helping him fight a war against an enemy that had fallen upon his country. Nothing seemed simpler than that. But Chiang was waging this war against Japan in alliance with the communists, whom he considered his real enemy. I was going to a broker, a money changer, who under the right set of circumstances would sell out his country and people without a second thought. I was to teach him patriotism? No, I was going to China to help its people drive the foreign invader from their land.

There are those who will say: So, you're a benefactor, but weren't you using China to fight a war against Japan on your behalf? I heard this comment at the time and have heard it since. But Japan did not attack the Soviet Union, not even during the darkest days of the German invasion. It was China that was drowning in blood and needed our help. Those who wish to be objective must admit to the obvious and indisputable facts.

Chapter 3

The Tiger's Tooth

I could have spent months preparing for China, but I had to hurry. My departure was set for December 1940. My predecessor as military attaché to China, P. S. Rybalko, was already back in Moscow.

To be honest, I was leaving for China with mixed feelings. I believed major events were about to happen on our western border, so of course I wanted to offer my experience as a commander there. It was also difficult to leave my family. My newborn daughter, Irinka, had just taken seriously ill. I consoled myself with the thought that I might be of use to my homeland in the highly complex world of China, even though I could not rid myself of the feeling that Chungking was very much a backwater, far from the important crossroads of the world. Here I was to be mistaken.

In accord with protocol, I called on the Chinese embassy and the Chinese military attaché before departing from Moscow. I did not expect to learn anything from either of these formal visits. In all likelihood, the Chinese themselves knew little about what was going on in their country. Still, from allusions made by the Chinese military attaché I could see that the embassy was worried about political developments at home, especially in regard to relations between the Chinese Communist Party and the Guomindang.

Fifteen military advisers and technical specialists left for China with me. None of them, unfortunately, knew a great deal about China, and none of them had a command of the language. In their own fields, of course, they were highly qualified. Our government was also sending Chiang Kaishek a large amount of military aid: 150 fighter planes, 100 SB high-speed bombers, some 300 artillery pieces and 500 ZIS-5 trucks, along with spare parts and other necessary items.

EN ROUTE TO CHUNGKING

In December 1940 our group left Moscow by train. Five days later we reached Alma Ata, the capital of Kazakhstan. From there we were to fly to Chungking, which meant taking one of the most difficult air routes of the time. The flight through the snow-covered mountains was not an easy matter for either civilian or military aircraft. December was a month of rain, fog and snowfalls. We had to wait several days for flying weather. But, as always, all delays come to an end. Our plane took off, accompanied by twenty SB bombers we were delivering to Chiang Kaishek. Our squadron crossed the mountains marking the border with Xinjiang province and landed at a small airfield at Shihezi. Here there was another delay. The mists once more had closed the passages through the mountains. Finally this delay passed. In the air again—and new problems: the wings of our plane iced over. But, happily, within a few hours we landed in Lanzhou, the capital of Gansu province.

At the airfield we were met by General Zhu Shaoliang, commander of the Eighth War Zone. An honor guard was drawn up for our reception. This clearly meant that the general had been forewarned of our arrival and given detailed instructions. From this moment my diplomatic work in China began.

Talks, banquets and reciprocal courtesy visits followed from that first day. General Zhu was a man trusted by Chiang Kaishek. He belonged to the inner circle of Whampoa Academy officers who had helped Chiang mount his counterrevolutionary coup against the communists in April 1927. Chiang put him in charge of an army to guard the land and air routes between the Soviet Union and China. This force constituted Chiang's defensive reserve in Xinjiang. It also served to complete the encirclement of the CCP Special Region in northern Shaanxi.

From my solicitous host I tried to learn about the situation in China and to discover here, far from the center of things, what he thought of the progress and long-term prospects of the Sino-Japanese War. Zhu Shaoliang, in turn, was anxious to learn "firsthand" of conditions on the Soviet Union's western borders and to inform himself of the present relationship between the Soviet

Union and the Chiang regime. In short, at this crossroads two would-be diplomats met, each determined to make a display of his talents. The situation had its humor. For the Chinese general this was a fleeting encounter. When I left, that would be the end of it. But for me it was my first lesson in how to conduct myself with Chiang Kaishek's generals.

If someone were innocently to suggest that the smile of the Chinese official was a mark of his friendship and candor, that person would be badly mistaken. They say that a diplomat is given a tongue to conceal his thoughts. General Zhu was not a professional diplomat, but he knew how to conceal his thoughts more skillfully than the most subtle diplomat of the old European school. He could not draw anything out of me, of course—I knew how to be silent, or else, if somewhat brusquely, to simply evade the question. But the general talked on, speaking even more ingratiatingly, smiling amiably, and pouring out a powerful raw Chinese brandy into my glass.

Our mutual visits continued. Day after day the airfield staff told me the same thing: it was not flying weather. My own plane had already returned home. According to the agreement, a Chinese aircraft was to bring us from Lanzhou to Chungking. We felt that Chiang Kaishek must be impatiently awaiting our arrival, especially as we were bringing him sorely needed equipment. Meanwhile, I was hearing from our pilots that the Chinese were bluffing about the weather. It was clearly not because of bad flying conditions that we were being detained. Could it really be that our host wanted personally to scrutinize the Soviet envoys to China?

I then received some news whose disturbing import I could not really gauge while I was in Lanzhou. Our local consul had learned of a suspicious regrouping of Chiang Kaishek's forces in the vicinity of the communist Special Region in northern Shaanxi province. The motives of the Chinese high command remained hidden. The consul expressed fear that Chiang might again be moving toward a civil war. I had heard nothing of this before leaving Moscow. Reports from our military advisers in Chungking contained no such suggestion. My understanding was that Chiang harbored no hostile intentions toward the CCP. The situation at the front had been going badly for him up to this point. I knew that he was very much pleased to learn of our most recent offer of assistance. If he launched a campaign against the Special Region, not only would this draw him away from resisting Japan but it would also cause him much new trouble, as the Soviet Union would terminate its military aid.

Under such circumstances, we could not drift along further in Lanzhou. I had to tell General Zhu quite plainly that, according to information I had received, good flying conditions now prevailed and that further delay in our departure would not be the result of the weather. General Zhu received my remarks with some irritation. I insisted on leaving immediately for Chungking and was right in doing so. Chiang Kaishek and his staff apparently had become concerned about our delay. From Chungking a single-engine, three-seater plane came for me and my assistant, G. M. Gorev. We were given a send-off from Lanzhou as festive as our arrival had been. Our Chinese pilot then expertly navigated the difficult passage through the mountains. Several times our wings froze over, but with a skillful maneuver he shook off the ice by diving down into warmer currents of air. We watched as the ice fell off.

In Chungking we landed to a grand reception. As the faces of our welcomers passed by in quick succession I could not immediately recognize anyone I knew. The military had a strong representation, but there were civilians present as well. Then with some surprise I caught sight of a number of men in general's uniform who were known to me from my work in Khabarovsk in 1930–32. They undoubtedly recognized me but acted otherwise. I too made the pretense of meeting them now for the first time. I could not begin to determine what this meant. Were they at the airfield as representatives of the Chinese communists, or were they there, for reasons known only to them, as members of Chiang Kaishek's military entourage? I did not know and did not try to find out. I must say things often seemed confusing. People not infrequently moved from the CCP to the GMD, and there were those who went from the GMD to the CCP. Sometimes this was done intentionally to place agents in the ranks of the other party.

From the airfield Gorev and I set off to the embassy. There I first met Aleksandr Semyonovich Panyushkin, our ambassador to China. Almost forty years have passed since then. During all the years I knew him, right up to his death, nothing interrupted our friendship, even though we often disagreed heatedly during our time in China. Panyushkin was young and energetic. He had entered the diplomatic service after graduation from the Frunze Academy. At the time of my arrival in China, he had been there two years and was fully conversant with the local situation. He was adept at reading the intentions of China's leaders, many of whom he knew personally, and he was an accurate judge of their character, abilities and political loyalties.

I introduced myself to our fine staff in the military attaché's office. My deputy, Colonel N. V. Roshchin, was a brave and intelligent officer who knew the country well. He had built up reliable connections with the Chinese as well as with the Americans and British. Our interpreter, Stepan Petrovich Andreev, was the consummate expert, completely fluent in Chinese and more than adequate in English. Andreev had skillfully developed contacts with officials and staff members in many government departments. He associated with these people in a friendly and unassuming manner. Roshchin and Andreev gave me great help, especially in understanding the current situation in China. All of the people in our office were ready to use their experienced judgment to take the initiative rather than sit back awaiting detailed instructions.

FIRST MEETING WITH CHIANG KAISHEK

We arrived in Chungking on the last day of 1940. That evening I was introduced to Chiang Kaishek at a New Year's eve banquet he was giving for our military advisers. I understood Chiang wanted to meet me right away in order to find out what we were bringing with us and when it would be arriving. Chiang was also very much interested in events in Europe and wanted to find out how the Soviet Union viewed the current situation there. He tried to squeeze out of me everything I knew, but I was ready for this. I did not say much about our western borders; instead I talked largely of Hitler's unresolved problems in the West, in particular Great Britain.

My first meeting with the supreme ruler of China was brief. The occasion was more one of protocol. All the same, it was helpful to me in forming an impression of Chiang Kaishek. He was short in height, thin of frame and dressed in a regular-issue uniform. He was not wearing epaulettes, only some medals in the buttonhole of his tunic. There was a cunning look in his dark, slanting eyes. His false teeth protruded sharply. He was a man predatory by nature, expert in marching over the bodies of the dead toward his goals, willing to use blackmail and deceit. Among the common people it was said that at night Chiang Kaishek placed a tiger's tooth under his pillow. His frequent interjections of "Hao, hao" (Good, good) grated upon the ear.

As mentioned, on this occasion Chiang was concerned most of all with our military aid and with the situation in Europe. But Chiang's words also conveyed an unspoken message, which seemed to say: "Don't regard yourselves as our benefactors: it will be my friendship, or simply my neutrality, that you will need when Hitler turns against you." I emphasized to him that the Soviet government practiced and would continue to practice the politics of peace, and that it would do everything possible not to become involved on anyone's side in the conflict. We had the most peaceful intentions toward Germany, but if Hitler should suddenly lose his wits and launch an attack on Soviet territory, he would encounter a ready army and would meet a response the like of which he had never yet encountered.

Chiang assumed an air of concern and said: "Who would have thought the French and British armies would go down to defeat in only a few weeks?"

He was far removed from the fates overtaking Europe, but one sensed in his tone and the way he pronounced his words a certain liking for Hitler. I answered: "If Hitler had not made his surprise attack through Belgium, or if the Anglo-French air force had struck his tank divisions when they were stretched out thin as a wire in the

Ardennes, the war would have been over in several days and quite likely with different results."

"There are three powers that have not been drawn into the present [European] conflict," Chiang observed, "the Soviet Union, the United States, and China. These three powers will determine the future. In other words, three people will decide the destiny of the world."

I took advantage of our meeting to ask why China had held out so long against Japan. There were many times later that I thought of Chiang's answer to this question. Even now it gives me cause for reflection.

"Japan cannot conquer China!" After a short pause, Chiang added: "China cannot be conquered. For China the war is an illness, that is all. And every illness passes."

"But illness can lead to death," I objected.

"No! We do not believe that illness means death. Death is not an illness—death comes of its own, regardless of illness."

This Chinese leader is clever, I thought. He is not so simple. Yes indeed, not simple. To begin as a money changer, a petty broker, and then to gain power over a huge country! He is talented, but his talents serve evil as well as good. And no, he is not a puppet in the hands of some unknown power. Here in China he himself is power, and only by power will he be destroyed. Not by plots or schemes or government coups, but only by the tide of the people's wrath.

FIRST IMPRESSIONS OF THE MILITARY SCENE

And so passed the first official meeting between Chiang Kaishek and the military attaché of the Soviet Union. Chiang asked me to convey his appreciation to my government for the aid it had sent. He recommended that I begin studying the current situation in China. I asked him then and there for a directive in order to study conditions at the front. I was promised the cooperation of the General Staff, but none of the senior Chinese generals proved in a hurry to be of assistance.

It was my colleagues in the embassy and the chief military advisorate, and my immediate co-workers in the military attaché's office, who enlightened me on current Chinese matters. Disagreements arose among us on a number of issues, which I need not go into here. (I should mention that our various military representatives in Chungking were not under one unified command. There were no administrative links between the offices of the military attaché, the chief military adviser and the deputy director of intelligence work. All three reported directly to the center, Moscow.) Our main problem was not differences among ourselves; rather, it was Moscow's unwillingness to believe that the GMD was moving toward a crisis with the communists. Moscow saw the lack of frontline Chinese military activity as the main problem with which we had to contend. But in Chungking everything was much more complicated.

In regard to the situation at the front, the Japanese up to this time had prevailed in every engagement, even when outnumbered by the Chinese—and even though the Chinese were gradually reducing their material disadvantage. The head of the Special Intelligence Office of the Military Affairs Commission, Admiral Yang Xuancheng, readily produced figures on the size of the Japanese army in China. It must be said that Chinese intelligence functioned not that badly. When I was later able to compare his numbers with the official record, I found hardly any discrepancy. At the end of 1939 the Japanese had had thirty-five divisions and 1.1 million men in China. If we add in the Chinese warlords and militarists who had gone over to the Japanese, overall enemy strength would approach 1.5 million. A million and a half well-armed and well-trained soldiers was a huge force.

It cannot be said that the GMD and communists had done nothing to resist Japanese aggression. If the Chinese army had not resisted, there would have been no need for the Japanese to build up such numbers. Their army would have marched from one end of China to the other, completely subjugating the country. The Chinese had checked the Japanese invasion with their defensive warfare. The enemy was now tied down. Each forward advance by the Japanese demanded another "island" of occupying troops. Furthermore, because of the reverse suffered at the hands of the Soviet Union at Nomonhan (Khalkhingol) in 1939, the Japanese found it necessary to keep the large and well-trained Kwantung Army permanently stationed in Manchuria.

THE WARTIME CAPITAL

Chungking, the provisional capital of Chiang Kaishek's government, was located on the steep left bank of the Yangtze at the point where the Jialing River flowed into it. Here the Yangtze Valley was closed off on all sides by high ranges. Few roads led into the city, and there were no bridges across the river. There was no heavy industry in the city or its outskirts: almost everything was made by hand or by means of hand-operated machines. All of Chungking's energy needs were provided by one small electric power station, which somehow supplied the city with lighting and water.

What struck me first of all were the dirt and the large number of rats to be found even in the city center. You could walk along a street in daytime and see dozens of the rodents scurrying past your feet. Dogs and cats meant nothing to them. On the main streets modern-style homes of three to five stories stood alongside the hovels in which the common people lived, worked and traded. There were no trams, though a few automobiles of different makes from various countries were to be seen. For the great mass of the working population, their feet provided their transportation. The automobile was preferred by the high officials and the rich, but its use was limited, as so many of the streets were connected to each other by ladderlike staircases, on which even rickshaws could not move. As a result, sedan chairs were to be seen everywhere.

The Yangtze River appeared to the eye like a reddish yellow mass. Bodies of dead animals floated everywhere in it, and sometimes even those of human beings. Without chlorination, water from the river could not be used for drinking unless boiled. But what could be used to boil it? Where could fuel be obtained? This was the kind of problem that confronted every family. For the workers, clerks and petty officials, living standards were so low that even government employees would change clothes after arriving home from their office and hire out a cart or sedan chair to serve the well-to-do as porters or rickshaw coolies.

From time to time Chiang Kaishek would step forth as the guardian of public morality. He would issue decrees shutting down brothels and places of pleasure. They were officially closed, but underground ones soon appeared in their place. Chiang ordered an end to opium smoking, threatening the death penalty, but on the streets you could see opium smokers lying there in ecstasy, counting the stars in the clear sky of a bright, sunny day. The city was crowded with beggars, lepers and cripples, all stretching out their hands for alms.

The food situation in Chungking was very serious. The best the city could do was provide one-quarter of its rice needs. In order to provide for those working in state institutions, such as officials, war workers and teachers, the government supplied rice at low cost. The great majority of the population (craftsmen, petty merchants, coolies, rickshaw pullers and even independent professionals such as doctors, writers and artists) were not covered. They had to buy their rice on the open market at extremely high and constantly rising prices. In June 1941 the price index stood at 3,214 percent, based on July 1937. The continuing shortages and the high cost of rice led to endless talk and rising dissatisfaction among the population. Long lines formed in front of the rice shops. People stood for hours or days, waiting for the delivery of rice. There were outbreaks of violence in the lines, leading to a number of deaths at police hands.

The government was forced to cut down on the number of institutions whose workers could buy rice at reduced rates. But conditions were exceptionally bad even for those working directly for the government in schools, universities and hospitals. Students suffered from malnutrition. Death from physical exhaustion was a common occurrence. Hospitals could not feed their patients. The average office worker barely managed to get by. Most of the manual laborers lived in want, earning only three or four dollars for a twelve-to-fourteen-hour day. Life for the coolies and rickshaw pullers was especially bad. There was a common saying at the time: "The general beats the officer, the officer beats the soldier and the soldier beats the rickshaw man." At the top of the social ladder stood the financial and industrial bourgeoisie, the big landlords and the upper levels of officialdom.

Speculation flourished. Goods were brought in from Shanghai, Canton and other cities occupied by the Japanese, as well as from Hong Kong, which was cut off from Free China by the Japanese army. In Chungking, as in every other large city, you could buy Swiss Longines watches, American Gillette razors, Kodak cameras and all sorts of other goods—but, of course, at outrageous prices. These items came in along the Burma Road (which ran from Rangoon to Kunming) or else made their way in from the Japanese-occupied seacoast. They found an avenue through the whole of China.

You could find everything you wanted in the right food stores: meats and sausages, poultry, and spirits of all kinds, from Jamaican rum to Chinese maotai. These goods adorned the tables of the well-to-do. There was one part of the city where the smells of food cooking in restaurants, or more often in cauldrons standing in the street, overwhelmed the passerby. Without fail, a "salesman" stood nearby, loudly proclaiming the praises of the dish and inviting everyone to sample it. The working people, however, had to be satisfied with rice of the poorest sort, taken with some garlic and vegetables.

In the spring of 1941 the Japanese launched a massive air offensive against Chungking. Their intention was to sow panic among the population and break the Chinese will to resist. The Japanese were so brazen that they would announce in the press when they were going to bomb Chungking, knowing very well that their planes would not meet any strong resistance. For example, the Japanese might give notice of a four-day bombardment of the Chinese capital. Although such operations were not mounted on a major scale—formations of three, five or nine enemy planes were the routine—they put the whole population under a state of constant pressure and forced people into sitting out the raids in bomb shelters. The Japanese always maintained that they were destroying military targets. But during my time in Chungking neither the War Ministry nor the

General Staff headquarters was hit even once. Since these would hardly be considered nonmilitary targets, I thought something else must be at work here.

In the favorable summer weather the raids might occur at any time of day. All life in the city came to a halt. The power station turned off its boilers, and the water pumps stopped. After a bombing raid, and especially after any damage to the electricity supply, the inhabitants of the city faced difficult days. Electric lighting and the water supply were cut off. Porters now went to work, drawing water out of the river and carrying it up to the city on poles over their shoulders. Not only the Chinese suffered during the bombing—the foreign embassies did as well, our own mission among them. Over the course of my stay in China I moved five times, as five places in which I lived were destroyed down to the very foundations. During the summer months we lived several miles out in the country, from where we watched the city under attack. So things went until the change of weather in the autumn brought a respite from the raids.

During the bombing the ordinary citizens usually took refuge in huge shelters, while the well-off left the city by car, taking their valuables with them. Most of the bomb shelters in the city did not have ventilation, light or benches. People had to stand on their feet for hours, unable to sit. Many shelters did not have doors. The detonation of a bomb in the immediate vicinity meant many fatalities. There were cases of incendiary bombs setting fire to buildings nearby, with the people in the shelters dying from either asphyxiation or the intense heat. The most notorious example of mass death occurred in the course of a Japanese night attack on June 5, 1941. Into a shelter of the tunnel type, intended for twenty-five hundred people, more than five thousand were packed. The shelter had neither ventilation nor lighting. The alert lasted approximately four hours. People soon began to suffocate from lack of air. Their attempts to get out were blocked by police guarding the entrance. When those inside became desperate, the police locked the doors and made off. As a result, everyone in the shelter perished from suffocation. This mass tragedy aroused great indignation in the population. Chiang Kaishek, however, confined himself to a token response. Garrison commander Liu Zhi and the city mayor were formally relieved of office, as they were deemed responsible for the shelter tragedy. In fact, both men were kept on in their administrative capacities.

The harsh and arbitrary behavior of the authorities came out in another way during the raids, and this too had a detrimental effect on overall public morale. In order to remove excess population from the city during the summer raids, the government forcibly evacuated people whose presence in the city was deemed nonessential. The relocation was carried out brutally. There were cases of children who returned home from school and were unable to find their parents, who had been loaded onto trucks and removed. Tragic accidents occurred. In May 1941 a clash between police and evacuees due for removal resulted in their boat overturning and many drowning.

The Japanese air raids had an oppressive effect upon the inhabitants of the city. The poor and middling levels of the population suffered most severely from the loss of homes, life and property. But, all told, one must give the Chinese people full credit for their endurance. They steadfastly held up under the unceasing attacks. Their spirit was not broken.

CHAPTER 4

TAKING STOCK OF THE WAR EFFORT

THE NATIONALIST ARMY

At the summit of the Chinese military structure stood Chiang Kaishek. He had awarded himself the rank of generalissimo, but we in the Soviet mission always addressed him as marshal. The Chinese referred to Chiang as chairman of the military commission *(weiyuanzhang)*. Army administration was handled by the General Staff office under General He Yingqin, who was concurrently minister of war.

In April 1941 Chiang had under his command approximately 290 infantry divisions. These were supported by 14 cavalry divisions, 22 artillery regiments, 6 howitzer divisions and some specialized units. (A Chinese division, it should be noted, was rated at about 7,500 men, half the size of its Japanese counterpart.) The official strength of the Nationalist army stood at 3,856,000 men. However, some Chinese armies and divisions existed in name only. The roster carried a good number of "dead souls."

By 1941 most of the major industrial and commercial centers of coastal China were under Japanese occupation. The principal railway lines and water routes were also in enemy hands. In all, the Japanese controlled 22 percent of China's land area, where 42.5 percent of the population lived. However, this still left 57.5 percent of the population—270 million out of 470 million people—in Free China. If we calculate the potential for conscription as 10 percent of the male population, Nationalist China could raise about 12 million men. Whatever the actual strength of the Nationalist army might be, it appeared that another 8 million men could be mobilized. This was more than enough for continuing the war.

The government had passed a general military service act in 1938. Provincial, divisional and regimental mobilization districts were established, and men between the ages of eighteen and thirty-five were made subject to call-up. Training consisted mainly of rifle drill and political lectures. The latter consisted of rote memorization of the most elementary phrases. For example: "Who are the murderers of our parents and brothers? Who are the violators of our wives and daughters? Who are the destroyers of our homes and our factories? If it is the Japanese, are they or are they not our enemies?" And so on. There was, of course, only one answer. China's misfortunes were completely due to the Japanese. Class enemies and class struggle did not exist in China. Any internal disorder was the work of troublemakers—in other words, the communists.

The highest operational body under the Nationalist command was the war zone *(zhanqu)*. Nine of these had been set up since the outbreak of the war. (The war zone corresponded to our definition of a front.) Chiang Kaishek also held a number of armies in reserve. Hu Zongnan's 34th Army Group, for example, was based in southern Shaanxi in order to cover the communist Special Region in the north of the province. Certain armies, such as the 5th and 6th, were accorded special treatment, as they were mainstays of Chiang's power. They were deployed behind the lines, usually to garrison large centers of population or guard major points of communication.

The War Ministry administered a number of military schools, including a central officers' academy. Chiang Kaishek was nominally principal of each, but actual authority lay in the hands of the deputy directors. As a rule, the Nationalists carefully selected the young men who attended these schools. Communists were not to be admitted, but it proved impossible to keep them completely out or to shield the cadets from their influence. These schools guaranteed the army a steady supply of officers. Our advisers provided considerable assistance in operational and tactical instruction. Of course, manpower reserves and officers' academies alone would not ensure China success in its struggle with Japan. That would largely depend on how well trained and well equipped the men were, how well instructed the officer corps was and how willing the army was to implement the most up-to-date methods of war. But in these respects, as we have seen, the situation stood much to the worse.

One of the most acute problems for wartime China was the supply of weapons and ammunition. This was particularly so in regard to artillery and aircraft, neither of which China produced. The nation's many small workshops turned out only light weapons, which were of amazing variety. Since local production did not meet army demand, the government had to buy from abroad. In 1940 the Nationalist army had an artillery inventory as follows: small-caliber weapons, 1,250; medium-caliber (75/76 mm), 997; heavy (over 75 mm), 171; mortars of various sizes, 5,795. Rounds of ammunition were as follows: small caliber (antitank included), 4,680,000; medium caliber, 278,600; heavy caliber, 68,000; antiaircraft, 75,000. All heavy and most medium artillery was kept in the rear area and not used in battle. If one considers that Chiang Kaishek was holding back a good part of his artillery for a possible offensive against the communist Special Region, then one can see why so many Chinese armies lacked the firepower necessary to reduce enemy defenses or neutralize enemy weaponry.

I have not mentioned tanks, since these were old models, used only for show. Warplanes were of various sorts from different countries. The air force was small in size and played little role in military operations. Much effort had gone into training pilots, and the Chinese had mastered their tasks well. But whenever the Japanese launched an air raid, Chinese planes, as a rule, flew off to airfields further to the rear and did not go into action. Air units were not assigned to the war zones or to individual army groups, so air support rarely could be counted upon in battle. The army was deficient in motor transport. Since China lacked an auto industry, this remained a problem. Repair facilities for vehicles were of poor quality. A general shortage of gasoline compounded the transport problem. Repair shops for aircraft were primitive. I visited some of these in Chengdu. They were little more than sheds with straw roofs and wicker walls.

THE RELATIONSHIP OF THE COMMUNIST FORCES TO THE NATIONALIST ARMY

Communist regular forces were theoretically subordinate to the Military Commission in Chungking. The Nationalists officially recognized two communist armies. The 8th Route Army, redesignated by the Military Commission as the 18th Army Group, was based in northern Shaanxi. The New 4th Army was concentrated in the lower Yangtze Valley. They resembled their Nationalist counterparts in externals but differed in certain important ways. For example, the Nationalist government had limited the New 4th Army to one division. But this division was more than 60,000 strong, exclusive of thousands of guerrilla fighters. The War Ministry in Chungking knew of this, as did Chiang Kaishek, but nothing could be done about it. They were powerless to block the growth of communist strength.

Inside the Special Region were schools for training army officers and political cadres. We had no advisers in any of them, however, as the Nationalists restricted our activities to their own war zones. Our only people in the Special Region were a few news correspondents. Entry into the communist area required approval from Chiang Kaishek. I was constantly sending him requests for travel clearance: for a shipment of medicines, next for a party of war correspondents and Comintern representatives, then for a planeload of 18th Army Group officers on their way back from one of our military institutes. Chiang never refused my requests, but he always intimated the greatest displeasure in agreeing to them.

Chiang kept control of all weapons coming into China from abroad, whether purchased or received as aid. Since the communists, in his view, were his principal rivals, he gave them nothing when distribution took place. As military attaché, I could not interfere in the allocation of equipment to the Chinese armies. The communists, nevertheless, were able to arm themselves very much at the expense of the Japanese. But the larger the communist armies became, the less the capture of weapons from the enemy counted. The CCP had to resort to every possible means to acquire weapons for their troops and money for their politico-administrative apparatus. Thus when their intelligence learned of Nationalist shipments of arms or cash to units in isolated areas, special communist detachments would be sent to seize them. Many people knew of these "expropriations," including Chiang Kaishek, but they could do nothing to stop them.

The political differences between the GMD and the CCP were clearly reflected in the army leadership. GMD commanders and officers were drawn for the most part from the propertied classes. They were in no hurry to coordinate military operations with the communists. As for the CCP, I had no direct links with either its political or military leaders, so I could determine Mao Tsetung's position on any issue only by noting the GMD response or by observing the conduct of the CCP liaison representative in Chungking, Zhou Enlai (though he generally preferred to keep matters to himself). I came to the conclusion that Mao and his associates were not much interested in working with the Nationalists but were intent instead on building up their strength for the eventual struggle for power in China.

THE STATE OF MORALE IN THE NATIONALIST ARMY

In studying our advisers' reports on the Nationalist army, I could see that its combat quality and general morale were at a very low level. Most soldiers served only for a bowl of rice and a few copper coins. On average, the Chinese soldier was paid 12 dollars a month. He was provided with about 650 grams of rice per day. However, with rare exceptions, he never received his full entitlement. Transport problems, food shortages or plain robbery reduced his rations. Men were often forced to fall back on their own resources. Not infrequently one saw the following picture: a group of soldiers scattered about the rice paddies, catching snakes and small creatures with which to embellish their scanty dinner. The poor sanitary conditions and systematic malnutrition led to illness and high mortality rates, and left the survivors weak and passive in the face of any challenge. In the 102nd Infantry Division, for example, 50 percent of the men suffered from malaria.

To the poor material conditions of the soldier's life should be added the harsh treatment meted out by commanders and junior officers. Corporal punishment was widespread, and there were cases of men injured as a result. Offenders were often beaten with sticks. One could only marvel at the forbearance and patience of the Chinese soldier, stalwartly bearing his afflictions—bad food, poor clothing, exhausting marches and the rough, often inhumane, behavior of his superiors. The middle and junior ranks of the officers also lived very badly. There was little material security for officers below the battalion level: they were shabbily dressed and lived in poverty, enduring their privations and separated from their families for years. Sometimes there were expressions of discontent with official policy, leading usually to arrests on the grounds of "purifying the army of undesirable elements."

Corruption and embezzlement flourished in the Nationalist armies. Divisional and regimental commanders received pay and provisions according to their muster rolls, which diverged widely from the actual complement of men. The commanders made money even on funeral expenses. A sum was allocated for burial of soldiers who died on duty, about 10 dollars for the purchase of a coffin. The officers worked out this scheme. They would not bury the dead man right away but would wait until there were ten or fifteen bodies for a group burial. The commander received money for that number of coffins but purchased only one, which was built with a collapsible bottom. Each body would be brought separately to the burial site, the bottom of the coffin opened, and the body dropped into the common grave. The empty coffin would be brought back for the next occupant. Only the last to be buried would be put into the grave with the coffin. The commanders thus made a profit on the coffins while helping themselves to the entitlements of the deceased by keeping them on the active roster.

Corruption also made it difficult for us to obtain accurate figures from the General Staff regarding the size of the army. Was this information secret? Did the Chinese mistrust us? Not so. It was rather that the General Staff itself did not possess such information. In traditional manner, each commander saw his appointment as a sinecure, which was to be used for his own personal enrichment. The quickest way of becoming rich was to send inflated numbers of soldiers up to the higher authorities. Government allocations for these "dead souls" went straight into the commander's pocket. Lined up behind the commander were his senior officers, practicing the same methods. And should officers not wish to risk padding the roster with nonexistent troops, they certainly knew how to profit by concealing every fatality or desertion that reduced the real number of their men. The total strength of the army was therefore difficult to determine. Whenever I took part in planning operations, I always made a discount for these "dead souls." There appeared to be no way, however, of changing this fraudulent system.

The Chinese soldier's good fortune was the absence of winter conditions in the southern parts of the country. Warm clothing and special living quarters were not needed, and this reduced the demands on the army. Officers up to the company commander walked about in shorts, wearing light sandals on bare feet. One often saw a company on the march with the officers up front riding in palanquins, falling off to sleep from time to time. The camp infirmary brought up the rear. The sick were carried in stretchers or on the backs of their comrades. Many of them were suffering from dysentery.

Despite all the above, I could not but note the general fortitude, good military bearing and well-maintained discipline of the ordinary soldiers in the Nationalist army.

A MILITARY REVIEW

In order to learn more of the army's state of preparedness, I attended a number of the regular official military exercises. In mid-June 1941 our advisory group was invited by Chiang Kaishek to a review of the Chungking garrison. Serious differences had recently emerged between Chiang and the local Sichuan militarists, so the review was called in the first instance to put some fear into the refractory generals. Taking part in the three-day exercise were the war minister, He Yingqin, who was deputizing for Chiang Kaishek (earlier it had been proposed that Chiang himself would conduct the review); the deputy chief of the General Staff, Bai Chongxi; the chief of the Political Department, General Zhang Zhizhong; the Chungking garrison commander, General Liu Zhi; and various "high priests" of the Guomindang.

On June 14, at the Beishi aerodrome outside Chungking, we first of all watched a demonstration of heavy weaponry, featuring a battery of three 105 mm howitzers of 1934 German make, mounted on a tractor truck. Their range, we were told, was 14 kilometers. It required thirty minutes, however, to make them battle-ready once they arrived at their destination. Also on display was a platoon of six armored cars, likewise of 1934 German make. Each was armed with only one 20 mm machine gun. The cars were open, covered only by metal netting, and had a speed of 60 km per hour. The centerpiece of this part of the review was the tank platoon—three old light tanks of the Vickers type.

Next came the inspection of the infantry units. In conducting this, He Yingqin neither greeted nor saluted the troops, but only walked past them. He then gave a speech on the tasks of the moment, in which he expounded at great length on how vital it was to have full trust in Generalissimo Chiang.

During arms inspection, the war minister and his party went from one unit to another, taking a random look at rifles and machine guns. They confined themselves to examining the barrel. I noted that almost none of those doing the inspection found any shortcomings, yet the majority of the soldiers did not know how to dismantle and reassemble the breech of the rifle! The company and platoon commanders and NCOs were next tested on their knowledge of regulations. Demonstrations of weapons firing followed, then rifle maneuvers (bayonet thrusts on the spot to the cry of "hurrah"), grenade throwing and finally tank maneuvers and marksmanship. When the tanks, armored cars and artillery were inspected, questions were confined to the weight and year of production of the vehicles and the type, muzzle velocity and range of fire of the howitzers.

For my part, I noticed that the police units were equipped noticeably better than the rest. They wore leather boots, while the soldiers wore straw sandals. Only the police possessed a truly military appearance! The rest of the troops looked quite pitiable, despite the fact that top units had been chosen for the review and soldiers even had been borrowed from other regiments. The junior officers wore the same uniforms as the enlisted men and were hardly to be distinguished from the rank and file. The troops were badly fed. Their appearance testified eloquently to this. In his address He

Yingqin called for provisioning not only with rice (which was actually hard to come by) but with other staples as well, corn in particular. To judge by their appearance, the police ate decidedly better.

Most infantrymen were armed with rifles of Czechoslovakian (Brno) make, but one regiment was equipped with German Mausers, and a few smaller units had rifles of Chinese manufacture, based on Czech models. The guns appeared to be of recent issue, but the care given them was appalling. Many of the rifle barrels were covered in rust. Staff officers were supposed to be equipped with Mausers, but in fact it appeared that only the police had them. There were also light machine guns of 1937–39 Czech and Belgian make. These were by no means poor weapons. In rate of fire, steadiness in operation and simplicity of assemblage, they approximated our Degtiarevs.

The inspection exposed striking deficiencies in weapons handling. Mistakes in aiming and loading were apparent. Men were unable to fix the sight without looking through it; they incorrectly positioned the rifle butt at the shoulder and insecurely placed the rifle when firing from a sitting position. The machine gunners showed even greater shortcomings in their training. The machine gun crew was given a most elementary exercise—to fire upon an enemy emplacement. For fifteen minutes the crew fumbled about, not only failing to open fire but unable even to aim the gun more or less accurately. Their performance showed that training in this technique was assigned no importance in the Chinese army. Furthermore, when the simplest questions on ballistics were put to the machine gun company officers, they could not answer any of them. Once again, it was the police who stood out in military bearing and precise execution of their drill, though they did not know how to attack with the bayonet.

When examined on their knowledge of regulations, officers were judged on the literal accuracy of their reply, with the number of words omitted in their answer noted. As it was, the officers knew the regulations poorly. Their field training was no better. They demonstrated a striking inability to master conditions on the spot and to use a map. For example, on the first day of the inspection, it took thirty minutes before the chief instructor and the chief of staff were able to get the war minister to the command post. The following day the same thing happened.

The next stage of the review was a tactical exercise. The assignment given a platoon was to defend an area 150–200 meters wide and 100–150 meters deep. The platoon commander positioned two squads on his front line and one in the rear for potential counterattack. The third squad did not play an active role in the engagement since, due to the terrain, it could not open fire except through the territory occupied by the first two squads. The heavy machine guns were so placed that they could not open fire until the attackers had penetrated the platoon's defensive perimeter. The firepower of the platoon was reduced to a minimum, and this obviously had an adverse effect on the platoon's conduct of the frontline engagement. The enemy now had the opportunity to attack with a small force, taking minimal losses. They did not delay in doing so. I now saw something most astounding—an assault by only two squads on the front line of a defending platoon. This was possible only in the Chinese army exercises I was watching!

During the exercise the platoon officers did not reconnoiter the area. They gave the order to take up a defensive position on the place where they stood. They could see neither the area they were to defend nor the whole of their front line. For both attackers and defenders, battle directions were given by the platoon commander solely by word of mouth. What struck me from the beginning was that no subordinate officer showed any initiative until he received a command from above. Later I learned that this was common throughout the Chinese army. The enemy, of course, could easily determine the location of the commander and his men from the shouted orders. Under conditions of heavy fire, commands might not be heard. As a result, contact would be lost and the squad left directionless. Yet no use was made of prearranged signals.

We had been given to understand that the Chinese practiced a tenacious defense. But something quite different was observed by us in another exercise. A platoon placed on the right flank of a company for defense abandoned its position without any pressure from the enemy. No one was to be seen advancing on the platoon's front line.

This withdrawal resulted in the enemy taking the platoon's vacated position without any losses. It also placed the entire company in a dangerous situation, especially the men closest to the platoon's previous location. Yet the defenders had been in occupation of a comparatively advantageous position. In front of their forward line was a depression about 100–150 meters long, which the enemy could traverse only with much effort and many losses. The enemy launched their attack across the depression. When they failed to meet with opposing fire, they at once realized that the defensive position was unoccupied. Just the same, with a cry of "hurrah," they attacked the hill formerly occupied by the platoon. The defending commanders took great delight in this: they had fooled the enemy into attacking an empty position!

It is obvious that deception of the enemy does not proceed this way in modern battle. In order to actually mislead the enemy, it is necessary to keep some firepower in the defensive area in order to give the impression that the defense is still active. Only at the very last moment, just before the attack begins, do the defenders slip away. This is what deception of the enemy means.

The tactical exercises I observed covered a wide range of field situations. But a significant number of them were not undertaken with clear tactical gain in mind. Instead of producing positive results, they resulted in the opposite, often to an absurd degree. In this regard, I witnessed a further example of the unthinking application of textbook tactics. In one of the exercises, the defenders decided to make use of a smoke screen. Smoke was released along the front line of their position. However, the wind was blowing toward the attackers, with the result that the smoke screen settled to the front of the defenders' forward line. The question then was: who was using the smoke screen? The Chinese officers answered: the attackers! One might have agreed that it was to the enemy's advantage to minimize its losses by advancing toward the front under cover of smoke. But if that was so, why release smoke from the defenders' position, thus easing the enemy's path toward it? The answer to my question was that this was the "convention." Then I was given another justification of this purposeless operation: "smoke was released to cover the withdrawal of our troops and their regrouping inside the defensive zone." This explanation also had no connection with the circumstances.

On the following day, smoke was directed at the attacking side. The weather was still, and the smoke released from the smoke box rose in a column overhead. The question now was: what was the purpose of using smoke under such conditions? However, none of those present gave this any concern. Once again I had the chance to confirm how mechanistic training was in the Chinese army. If the job was to make use of smoke, then it was obligatory to do so, even if this was detrimental to the actual operation. What was apparent from this was that Chinese army staff had likely read about a particular tactic in German or Japanese military manuals but had never genuinely translated it into practice. In the case at hand, if a smoke screen was to be employed, then it was done in the ill-judged manner described above.

As is well known, the basic task of a military review is to expose inadequacies in battle preparation, which can then be rectified by a program of training based on the information gathered. Nothing of the kind took place here. The adjudication of battle readiness amounted to mere show, to a superficial examination of the units involved. The level of training was obviously low. The mechanistic and formal observance of regulations did not conceal the lack of preparation on the part of the commanders, nor their inattention to conditions and terrain during the field exercises. In sum, the tactical performance of the company and platoon did not answer to the demands of modern war.

CONCLUSION: GUARDED OPTIMISM

Despite the major financial difficulties faced by the Chinese government, we were prepared to conclude that the war could be supported by taxation and heavy borrowing (though with consequent inflation) at the same level through 1941, or at an even higher level if expected foreign loans came through. Sources of war financing had not been exhausted. As for food supply, the loss to the enemy of major agricultural areas had certainly had a serious impact. However, during the war years the local harvests were quite good, and with proper distribution the needs of the army and general population might have been met effectively. The government tried to control prices on a number of foodstuffs, rice above all. Unfortunately, these efforts were compromised by the machinations of big merchants, who worked hand in glove with local power holders.

The Chinese army was poorly equipped to undertake offensive operations on a major scale against the Japanese. It disposed of little firepower and lacked adequate transport. It was, however, capable of mounting offensive operations of a limited nature, though these required long and careful preparation. It could also launch raids against isolated Japanese garrisons of less than divisional strength. The Chinese army was quite capable of carrying out "active" defense, through taking advantage of the rugged terrain. To mount this kind of defense it possessed sufficient men and weapons, as was demonstrated in the course of the 1941 Japanese offensives.

For the common soldier a constant source of worry was the desperate condition in which his family and dependents were living. By 1941 war weariness was beginning to affect the middle and lower ranks of the army. Alongside went a growing loss of belief in the high command's commitment to fighting the war to a finish. These sentiments had their origins in the passivity of the Guomindang leadership and the defeatism of the high-level commanders, who were terrified of the Japanese. The lack of any major success on the part of the Chinese, in contrast to the many victories of the Japanese, also shook the resolve of the Nationalist army. Various symptoms of demoralization began to appear. Pilfering and black-marketing of war matériel were increasingly evident, as were individual cases of desertion.

Nevertheless, despite indications of war weariness and, on the part of some officers and men, of loss of faith in ultimate victory, and despite the disillusionment in both front and rear lines because of the serious material shortages, the fighting capacity of the Chinese army was not undermined. The absence of wide-scale desertion to the enemy, or of attacks by men on their officers, or of soldiers refusing to go into battle serves as evidence of this fact.

Furthermore, the middle-ranking officers, who lived under extremely hard conditions, still remained committed to decisive action, despite their loss of confidence in the willingness of their senior commanders to fight on to final victory.

My overall conclusion was that the Chinese army as I found it in 1941 was capable of undertaking active military operations against the Japanese enemy. However, the Chinese high command deliberately held to a defensive policy so that it could pursue other goals. Chiang Kaishek and his circle were pinning their hopes on the Anti-Comintern Pact, as they believed it was only a matter of time until Germany and Japan attacked the Soviet Union. This would lessen Japanese pressure on China and free their hands for battle with the communists. I believed tensions between the GMD and the CCP were going to intensify. For the present, however, the situation was quiet. The two sides were hoarding and strengthening their forces, until decisive events in Europe intervened.

Chapter 5

Events in Southern Anhui

Growing Communist Military Power

When I stopped in Lanzhou, our consul there had told me of the buildup of Guomindang troops close to the Special Region. His concern about the developing situation was soon to be proven correct.

By the fall of 1940 relations between Chiang Kaishek and the communists had become badly strained. As would soon become apparent, Nationalist forces in the lower Yangtze valley were readying themselves to attack the New 4th Army. Chiang already had the southern border of the Special Region blockaded by well-supplied units under his loyal protégé, General Hu Zongnan. None of the foregoing was known to the China specialists in Moscow. In Chungking, the military attaché's office was also in the dark, as were all our advisers.

To better understand what was going on, I sought out the CCP representatives in Chungking, among them Zhou Enlai, Ye Jianying, and Dong Biwu. Zhou and Ye spoke heatedly about Chiang, whom they deeply mistrusted. The first thing they told me was that Chiang regarded the communists, not the Japanese, as enemy number one. They confirmed that most of the guerrilla detachments active in the Japanese-occupied areas were under CCP control. But when I asked about what operations their forces were currently undertaking, they limited themselves to complaints about Chiang Kaishek and the serious problems faced by their troops in regard to equipment and supplies. Neither Zhou nor Ye gave me a clear answer when I asked them what the united front had achieved. From my talks with them, I believed that a serious rift already had opened up between the GMD and the CCP.

Chiang Kaishek, of course, was aware of the strength of the CCP. He took every possible opportunity to reduce its influence. Drawing on his authority as supreme commander of all anti-Japanese forces in China, Chiang endeavored to put communist units into direct combat with the enemy, or else he assigned them tasks which were impossible because he withheld all support. In sum, Chiang's maneuvers were intended to weaken the communist forces so that he could then bring about their liquidation. With the picture now clear, I thought it essential that I influence the situation somehow, in order to prevent any further worsening of relations between the GMD and CCP.

My impression, which later events confirmed, was that Mao Tsetung and his circle were also of the opinion that enemy number one was not the Japanese army; rather, for them, it was the GMD. There was a covert and bitter struggle taking place between the two parties, and it was sensed by many in China. I became increasingly convinced that both Chiang and Mao believed the Second World War would be decided by the Great Powers and that they should avoid major battles with the Japanese in order to conserve and expand their forces for the future showdown.

THE NEW 4TH ARMY "INCIDENT"

The Nationalist army command had carefully concealed from us the fact that starting in the spring of 1940 troops under General Li Zongren had been making regular attacks on the New 4th Army, pushing it out of areas it had liberated from the Japanese. Now, in the first days of 1941, tensions between the GMD and CCP reached the point where Chiang's forces launched an attack on the New 4th Army. A number of its units were destroyed. This happened just at the time of my arrival in China. From what I learned later, this is how events developed.

In October 1940 the Military Commission in Chungking expressed its dissatisfaction with the New 4th Army's establishment of base areas in the Nanjing-Shanghai-Hangzhou region. The commission stated that this altered the balance of power between the GMD and CCP and ran counter to the orders of the supreme commander on the disposition of forces in China. This charge seemed absurd to the outside observer, as the New 4th Army was liberating territory from the common enemy. The explanation, of course, was easy. Chiang Kaishek feared that the communists would consolidate themselves in the lower Yangtze, where much of China's industry was concentrated, and become the dominant power there. Easy to explain, but hard to understand. It was certainly clear, however, that the communists were coming to be of greater concern to Chiang than the organization of resistance to Japanese aggression.

In December 1940, shortly before my arrival, an important meeting between Chiang Kaishek and Zhou Enlai was held regarding redeployment of the New 4th Army. The area in which the communists were active—the Nanjing-Shanghai-Hangzhou triangle—fell within the Nationalist Third War Zone, under General Gu Zhutong. Chiang presented Zhou with an ultimatum and demanded that all communist forces, New 4th Army included, submit to his direction. Chiang declared that the CCP "had recently given a bad account of itself: it had moved without authorization into new territory, it was expanding the territory under its control, increasing the size of its armed forces, organizing guerrilla units, and positioning its units around those of the central government."

To "settle" the issue, Chiang ordered the transfer of the New 4th Army to the north bank of the Yangtze. If this was not done, he would move against the army immediately and destroy it unit by unit. "You will meet defeat at our hands, not at those of the enemy," Chiang told Zhou Enlai. Communist forces were to regroup in a designated area, and their numbers were not to exceed 80,000 men. Chiang promised that when this was done, the war minister, He Yingqin, would supply the CCP with money and ammunition. Chiang thus gave the impression that he wished to avoid an armed confrontation, although clashes already had occurred in a number of areas and preparations were already under way for the main strike against the New 4th Army.

On December 1 Zhou Enlai reported that the New 4th Army "has now reached the south bank of the Yangtze and is preparing to cross to the other side." This statement had no influence whatsoever on Chiang and his generals. None of them wished at this point to stop the forthcoming attack. It was He Yingqin who signed the order to attack, not Chiang Kaishek. Should it prove necessary, Chiang could deflect responsibility from himself by referring to "precautionary" measures arbitrarily taken by his commanders.

The New 4th Army required time to carry out the Military Commission's directive (more accurately, Chiang Kaishek's ultimatum)—time to execute a skillful military withdrawal. The New 4th Army complied with orders and began to transfer its troops to the north bank of the Yangtze. But later in December Chiang expressed to Zhou Enlai his dissatisfaction with the slow progress of the communist withdrawal. The discussion was sharp in tone. Chiang assumed the pose of a dictator, master of the whole situation. He sought neither to persuade nor to request; rather, he demanded that the communists unquestioningly obey him. Chiang declared that power in China belonged to him alone and that he did not intend to share it with anyone else.

Zhou demanded in return a guarantee from Chiang that he would not take advantage of the current remarshaling of the communist forces to attack them from the rear. Chiang again declared that he had no intention of destroying the CCP and that he stood for close cooperation between the two parties. He reiterated his complaints: the communists had moved into an area not specified by prior agreement, where they had extended their influence and increased their armed strength, thereby threatening both the central government army in the region and overall national unity. Chiang once again insisted on immediate removal of CCP forces to the north of the Yangtze. Zhou Enlai assured Chiang that the order would be met. Zhou did not know, nor did we in the Soviet mission, that the "incident" already had been arranged. On December 19 He Yingqin signed the order for destruction of the New 4th Army.

Twelve divisions from the Third War Zone, commanded by Gu Zhutong, fell on a 9,000-man detachment of the New 4th Army. The unexpectedness of the attack made the task much easier for the government forces. They succeeded in wiping out most of the New 4th Army's staff column. Ye Ting, the commander, was captured, along with many of his senior officers. Ye Ting's deputy, Xiang Ying, was wounded in battle and brutally killed by his Nationalist captors.

Without doubt, this "incident," as it was termed in Chungking ("act of treachery" would be more correct), was intended to break the revolutionary spirit of the New 4th Army and strike a blow at the Communist Party. But this conflict arising between the GMD and the CCP would bring to naught the common struggle against the national enemy. It was obvious to us that the Nationalists, who enjoyed great superiority in numbers compared to the scattered units of the New 4th Army, had seized the opportunity to destroy Ye Ting's staff column. But while this may have been obvious to us, it demanded tangible or documentary confirmation. At this early stage, our military advisers had neither. The Nationalist commanders simply engaged in deception. The situation demanded the greatest caution so that we did not make a false step in our response to the government.

The worsening situation between the CCP and the GMD was marked by political offensives launched by each side against the other. The GMD stepped up its repression of the CCP. Offices of the 18th Army Group were closed down in Guangxi and Xi'an (and destroyed in the latter case). In Chungking the left-wing publishing house New Life (Xin Sheng) was suppressed, while the official communist organ *New China Daily (Xinhua Ribao)* was subjected to slander and baiting. Young activists were arrested in the Sixth War Zone, while left-wing figures in Chungking, Chengdu, Xi'an and other cities were persecuted and arrested, and police observation of leftist activities was stepped up. The CCP replied through pamphlets detailing the recent course of events and exposing the reactionary practices of the GMD. On the outskirts of Chungking a number of meetings were held opposing government persecution of leftist organizations and the party newspaper. These protests, however, did not develop into a mass movement. The CCP already had evacuated local leftist personnel from the city, so now, when leadership of the protest movement was needed, there was in effect nobody to provide it.

Talks began at this time between the GMD and the CCP. At the outset the head of the Political Department of the GMD, General Zhang Zhizhong, attended. Subsequently he removed himself from the discussions, and Zhang Chong, a second-ranking figure with a police background, took over negotiations with Zhou Enlai. This permitted Chiang Kaishek to declare at a session of the People's Political Council that neither he nor the administration knew anything of the CCP demands.

The New 4th Army was not destroyed in the January attack, but it took heavy losses. The incident was also a setback for Chiang Kaishek. Casualties among his forces were high as well. Progressive opinion in the nation saw that, as a result of the provocative actions of the GMD leadership, China was again on the brink of a serious political crisis, threatening to erupt into a civil war. Influential members of the GMD such as Song Qingling and He Xiangning spoke out in public, protesting against the actions of the government. Liberal circles within the ranks of business and the intelligentsia founded the China Democratic League. In its manifesto the League subjected Guomindang policy to harsh criticism.

WE MAKE OUR PROTEST

The time had come for us to say something. But to do this would require careful preparation, lest our remarks be taken as interference in the affairs of a friendly state. I still had not received my appointment as chief military adviser to Chiang, so anything I said as military attaché would be taken as representing my own government. Without Ambassador Panyushkin's sanction, there was nothing I could do. The ambassador and I gave long consideration to how we should act in order to avert the growing crisis and redirect Chiang toward the struggle with Japan.

The situation was not an easy one for us. We had treaty obligations to Chiang's government, but our spiritual sympathies lay with the Chinese communists. However, if we gave open expression to these sentiments, we might alienate Chiang. I had no doubt that Chiang fully realized where our sympathies lay, but inasmuch as we did not give tangible expression to them, he could remain silent on the issue. What concerned Chiang was our military aid. If we openly declared our support for the communists, he would be put in a most awkward position, under pressure from the GMD and his Western patrons to break with us. This would be much to the advantage of the Japanese. There was only one avenue open to us—to make Chiang understand that any aggressive actions on his part against the communists or any redirection of his forces against the Chinese people, rather than against the enemy, would have a serious bearing on the supply of military aid from the Soviet Union.

It was necessary for us to delay our protest, as we intended to work on Chiang through his close associates. According to protocol, I was to make my first call on the minister of war, He Yingqin, who was also chief of the General Staff and author of the command setting in motion the attack on the New 4th Army. Among the army men surrounding Chiang Kaishek, He Yingqin stood out prominently for his knowledge of military matters, his remarkable ability and his cunning. His political position was on the extreme right—he was an ardent anticommunist, an opponent of any kind of revolutionary change in China, and a supporter of a military dictatorship of the feudal and big business interests. He sought to outwit the Soviet diplomats. He wanted increased Soviet military aid but hoped that an understanding could be reached with the Japanese. He considered Japanese occupation of Chinese territory to be temporary. Japan, he thought, would come into conflict with the Western powers. This would force a Japanese withdrawal from China, or else bring about a settlement between the two nations.

He Yingqin and I met as if we were old friends. A crafty smile played about his lips. I too assumed a friendly, pleasant-faced manner. I presented myself as a man who would take on faith everything he was told and who might ask unexpected questions only through naive honesty—by chance, as it were. He Yingqin opened with expressions of gratitude to the Soviet Union and the Soviet people, and to Marshal Timoshenko in particular, for the assistance given China. He praised the advisers for their knowledge, ability and assistance in military operations—not mentioning, however, that his commanders never fully executed the plans worked out with our advisers, or that some plans, while not rejected, were simply shelved.

I waited patiently for this cascade of thanks to end and then asked him if weapons supplied by us had been used in battle with the New 4th Army. He Yingqin immediately assured me that not a single weapon of ours had been so used. Here was confirmation from a senior Chinese leader of what I had been waiting for—that an engagement actually had taken place. It would have been very difficult to pursue the matter if the minister had denied everything or feigned ignorance. With his admission I could continue the discussion.

I now put my second question to him: how was I to report this clash to Moscow? He Yingqin obviously had prepared his reply beforehand: Chiang Kaishek had told Zhou Enlai of the warnings issued since October to the New 4th Army by the Military Commission. I was indignant at the effrontery with which He offered his ready speech, though I kept my feelings to myself. The war minister said quite amicably, with an ingratiating smile, that the New 4th Army had not carried out Chiang's orders and that the Supreme Command had therefore decided to discipline it. This answer confirmed that the order for the attack on the New 4th Army had come from Chiang.

To be honest, it was hard for me to say what He Yingqin had in mind in giving this explanation of the incident. If he was trying to hide behind Chiang, he was doing his superior a disservice.

"Let us suppose this is so," I answered. "Let us suppose that the New 4th Army was tardy in carrying out its orders for one reason or another. What should the Supreme Command do under such circumstances? It should remove the commanding officer and put him on trial or discipline him. But it should not open fire on his troops, against the rank-and-file officers and men who in no way were guilty of their commander's mistake. There is a war going on against an invader, and if this war is to be won, the people must be united. Why wage war against your own men?" He Yingqin could not give me a clear answer. He assured me that the government did not wish a renewal of the civil war and that this was merely a passing difficulty. And once more he came forth with effusions of friendship for the Soviet Union.

The next day I paid a call on the deputy chief of staff, General Bai Chongxi. His influence in the government was due to more than his official position. He was head of the Guangxi military clique, which was closely attached to Chiang Kaishek, and he was one of the nation's foremost anticommunists. My visit was for reasons of protocol, so there was no obligation for either of us to make a formal statement. Once again the meeting began with thanks for our military aid, but not expressed in He Yingqin's cloying manner. Bai Chongxi was a sterner, rougher and more direct man. He immediately began to talk about the New 4th Army incident. He spread out a map before me that was to serve as documentary proof of the CCP's culpability. The gesture was significant. The questions I had put to He Yingqin had produced an effect. Now, right in front of me, they were hastening to justify themselves. They had become worried. They needed Soviet military aid and were looking for a way out of the corner in which they had put themselves.

Bai Chongxi's gesture did not make it any less necessary for me to remain on guard. Without looking at the map, I said that I had just arrived in China and had not yet become familiar with the situation. I had not studied the deployment of forces at the front and could not make a judgment on the appropriateness of the supreme commander's decisions. However, to my mind there was no way of making sense of what had happened. For a government to engage in any kind of armed conflict with its citizens in the face of the enemy appeared most astonishing. I said I would have to make a detailed report to Defense Minister Timoshenko about this prearranged attack by government forces on an army that had accounted itself well in battle with the enemy.

In subsequent meetings with lower-level members of the government, I made the same point: civil strife could only weaken the struggle against the invader. I gave the impression that such conflict might well lead to the termination of Soviet aid, as our people and soldiers would find it incomprehensible that Chinese troops were fighting each other rather than the common foe. I noted that everything I said in these conversations came to the knowledge of the high command and in all probability was reported to Chiang Kaishek himself. With the senior civilian officials of the Chungking government I was more careful. I did not raise the New 4th Army incident with them but continued stressing that only a united people, aided by friendly nations, could stop the aggressor. Parallel with the protests I conveyed as military representative, Ambassador Panyushkin did good work with the civilian ministers. The president of the Legislative Yuan, Sun Fo (son of Sun Yatsen), made a point of receiving us and declared that the year 1941 had begun very favorably for China. Thanks to the military assistance of the Soviet Union, the Chinese had succeeded in stabilizing the front. With their larger army they would be able to undertake new offensive operations. Sun Fo assured us that China would fight on against the invader until the final victory.

From these meetings, formal and informal, with our Chinese counterparts, it would have become clear to Chiang Kaishek that the Soviets had taken note of his belligerent handling of the communist forces. Protest was also building in China at this time. I was given to understand that Chiang's actions had not found support among the officer class. After stating our position, it remained for us now to settle the question of whether Chiang would further intensify his conflict with the CCP. This was an important question, upon which another very much depended: would Chiang make a deal with the Japanese or would he continue to resist?

LOCAL POLITICAL REPERCUSSIONS

On January 22, 1941, the CCP had presented the government with "twelve demands" for settling the crisis. The opening of the People's Political Council (PPC), in which the CCP had representation, was set for the beginning of March. The CCP had not yet received a reply to its demands. It thereupon informed the PPC secretariat that it would not take part in the session.

Government ruling circles became nervous, as the absence of the CCP would reveal serious national divisions the GMD wished to conceal. The secretary-general of the Nationalist Supreme Defense

Council, Zhang Qun, and PPC secretary Wang Shijie had long discussions with Zhou Enlai about CCP termination of its boycott. The CCP refused to do this and insisted on the fulfilment of its January set of demands. Chiang then decided to open the PPC session without the communists, and see what effect communist nonparticipation would have within China and abroad. The first four days of the session were devoted to hearing the reports of various ministries. The CCP demands were not discussed. At this time major Nationalist military buildups were taking place in the immediate vicinity of the Special Region as well as in central China

When the People's Political Council opened on March 2 the CCP handed the PPC secretariat a new set of twelve demands. Among them were the following: (1) immediate termination of all military action against the CCP; (2) recognition of democratic government wherever it was in place in the occupied areas; (3) recognition of the status quo in northern, central and northwestern China; (4) creation of a new army group to complement the 18th Army Group and expansion of overall CCP military strength to six divisions; (5) release of Ye Ting and his reinstatement as New 4th Army commander; and (6) release of all prisoners and return of all weapons captured in the southern Anhui engagement. If the government accepted the twelve demands, the CCP would participate in the session. However, the CCP did not receive an immediate response. Guomindang leaders were increasingly sure of themselves, since the refusal of the CCP to take part in the PPC had not led to widespread dissatisfaction either at home or abroad.

On March 6 Chiang Kaishek, addressing the Guomindang Political Council, gave his reply to the CCP. He declared the CCP refusal to take part in the PPC a hostile act. The principal demands of the CCP were untenable. Acceptance of them, he said, would be the same as granting recognition to the traitor Wang Jingwei's puppet regime. Chiang charged the 18th Army Group with engaging in illegal activities and with not prosecuting the struggle against the Japanese. He bluntly stated that the government had had no alternative but to marshal large forces to keep it in check. Chiang rejected the communist claim that the central government was organizing "punitive campaigns" against the party. He called on the CCP and the 18th Army Group to "reconsider their position" and to cooperate with the government on the basis of the CCP Central Committee declaration of 1937. At the same time, he declared that the government would use every means at its disposal to ensure fulfillment of its decisions.

Following Chiang's statement, the PPC passed a resolution expressing its readiness to discuss all questions raised by the CCP, with the exception of those of a military nature. Once more the conference invited the communist delegates to participate in its work. In reply, the communists restated the facts of Guomindang repression. They emphasized their party's continuing commitment to unity. But since CCP relations with the GMD had not been "regularized" on the basis of the twelve points, the party would not take part in the PPC. The communists held to their position, and the session ended with the dispute unresolved.

Given the rising discontent in the country, concessions on the part of the CCP might have generated support for their position. The party, however, was unable to organize a mass movement, either in Chungking or in the nation at large, that might indicate to Chiang the dissatisfaction of wide segments of society with the Guomindang.

CHIANG HAS TO DESIST

As of March 1941 Chiang had two major military concentrations in place against the communists. One was in the northwest, facing the Special Region; the other was in Anhui-Jiangsu, in the lower Yangtze Valley. The nucleus of the former was the 34th Army Group, consisting of sixteen infantry and three cavalry divisions, under Hu Zongnan. The latter was composed of the 21st Army Group, under Li Pingxiang, and the 31st Army Group, under Tang Enbo. Their combined strength stood at fifteen infantry and two cavalry divisions. The placement of such major forces on the borders of the communist regions in northwestern and east-central China, together with the New 4th Army incident and the destruction of leftist organizations, all served to stoke the ambitions of the GMD to finish off the CCP in a final decisive blow.

The situation was becoming serious. At a minimum, the events in southern Anhui had shown the readiness of the Nationalist government to begin elimination of isolated communist army units. However, because of the conflict with Japan, Chiang Kaishek could not openly break with the united front and initiate a civil war against the CCP. In the first place, this would have meant an abrupt worsening of relations between the GMD and the Soviet Union. In the second place, the political and social situation in China would not have permitted this. The masses were weighed down by the economic burdens of the war, which government incompetence worsened. Dissatisfaction with the regime was to be found at all levels of society. The arbitrariness, extortion and corruption common to the basic organs of power made the burdens of war heavier. Even the intelligentsia was alienated from the regime by its repressive and despotic policies.

Under the circumstances, Chiang Kaishek did not want to unleash a civil war, as this not only would worsen China's international position but also might set off a great internal explosion. In my opinion, these were decisive days for the government. We reached the conclusion that, for the present at least, Chiang Kaishek would not escalate his struggle with the communists further.

Chapter 6

Chief Military Adviser to Chiang Kaishek

Our Work Style in China

In undertaking my new assignment, I wanted to see how our advisers, both those in Chungking and those at the front, worked with the Chinese. This was not a simple task, particularly since our people in the field were dispersed over such a wide area. I already knew from my predecessor's experience that it had not been easy for our people to work with Chinese officialdom.

Our outgoing chief military adviser was Divisional Commander K. M. Kachanov. From talks with him and other staff members, I concluded that my comrades had not always built the right kind of working relationship with the War Ministry and the Chinese commanders in the field. Our advisers were anxious to help the Chinese people inflict total defeat on the enemy, and to this end they were risking their lives. But the weak spot for many was their inadequate understanding of China and its ways. From my earlier time in the country I knew how important such knowledge was. Thus my assistants and I had to make our people understand how best to work with the Chinese. Our senior advisers were brought from the outlying districts to Chungking and given explicit instructions. Those who learned the proper approach not only were less likely to make mistakes in working with the Chinese but also were more likely to better serve as advisers.

Our people had to be exceptionally careful in their work. They had to keep in mind the high premium placed by Chinese commanders on established practice, and their impatience regarding the most reasonable criticism. Special techniques were necessary. Let us suppose that a Chinese general decided to launch an offensive (or go on the defensive) and that his battle plan was, to say the least, seriously flawed. If the adviser offered candid criticism, he would either gain himself an enemy or else be ignored from then on. Thus, whether or not the plan had any merits, the adviser first had to admit to its excellence, if not genius, and make this known to everyone. But under the pretext that the commander's subordinates might be able to better execute the plan, the adviser would request permission to introduce a few clarifications. It may be taken for granted that, after the adviser's earlier high praise, the commander would permit a "few" adjustments to be made. The adviser's proposals could then be carried out as if they came from the commander himself.

Should the plan meet with success, the adviser would remain in the background while the commander publicly received the laurels of victory. In the event of failure, the adviser had to find reasons justifying the commander and his men, or he might even compliment them on a victory. When I was first introduced to Chiang Kaishek at the New Year's eve reception, I began the conversation by congratulating him on the successes of the Chinese army, even though these in fact did not exist. But Chiang appreciated my gesture.

I BECOME CHIEF MILITARY ADVISER

Upon arrival I informed Ambassador Panyushkin that I had not only been appointed to our embassy as military attaché, but was also to be named chief military adviser to Chiang. After the events in southern Anhui I believed that I could not delay my assumption of the latter post. Both Commander Kachanov and our advisory group in the Third War Zone had found themselves in a difficult position, as the Chinese were obviously keeping all important military matters from them. As the newly designated attaché and adviser, I thought that somehow I would be able to influence the Chungking leaders and prevent a further worsening of the conflict between the GMD and the CCP. As chief adviser, I would be speaking as a "volunteer" serving in the Chinese army. As military attaché, I would be speaking as an official representative of the Soviet Union, which was sending Chiang Kaishek aid in order to resist Japanese aggression, not unleash a civil war. Since political and military questions were so interwoven in China, I needed to approach my duties in both capacities. Ambassador Panyushkin agreed with my position. A directive soon followed from Moscow, instructing us to inform Chiang Kaishek of my new appointment.

Panyushkin, Kachanov and I then asked to meet Chiang. The Chinese were clearly quite perplexed by this request coming from the three principal Soviet representatives in Chungking. More than likely they thought our visit was connected to the attack on the New 4th Army and that a sharp comment or protest would be coming from our side. Chiang naturally would want to be prepared for this. For about a week he delayed responding to our request while he tried to find out through his officials precisely what we had in mind.

During that week Chinese political and military leaders wore me out with receptions and banquets honoring me as the newly arrived military attaché, all the while trying to discover why the three of us were set upon a meeting with Chiang. After giving the Chinese time to become a little agitated, I informed the secretary-general of the Supreme Defense Council, Zhang Qun, that our intended visit was not in order to discuss matters of grave import to our two countries. I assured him that the betterment of mutual relations and the continuation of our common efforts were the topics we wished to raise. This proved sufficient. The purpose of the meeting, then, would not be what they feared. Shortly thereafter we were received by Chiang.

I had spoken honestly to Zhang Qun, knowing that he enjoyed the personal confidence of the generalissimo. Through my candor I gained, as it were, an advance on the future. By giving Zhang the opportunity to offer Chiang Kaishek information that only he was privy to, I sought to indicate to Zhang my wish to develop him as a contact. I calculated that he would later repay the debt with information of use to us. This turned out to be the case.

I had in fact disclosed no secrets of any sort to Zhang Qun. When Panyushkin officially stated at a reception that Commander Kachanov was returning to the Soviet Union now that he had completed his term, and that our government was recommending me as chief military adviser, Chiang Kaishek's spirits at once lightened and he looked approvingly at Zhang Qun. A broad smile appeared on Chiang's face, and the words "Hao, hao" (Good, good) fell from his lips. Chiang understood that he was acquiring in the person of the military attaché an adviser who, as official representative of the Soviet Union, could offer him direct assistance in the struggle against Japan. At a banquet to honor Kachanov on his departure, Chiang and I traded compliments and promises of support and proclaimed our faith in the friendship of the Soviet and Chinese armed forces. All this, it seemed to me, brought further pleasure to Chiang.

WORKING AS CHIEF MILITARY ADVISER

The building where I worked had as its neighbors the War Ministry, the General Staff administration, and the headquarters of the Chief of Intelligence. I saw it as my duty to establish good working relations with the people employed in these offices. But the more I entered into my work, the more I became aware of the vast depths of Chungking politics. I realized that without reliable sources of information it would be difficult for me to carry out my task. I received great help from my assistants, Andreev and Fomin, both of whom were fluent in Chinese. Both had extensive contacts with progressive-minded members of the Chinese public. Knowing that the Soviet Union was sincere in its aid to China, reporters, journalists and a wide representation of government officials came and talked over with us many domestic and international issues. This gave us the opportunity to assess the general state of mind in China, as well as learn about the problems affecting different sections of society. In turn, we sought to inspire in our visitors confidence that China would prevail over Japan in its national liberation struggle and that ultimately there would be a revolution in China. Our visitors responded to our words with genuine enthusiasm. In short, there were always many people calling on us, and the help they provided us in our work was immeasurable.

Our rivals in Chinese intelligence tried to plant agents among us. With the help of our Chinese friends we soon discovered who these people were. We decided not to distance ourselves from them; instead, we treated them with caution, to ensure that they did not find out anything of importance to us. We knew that listening devices had been planted on our premises, but we felt it would be pointless to neutralize or remove them. Instead, we endeavored to use these devices to pass on disinformation to Chinese intelligence. I never noticed myself being shadowed, but this was only because they carried out such work very artfully. I was not worried about being watched since, as chief adviser, I did everything in the open. My colleagues and I had no intention of interfering in internal Chinese affairs.

At the head of the Chinese secret services, whose agents were tracking us, stood Dai Li. This man enjoyed Chiang Kaishek's deep trust. None of our people, and none of the Chinese with whom we associated, knew Dai Li. He was highly secretive, an anticommunist, of course, and feared by all Chinese. No one boasted of knowing him personally. Since I was often in Chiang Kaishek's presence I might well have met Dai Li and exchanged pleasantries with him. He even may have accompanied Chiang when we went to inspect Soviet military aid. I honestly never sought out a meeting with this man and had nothing I wished to discuss with him.

Once a week the Central Military Commission met. Proceedings were conducted by He Yingqin, who was concurrently war minister and chief of staff. Chiang Kaishek was officially chairman, but He Yingqin almost always substituted for him. The presence of the chief military adviser at these meetings was obligatory, as he was considered a deputy of the chairman. Zhou Enlai was a member of the commission, as was Marshal Feng Yuxiang, but neither was present at any of the sessions I attended. I thought this a big mistake on Zhou's part. The public boycott of the military commission spoke to the continuing problems between the CCP and GMD and undermined the common struggle against the Japanese.

When I made my first appearance at the Military Commission, the Chinese did not want to allow my interpreter, Andreev, into the meeting with me. My predecessor had used an interpreter provided by the Chinese. This, of course, had a detrimental effect on our work. The Chinese interpreter would convey to the chief military adviser only what his superiors wanted, overlooking everything else that was being discussed. When I was told that I could bring only a Chinese interpreter, I replied that I would not be attending, since I had to have my own interpreter, someone who understood me and I him. However, if it was necessary, a Chinese interpreter could join us in our work. The meeting came to a halt. Neither He Yingqin nor any of the Military Commission members knew what to do. As I later discovered, He Yingqin phoned Chiang Kaishek personally. The question was resolved in my favor. Henceforth I was served by two interpreters: my own (Comrade Andreev) and one provided by the Chinese. From this episode I saw how concerned Chiang was to maintain a cooperative relationship with us.

Meetings usually proceeded in this way. He Yingqin would produce an item for discussion. If I thought something was not quite right, I would immediately ask to see the document, which I would hand to Andreev for translation. Sometimes the Chinese interpreter was needed to help explain the context of the document and give the correct reading of it. I considered all information to be of vital importance. I was able to follow matters such as the continuing disputes erupting between the Nationalist and communist armies. I never expected that the Chinese would discuss in my presence any critical political or military issues. Since I had other sources to draw on, I could raise questions about these on my own initiative and ascertain the real situation from the reaction of the commission members. When I learned of any troop movements ordered by the General Staff that might pose a threat to the CCP, I would report these to Zhou Enlai or Ye Jianying (usually the former, as Ye was in Yenan most of the time as chief of staff to the 8th Route Army). I regarded this as necessary in order to avoid any further New 4th Army incidents.

As I became familiar with the Chinese scene, I came to the conclusion that Chiang Kaishek and his commanders were not really interested in prosecuting the war against Japan. They knew that Japan was preparing for a greater conflict [with the Western Allies], and they clearly did not want to do anything that might prevent this conflict from occurring. In the meantime, Chiang was keeping the communist forces under intense scrutiny. The Luoyang-Xi'an area, south of the Special Region, was garrisoned by some of Chiang's most dependable divisions, under General Hu Zongnan. There were no Soviet advisers accredited to Hu Zongnan, but we received intelligence on his army from our CCP contacts in Chungking.

Meetings with CCP representatives further helped me understand what was going on, especially in regard to Chiang Kaishek's political maneuvers. I learned how irreconcilable the differences were between the CCP and GMD and how unwilling the two were to coordinate operations against the common enemy. Zhou Enlai, Dong Biwu and other CCP representatives had established contacts with local GMD political and military functionaries, as well as with progressively minded people. Such contacts offered the CCP leaders much help, not least in alerting them to possible provocations or confrontations on the part of the GMD. Despite this, the danger of the united front breaking apart remained very real.

CCP-GMD INCOMPATIBILITY

During my stay in Chungking I frequently saw efforts to coordinate CCP and GMD military operations end in failure. Mao Tsetung and Chiang Kaishek were responsible for this to an equal degree.

For example, in early May 1941 the Japanese resumed active campaigning with an offensive in southern Shanxi. (See chapter 8.) Near Luoyang they forced the Yellow River at a number of points and threatened to sever the Longhai Railway, which ran through Henan province, just south of the river. Immediately the Military Commission was summoned into session. The chief of the Operations Section gave a detailed report on the enemy offensive. In my view, we were presented with a most favorable moment to mobilize Chinese forces in the region and destroy the advancing Japanese units. I took the floor and proposed the simplest maneuver—a solution that was apparent at first glance at the map. In their southward advance the Japanese had exposed a flank to the communist 18th Army Group, while their rear was open to attack from the Nationalist Second War Zone under Yan Xishan. I proposed immediate preparation of a combined counterattack to strike at the flank and rear of the forward Japanese units.

The commission members and War Ministry spokesmen listened to me attentively, without interruption. I waited for a reply. None came. It was difficult, of course, to say anything against such an obvious solution to our problem. But no one spoke in its favor. I would have thought the moment had arrived for coordination of CCP and GMD forces against the enemy. I concluded, however, that there was no thought of embarking on any such operation without first convincing Chiang Kaishek personally. I must say that my proposal to order both communist units and Yan Xishan's army into the attack brought a smile to the faces of those at the meeting. I was given to understand that no one would issue such an order, since it would not be executed. Right then I decided I would ask Zhou Enlai and Dong Biwu if they would move against the Japanese in the present circumstances.

Zhou and Dong readily offered me a detailed summary of the general situation. They proved well informed about Japanese politics and the Far Eastern military picture. Their assessment of the possible future course of Japanese aggression might well interest the listener. But they refused point blank to discuss communist troop movements with me, the chief military adviser. (In earlier meetings Zhou and Dong had constantly tried to convince me that the GMD was preparing a decisive attack on the Special Region, this despite the fact since the outbreak of the war the GMD had not directed a single operation toward that area.) I succeeded in getting from them only the statement that as far as joint action against the Japanese was concerned, the time for it had not yet come.

My efforts to link up CCP and GMD operations during the Japanese south Shanxi offensive were unsuccessful. Neither the CCP nor the GMD nor Yan Xishan (who was in fact independent of the Nationalist supreme command, despite formal subordination to it) intended to put aside self-interest in the common cause. It was fortunate, then, that the Japanese did not have sufficient reserves to make good their initial threat to Luoyang.

THE THREAT EMERGING IN THE SOUTH

I continued to study the political and military situation carefully. The possibility existed of prominent Chinese going over to the enemy. There were already examples of this. In the northeast, in Manchuria, the last emperor of the Qing dynasty, Pu Yi, stood as head of the puppet state of Manzhouguo. In Inner Mongolia, Prince De headed a puppet regime; in Beijing the North China Political Council had been set up under Wang Yitang; in Nanjing a pro-Japanese government had been established under Wang Jingwei. A sort of ragtag empire of pro-Japanese puppets serving the mikado had been created. In carving up the territory they had occupied, the Japanese had fallen back on the well-tried imperialist tactic of divide and rule.

By the end of 1939 the front in China had stabilized, as if frozen into place. The general course of events in Western Europe through 1939 and 1940, together with the specific intelligence I was receiving about East Asian matters, made me think that Japan might put aside the China war for the present and risk a move into Southeast Asia and the western Pacific. The Japanese evidently thought that with the imperialist powers tied down in Europe, and America increasingly distracted by European concerns, they were in a position to throw all their strategic reserves into battle locally. Japan could realize its long-term goals under such demagogic slogans as "Asia for the Asiatics," "Japan—Asia's defense against Anglo-American injustice," and "Forward with the Co-prosperity Sphere." The Japanese militarists also had not given up their plans of an attack on the Soviet Union. But, wiser from their experience of 1939, they were holding back in the hope that a Soviet Union weakened by war would present them with the right opportunity to move. As we now know, this was the approach they took in the "Outline of National Policy of the Empire in Regard to the Developing Situation," adopted by the Imperial Conference in Tokyo on July 2, 1941, shortly after the Germans launched their invasion.

During early 1941 the situation in the southern region began to heat up. There was much evidence of this. British embassies in the Far East began to evacuate their nationals home. The British mined the coastal waters of Malaya and Singapore and began to transfer troops (British, Indian and Australian) and aircraft to these same colonies. To guard against attack on Malaya from the north the British had placed some of their Indian regiments along the Thai border. The Americans had tightened security around their air and naval bases in Hawaii, Alaska and elsewhere. American banks were ceasing to supply credit for commercial transactions in the Far East. President Franklin D. Roosevelt had stated that in the event of the United States being drawn into a Pacific war, there would be no reduction of aid to Britain. But what was more significant than the above was the buildup of the Japanese position in Southeast Asia. The Japanese had compelled the French authorities in Indochina to grant Thailand its territorial demands on that country. Japanese influence in Thailand was growing. Japanese forces were already positioned in northern Indochina (Annam), which they had occupied in September 1940. The whole region was being transformed into a vital strategic springboard for a Japanese move against the British, Dutch and American colonial possessions.

According to information provided by the Chinese, the total number of Japanese planes in the southern region was about six hundred, of which some two hundred had been dispatched to Annam. The Japanese were engaged in intensive military construction on Hainan Island, where they were building airports, shelters, antiaircraft emplacements and a submarine base. We also learned that tank units had been concentrated on the island. In early March the Japanese carried out joint air, sea and land exercises there. According to information we had received, the Germans were putting strong pressure on the Japanese for a push to the south. One report stated that a joint army-cabinet meeting had been held in Tokyo in March to discuss the German request. It was decided that preparations for a move to the south should be completed by the end of the month. Statements by the foreign minister, Matsuoka Yosuke, and the Japanese ambassadors in London and Washington to the effect that Japan had no intention of using armed force to attain satisfaction of its claims in the southern region did not defuse the tense situation. Japanese military preparations contradicted such assertions.

GROWING ANGLO-AMERICAN WORRIES

In January President Roosevelt, acting upon the request of the Chinese government, sent Dr. Laughlin Currie to Chungking as his personal envoy. Currie was to conduct a wide-ranging study of the political, economic and military situation in China. The Americans considered accurate knowledge of what was going on in China essential to their overall policy formation for the Far East and Europe. They needed to know how reliable an ally China would be if they found themselves at war with Japan. Naturally, Currie could not do everything in the course of a short trip. It would appear that, apart from gaining on-the-spot impressions, his task was to verify data already in the possession of the American government. So far as I could tell from my conversations with the Americans, Currie's conclusions were unfavorable to the Nationalist government. Currie focused on China's critical financial and economic problems, which the government appeared incapable of managing, and the lack of democracy, which the patent Guomindang dictatorship made obvious. I felt, though, that regardless of Currie's conclusions, growing tensions between the United States and Japan meant that the Americans would soon be compelled to offer substantial assistance to China.

It was the British who displayed the greatest unease. This was understandable, as their Far Eastern possessions were under direct threat of Japanese attack. What most worried the British was China's economic condition. Some British diplomats believed that without aid from Britain and the United States, China would last only another six to twelve months. The British proposed the dispatch of an Anglo-American economic delegation to advise the Nationalist government. In February 1941 Chiang gave his consent to this.

Rumors were also circulating in Chungking about discussions between Britain and China regarding military cooperation. Great importance was attached to the mission led by the head of the Military Commission secretariat, General Shang Zhen, to Burma, Singapore and Malaya. It was speculated that General Shang had met with the British Far Eastern Military Command and had reached an agreement with them on Anglo-Chinese military coordination in the event of a Japanese attack on the British colonies. From information at my disposal, I knew that the question of Chinese military protection of the Burma-Yunnan Road had come up in the course of the mission. (The Chinese had created two new army groups in

Yunnan, the 1st and 9th, for defense of the south in case of war between Japan and Britain.) Meanwhile, the head of the GMD Overseas Affairs Department, Wu Tiecheng, was sent to Hong Kong upon his return from an extended visit to Chinese communities in Southeast Asia. By all appearances, the purpose of Wu's mission was to hold talks with the local British command. In sum, I was certain that talks on the subject of military cooperation were taking place, though what form this cooperation might take remained unanswered.

Thus the British and Americans began to link their China policy ever more closely to the rapidly deteriorating situation in Southeast Asia. The need to defend their colonial possessions in the Far East from Japanese encroachment now confronted them directly. But they had come to this realization quite reluctantly. It was not only the critical situation in Europe that explained this, but also their unwillingness to challenge or weaken Japan, whose forces might be useful at the right moment against the Soviet Union. The British ambassador to China, Archibald Clark Kerr, was open about this. It was clear to me that the tenser the Southeast Asian situation became, the more the British and Americans would urge China on in its war with Japan; the greater the threat of war in the south, the more substantial their assistance to China would become. Conversely, if Britain and the United States saw the prospect of an agreement with Japan, they would not hesitate to sacrifice China in their own interest.

The possibility of war between Japan and the Western powers had now become part of Chinese foreign policy calculations. Thus the Chinese government sought to draw itself even closer to Britain and the United States. At the same time China naturally assigned great weight to Soviet policy in the Far East. The news of Soviet-Japanese talks about a mutual non-aggression pact raised great anxiety in Chinese governing circles. This is what underlay renewed efforts by the Chinese to emphasize their friendship with the Soviet Union. Chiang Kaishek personally attended the Red Army Day reception at the Soviet embassy on February 23, while He Yingqin was host of a banquet given in honor of myself and the other Soviet military advisers. At the banquet He Yingqin took great pains to express his love for the Soviet Union, furthermore declaring that a counterattack against Japan was in the offing.

In Chungking both Chinese leaders and foreign diplomats were concentrating on events in Europe. In what direction would Germany move next? Would it be west, against Britain, or east, against the Soviet Union? (The Chinese had little interest in what happened to countries such as Romania, Bulgaria, Yugoslavia and Greece, which they regarded as having minimal influence on the greater military picture.) Everyone awaited the entry into the war of the two giants, the Soviet Union and the United States.

The British and American representatives were especially interested in the possibility of our involvement in the European war. The Americans asked me directly if we would be able to maintain our military assistance to China. The United States military attaché, Colonel David Barrett, and I gave each other to understand that continued Chinese resistance to Japan was in the interest of both our countries. China must not capitulate. From our meetings I concluded that the Americans would provide China with military as well as financial support. I also determined that they would oppose the outbreak of civil conflict in China, as it could only weaken national resistance to Japan.

CHAPTER 7

ENCOUNTERS IN CHUNGKING

A FAR EASTERN MUNICH?

Chiang Kaishek's change of attitude following the events in southern Anhui was first brought to our attention by the local American and British diplomats. The fact is that by early 1941 they themselves had begun to look differently at the Sino-Japanese War.

At this time the politics of a "Far Eastern Munich" still prevailed. Britain and the United States had not given up the possibility of instigating a Japanese attack on the Soviet Union, and to this end they continued to make concessions to Tokyo. And if the Japanese now found themselves bogged down in China, they still had realized major territorial gains. With their strong position in China, they could now take advantage of the French defeat in Europe and extend their tentacles into French Indochina. An advance into Indochina and the creation there of a military and economic base facilitating a further move to the south could not but trouble the United States. In the event of a British defeat in Europe, Japan would be able to appropriate Britain's Far Eastern empire with little expenditure of effort. From Indochina Japan would also be able to reach out and threaten American bases and communications in the Pacific.

The complete collapse of China would have meant a dangerous increase in Japanese power for all concerned. At the time, of course, no one could accurately predict where the Japanese militarists might next move: whether toward Siberia, the Philippines, Malaya or the Dutch East Indies. The Americans had known since the mid-1930s of Japan's program to expand its surface and submarine fleets. Having let the genie out of the bottle, the Americans hoped that it would remain submissive, but the genie, having raised itself to its full height, now threatened to turn on its patrons. It was indeed possible that the Far East would witness a repetition of Europe's experience with Hitler.

These concerns only gradually came to dominate the minds of Western politicians and diplomats. While continuing to pursue a "Far Eastern Munich," they now began slowly and carefully to change their attitude toward China. The first signs, still very timid ones, appeared of a definite interest in marshaling China's strength to beat back Japan. This became apparent in the approach taken by the Western powers to cooperation between the GMD and the CCP.

I knew already from my deputy N. V. Roshchin, who often met with the American and British diplomats and officers, that neither of those countries approved of Chiang Kaishek's hostile actions toward the communists. Here one must read between the lines. Every word, every gesture, had its own hidden meaning. Neither the Americans nor the British would have admitted to their earlier hopes of a Sino-Japanese reconciliation, in order that Japan might fall upon the Soviet Union, nor would they have let slip a word that following a peace settlement Chiang Kaishek would then turn on the communists. Up till this point our Western colleagues had been censoriously shaking their heads, affecting great distress that China was wasting its armies in a civil war rather than using them to resist the enemy. But this time, as Roshchin noted, their dissatisfaction with Chiang Kaishek was genuine.

MY AMERICAN OPPOSITE: COLONEL BARRETT

I arrived in Chungking with the rank of lieutenant general. According to protocol, the acting American military attaché, Colonel David Barrett, was to pay me the first visit. I knew that he was a seasoned, veteran intelligence officer—a specialist in the Far East, with more than ten years in China, complete mastery of the Chinese language, and extensive ties to the Chinese industrial and military community. He was always informed about what was taking place in Chungking government circles and what was being traded on the stock exchange or on the black market.

Our meeting gave me the opportunity to ask my American colleague to share his experience of working in China. In this way I could put various questions to him. It would have been naive to expect full candor on his part, but even misinformation sometimes has its uses: one can at least ascertain what the other side is concealing. I expected pointed questions from my visitor, due to the complicated nature of current Soviet relations with Britain and the United States. Our country had signed a non-aggression pact with Germany, Germany was at war with Britain, and the United States had made its sympathy for the British cause clear to the world.

Soon after my arrival Colonel Barrett requested a meeting. This indicated that the Americans were concerned about something and wanted to sound us out. My first encounter with Barrett exceeded my expectations. This American was not devious. He won you over with his way of freely carrying on a conversation. He did not seem under any restraint and expressed his views on any question without fear. I was interested first of all in how he viewed the tense relations between Chiang and the communists, and in what he made of the New 4th Army "incident." Barrett could have escaped answering by feigning lack of information. But he at once replied, saying that the differences between the GMD and CCP disturbed him greatly. He then gave our military assistance to China the highest approval and emphasized the importance of our advisers to the Chinese army.

"Tell me, Colonel," I asked directly, "how would your country react if the British used the weapons you were sending them not in the war against Hitler but, let us say, against India?"

Barrett smiled. "I understand and share your concerns, General. In the past we were not much concerned about disorder within China. To the Western mind, China cannot be imagined apart from its many internal divisions. Centuries and centuries of history speak to that."

I did not interrupt Colonel Barrett, even though I might have observed that China's divisions always suited the Western colonialists very well and that none of them would make any effort toward ending this state. In fact, one could cite many instances where the Western powers fueled the flames of disorder. What interested me, however, was the attitude of the Americans toward the current civil conflict.

"Now," continued Barrett, "we are aware of how unacceptable the traditional divisiveness is. We have conveyed to the Nationalist government our negative reaction to the New 4th Army incident. This prevents China from repelling Japanese aggression."

The colonel was careful how he spoke, just the same. Not once did he refer to Chiang Kaishek as the perpetrator of the incident; neither did he anywhere imply that the Japanese were to blame. His view on the matter was given not in so many words, but in the way he expressed himself on the overall situation.

"We are frankly interested in the Chinese putting up a real fight against the Japanese. We cannot let ourselves forget that Japan is militarily linked to Germany and Italy. But if the Japanese find the situation in China getting hot for them, they will have to ease up on their expansionist intentions in the north and the south."

In the north! I took note of this. Even though he had not touched on the issue directly, my opposite in this discussion had done little to conceal his hope that there would be no further worsening of Japanese-American relations. Yet by this time it was quite obvious how strained relations between the two countries had become.

I should remind the reader that these conversations with the acting military attaché of the United States took place in Chungking toward the end of January 1941. Thus Colonel Barrett could not help but show interest in my "personal views" on how relations between the Soviet Union and Germany were developing.

"Doesn't the Soviet government fear," he asked directly, "that this spring or summer Germany will move east?"

"Without having first finished off England in the west?" I put as a counterquestion to avoid giving a direct answer.

"A crossing of the Channel was possible last spring," he replied. "But both the British high command and our own military analysts are of the opinion that a crossing is quite unmanageable this coming spring. The British air force is stronger. The British have fortified their coastline and built up their army. Every day our assistance to Britain increases. Our military aid is in fact changing the balance of power [in Europe]. At the present moment, however, we cannot provide such aid to China."

"Wouldn't American aid to Britain be more effective if the United States were actually to enter the war?"

"The same goes in regard to the Soviet Union," he countered. "If you were to ask me in a private capacity, I would say that postponement of the war is as advantageous to your country as it is to mine, though it would be much to your gain if the United States declared war on Germany, while it would be to our gain if you were the ones to become involved in a war with Germany. I should add, though, that I personally think events are developing in such a way that neither the United States nor the Soviet Union will be able to escape direct involvement in the war. It is a matter of time. Our relations with Germany have worsened considerably because our aid to Britain has been so effective. And any change in the balance of power in Europe cannot but be reflected in other parts of the globe."

In response to his remarks, I expressly stated that the policy of the Soviet government was one of peace and that any attack on the Soviet Union would be repelled with the greatest force.

"According to information reaching me here," Barrett went on, "Germany is beginning to move troops from France to the east. I don't think this is connected just to German interests in the Balkans."

These words sounded like a warning being offered. It was possible to read them differently. Barrett himself did not hide the fact that certain circles in the United States wished to draw the Soviet Union into the war. His statement may have been made with the intent that I would transmit it to Moscow, where it might help prompt us in the direction of some ill-advised steps toward Germany. But I was inclined to value his frankness as genuine. I myself felt that the storm clouds were building up on our western frontiers. We still did not have any direct warnings. But I do think that our military intelligence by this time had sufficient information on the transfer of German forces to the east. Such movements could not be kept secret.

When I told Panyushkin of my meeting with Barrett, the ambassador remarked on how forthcoming the colonel had been and how different his tone was compared to that shown toward my predecessor. We now had further indication of the growing American concern over Japanese military preparations in the Far East.

MY FRENCH OPPOSITE: COLONEL YVON

It was in the spring of 1941 that I had the occasion to meet the French military attaché, Colonel Yvon. His position was not an enviable one. Since mid-1940 the Chinese had not paid much attention to the French delegation in Chungking. Yvon represented the Vichy government in China, but he detested the French defeatists with all his heart, regarding them as traitors. He was a true French patriot. He found it most difficult to conceal his true feelings, but he had to do so, as he did not wish to lose his official post, which he could use for the benefit of his homeland.

My close relationship with Yvon did not begin straightaway. Chance helped. In my dual capacity as military attaché and chief military adviser, I had two places of work. During one of the Japanese air raids on Chungking, the residence of the chief military adviser was destroyed. The Chinese government quickly arranged for me to take the building that had lodged the French embassy. I talked this over with Panyushkin, and we concluded that the Chinese were hoping to create discord between us and the French through this petty provocation. We decided not to move. I informed Colonel Yvon, who appreciated our gesture. From then on, Yvon became very open with me. He did not conceal his attitude toward the Vichy regime. And he did his best to share with us any information that came into his hands from the Americans and the British, especially in regard to Indochina.

Yvon often talked to me about the battle for France. He spoke of German military technology and the German coordination of tank formations with airpower. His analysis was expert, but it was too late. The French army no longer existed: the Resistance was now beginning to take its place.

Some of Yvon's reports in the spring of 1941 caused me to think further of the situation developing in the south, specifically in Indochina. The Japanese had occupied Annam and were building army and air force bases there. Large transfers of troops and equipment had taken place. None of this was necessary for the Japanese war in China, let alone a future attack on the Soviet Union. Through his private channels, Yvon had learned of Japanese construction of naval bases for operations aimed at the south. Evidently the French, and Colonel Yvon in particular, still retained a wide network of agents both in China and in Indochina.

"The Japanese are waiting to see how the war in Europe will develop," he told me. "They could undertake more vigorous efforts in China, but with the growing resistance here they're suspending operations. They are waiting."

"Waiting for what?"

"They are certain that war against Russia has already been decided. Depending on how the war develops, they will choose where their next blow will fall."

"And if Hitler, who has signed a nonaggression pact with us, does not move against us?"

"Then the bases in Indochina will still be useful. Japan will not sit on the sidelines. She will move against the United States. Japan can help Germany only in this way. A German defeat in Europe would be fraught with grave consequences for Japan."

Yvon made his remarks with great conviction. Naturally I was interested to know the reason for such certainty on his part.

"My friends in France report that Hitler has been withdrawing large military formations and transferring them to Poland."

Yvon revealed the sources of his information to me. German officers outside France corresponded with fellow officers in the French-occupied zone. A number of letters had fallen into the hands of former collaborators in the Sûreté Nationale. From the postmarks and contents of the letters, French intelligence agents established that they had come from Poland. The movement of huge formations of troops could not but leave tracks. Someone writes a letter, someone is overly talkative. Many French officers in the service of Vichy remained patriots in their heart. They hated the German occupiers and watched their every move. It was from these people that Yvon received his information.

INTRIGUES WITHIN THE CHIANG CAMP

As mentioned before, in February 1941 our military mission held a special reception to mark the anniversary of the Soviet Red Army. All the foreign ambassadors were in attendance, as well as military representatives from the Nationalist government. Chiang Kaishek's presence at the reception might be considered the crowning achievement, since this was his first visit to the embassy on the occasion of Red Army Day, a point all his officials emphasized. This was another sign of the change in attitude of the GMD ruling clique. Panyushkin and I concluded that the Americans and British must have been putting more pressure on Chiang to go on the offensive against Japan and to hold back from internal conflict with the communists.

For our part, we remained alert to the stratagems of Chiang Kaishek, who was doing everything possible to bring us into open war with Japan. Chiang saw this as one of his major goals, and he pursued it tenaciously. In this regard I had some opportunity to witness the maneuverings of Chiang's wife, Soong Meiling. She pretended to the role of a major political actor. (Comparison to Mao Tsetung's wife, Jiang Qing, comes to mind here.) Soong Meiling was ready to provide the Soviet military mission with reports on the Chinese domestic scene, the situation on the Chinese front and the plans of the Japanese high command. But there was more disinformation than information in what she gave, and her words more often than not conveyed provocative rather friendly sentiments toward the Soviet Union. She frequently made the point that the greatest support the Soviet Union could render China would be to declare war on Japan. Her "unofficial" position gave her the opportunity to make such remarks with impunity.

Soong Meiling did not just confine herself to the above rhetoric. There were occasions when she deliberately tried to provoke a collision between the Soviet Union and Japan. In the spring and summer of 1941, and especially after the German attack on us, journalists connected with her printed a number of reports in Chinese newspapers about Soviet military aid to China. These items contained statements of appreciation for the weapons China was receiving from the Soviet Union, and directed reproaches at the Americans and British for not providing China with military equipment even though they were no less able to do so. These articles caused me great alarm. I did not, of course, think that the Japanese high command, with its far-flung espionage network in China, was in the least unaware of the aid we were providing. But unofficial information was one thing, while open declarations in the Chinese press, and not from any ordinary person but from Madame Chiang Kaishek herself, were quite another. What stood behind this was the Chinese desire to provoke the Japanese: to show them that the Soviet Union was more dangerous than America or Britain. I at once suspected the hand of my colleague Colonel Barrett at work here. He would do his utmost to deflect the impending Japanese blow away from his own country.

Other government members were also not particularly reluctant to express their views. H. H. Kung (Kong Xiangxi), who was deputy premier and minister of finance, once "unburdened" himself in a conversation with me. Declaring his love for the Soviet Union, he tried to persuade me that it was in our interest to enter the war against Japan. I had to remind him of the eloquent testimony provided by the 1929 Chinese Eastern Railway conflict of the Chinese government's "love" of the Soviet Union. Kung changed his expression but said nothing in reply. More provocative was the behavior on one occasion of the minister of trade. By mutual agreement, China was to supply the Soviet Union with wool. This was needed in the manufacture of greatcoats. I was asked by our trade representative to remind the minister of China's obligations, since deliveries had suddenly stopped. My conversation with the minister took place in the presence of his subordinates. The minister ventured to remark: "You help us defeat the Japanese, and Chinese goods will reach the Soviet Union without hindrance. . . .What you want is to defeat Japan by using the Chinese. . . ."

"If I were a Chinese army commander," I replied, "I would send such an ardent patriot as you at once to the front line. The army is doing without a most valiant soldier!"

My joke was taken, and there was a burst of laughter. Those present were laughing at their minister. I did not doubt that I had just made a personal enemy.

OUR NEUTRALITY PACT WITH JAPAN

Ambassador Panyushkin had repeatedly told me of Chiang Kaishek's efforts to bring about a Soviet-Japanese confrontation. However, in March 1941 Chiang and his Western patrons saw their hopes of increased tensions between the Soviet Union and Japan suffer a serious reversal.

The news of the negotiations in Moscow in the early spring of 1941 between the Soviet government and Japanese foreign minister Matsuoka struck the Chungking regime like a thunderbolt. The Chinese noted particularly that Stalin had come in person to the railway station to meet Matsuoka and that he had chatted amicably with him and the German ambassador. Only someone myopic could interpret Stalin's presence at the station as a routine diplomatic courtesy. Whose position had changed? The Soviet Union's? Definitely not. The Soviet Union was pursuing a policy of peace and was not preparing for war against either Japan or Germany. On the contrary, it was the Japanese militarists who had been devising plans for an attack on the Soviet Far East. The Moscow talks signified that the Japanese were changing course and that what they now needed was the assurance of stability on their borders with the Soviet Union.

The question of Matsuoka's mission naturally interested not just the Chungking politicians but also the Americans and the British, who literally besieged us with requests for meetings. Colonel Barrett asked for one. I saw no reason to refuse him, as I was certain that he would not put any tactless questions to me, and that if he did, I would be able to handle them. I assumed that the reaction of such an experienced American intelligence officer as Colonel Barrett to the Soviet-Japanese negotiations would be of interest to Moscow.

I was not mistaken. One could do business with Barrett. Not once in the course of our meeting did he raise Matsuoka's name. Our talk was off the record, so I would not have found myself in a predicament if any leading questions had been posed. Barrett was quite candid when I put my questions. But I noted that while the colonel was in command of himself, he was very much ill at ease.

Barrett asked: "Are the reports we have received from American missionaries true, that heavy artillery of Soviet manufacture has arrived in Lanzhou?"

The question was a delicate one. Barrett appeared to be saying that we had reached an important agreement with Japan in Moscow, yet here we were continuing to give military aid to China. Such aid could not be concealed from the Americans, who in any case would learn of it from sources other than missionaries. Chiang Kaishek himself would see that the delivery of Soviet weaponry was not kept secret. Not hurrying to reply, I countered with my own question: "Is it true that the USA is preparing to dispatch P-40 fighters to China?" I had gotten this information from Chinese sources. Barrett answered that such an undertaking was fully possible in the immediate future. I then acknowledged that 150 75 mm guns had arrived in Lanzhou.

Barrett was satisfied. He understood that Matsuoka's trip to Moscow had not changed our position on Japanese aggression in China. For his part, he confirmed that the American government would assist China however possible until the Japanese were finally driven out of the country. He also hinted that pressure would be applied to Chiang Kaishek not to provoke a clash with the communist armies.

When our five-year neutrality pact with Japan was announced on April 13 the Nationalist government reacted with alarm, bordering on panic. The many high-level party and government meetings convened by Chiang testified to the confusion in Chungking. Even Chiang gave the impression of being at sea. But gradually this passed. In Moscow the meeting between Molotov and Chinese ambassador Shao Lizi helped greatly to clarify the Soviet position. In Chungking Panyushkin's meeting with Chiang had the same effect.

The official position of the Chinese government on the neutrality pact was expressed in a Foreign Ministry statement. Its key point was the denial by China of the right of any other power to decide questions involving Manchuria and Outer Mongolia. [The pact had specified these as regions of special interest to Japan and the Soviet Union respectively. —*Editor*] Within the government and party, the neutrality pact brought to light a strongly anti-Soviet group whose leaders came from the right wing of the party. At their head stood the reactionary Guomindang theoretician, Dai Jitao. Other major figures were Central Executive Committee member Zou Lu and the head of the GMD Propaganda Department, Wang Shijie. Opposed to this group were those who wanted to preserve and strengthen good relations with us. Apart from longtime "friends of the Soviet Union" such as Sun Fo, Yu Youren and Feng Yuxiang, this latter group included figures such as the commander of the Sixth War Zone, Chen Cheng, and the chief of the International Intelligence Bureau, Wang Pingxiang. They spoke up against Dai Jitao and his followers when the Soviet-Japanese question came up for discussion. Chiang Kaishek seemed to be wavering. In a speech to the Central Party School he went so far as to say that the supporters of the Soviet position did not really understand the politics of the Soviet Union. Whatever Chiang's personal reaction to the neutrality pact was, no indication of it was given in public.

The Nationalist government decided not to aggravate relations with the Soviet Union. The status quo would be preserved. The Chinese would work to see that our aid continued. Instructions were given to all newspapers and journals not to attack the Soviet Union nor refer to the circumstances surrounding the conclusion of the treaty. Chiang Kaishek preferred to wait and see how events unfolded in Europe.

The neutrality pact, it should be noted, meant that Japan, while a member of the Tripartite Pact with Germany and Italy, intended to follow its own foreign policy in the Far East. The Japanese now turned to major attacks, by land and air, on China's armies and cities. In May they launched the south Shanxi campaign; in June they renewed the summer bombing offensive against Chungking. The

Japanese goal, so it appeared, was to bring about the surrender of Chiang Kaishek or, failing that, to deprive him of the means of active resistance.

CHAPTER 8

CHIANG KAISHEK BIDES HIS TIME

THE STALEMATE AT THE FRONT

Following the capture of Canton and Wuhan in October 1938, the Japanese for all intents and purposes terminated their offensive and limited themselves to minor forays and counterthrusts. Some of our advisers were of the opinion that by the end of 1938 the Japanese had exhausted themselves and did not have the capacity to advance further. The China war obviously tied down great numbers of their troops. This, however, was not the only reason for the suspension of the offensive. The aggressive actions of the Japanese militarists at Changgufeng (Khasangol) and Nomonhan (Khalkhingol) on our Far Eastern border demanded a major commitment of men and weapons. The Japanese now set about establishing mastery over those parts of China they had occupied. They also began readying their industry and military, so it appeared, for a larger war against new opponents.

For his part, Chiang Kaishek aimed to conserve his army rather than use it actively against the enemy. His priorities were maintaining dominance over the provincial militarists and combating the forces of progress in China. Chiang's authority over his senior generals, especially the war zone commanders, was precarious. At the top level of the Nationalist government little cooperation was to be seen. Each commander strove to preserve intact his own men and weapons, especially the latter, as without these he would lose all influence. There was no doubt Chiang feared that any of his generals might go over to the side of the Japanese, following the example of Wang Jingwei.

Chiang Kaishek's passivity became much more pronounced in 1940, following Hitler's victories over the French and British and the diversion of American attention to events in Europe. Military aid from Britain and France, which in any event had never been much, now almost completely ceased. The United States, not wishing to strain relations with Japan, refrained for the time being from offering genuine assistance to China. Along with the British and French, the Americans were playing the politics of a "Far Eastern Munich," which only encouraged the Japanese aggressor.

When I arrived in China in late 1940 I found Chiang at a political crossroads. He feared the communists and their growing military power. If it came to a battle with them, Chiang expected he would obtain support from the imperialist powers, Japan included. But capitulation to Japan would mean forfeiture of all popular support and his designation as a national traitor. These considerations aside, the Japanese already had Pu Yi in Manchuria and Wang Jingwei in central China on which to pin their hopes. No end appeared in sight to the world war now under way. This also influenced Chiang to bide his time and wait on events.

Mao Tsetung also held to the same policy of accumulating strength for the coming struggle for power. Mao and the other communist leaders must have realized that their passive stance in the war would not strengthen their position but would in fact weaken it. The Japanese, having stabilized their front against the Nationalist army, now adopted the slogan "Pacification of the rear is more important than action on the front" and initiated an extensive campaign against the communist guerrilla areas.

It was in vain that we advisers offered the Nationalists plans for the destruction of specific Japanese troop formations. Chiang and his aides would give their approval, but they did not intend to act on our plans, preoccupied as they were with preparations for battle with the communists. The Japanese, whose ground forces were insufficient for extending their conquests in China, tried to force Chiang to a humiliating peace by launching massive air raids on Chungking in 1940. At this time, the Japanese completely ceased their air attacks on the communist Special Region.

Could the Japanese have continued their offensive in China through 1939 and 1940? This question begs a further one. What purpose would the Japanese have had in seizing more Chinese territory when they were already in possession of the major industrial centers and coastal areas of the country? Chiang Kaishek was left with only two routes to the outside world: Kunming to Rangoon in the southwest and Lanzhou to Alma-Ata in the northwest. To sever these two lines of communication, the Japanese would need to bring into China another dozen divisions, while several hundred thousand guerrillas were still operating to their rear.

The widening war in Europe was prompting Japan likewise to wait on events, inducing them to keep their main reserves— economic, military and human—in the highest readiness for future action.

SINO-AMERICAN RELATIONS WARM UP

Chinese foreign policy in the spring of 1941 was based on two firmly held suppositions. First, within the next six months war would break out in the Pacific between Japan and the Anglo-American bloc, leading ultimately, so the Chinese believed, to Japan's defeat; second, war would break out between Germany and the Soviet Union, bringing Japan, despite its neutrality pact, into the conflict on Germany's side.

In Chungking's view, these events would soon work to China's advantage. The Nationalist leaders therefore continued to await developments in Europe and the Far East. It would be more to their benefit to bide their time rather than go on the offensive, which would only bring further casualties and threaten their forces with partial destruction. The troops were ordered to limit operations to defense of the lines they already held. I was quite convinced that until the global picture became clear, Chiang Kaishek and the army high command would not take any action against the Japanese.

It was the complex internal situation that primarily dictated the Nationalists' determination to conserve their forces. After the New 4th Army incident, the Guomindang right wing and the more reactionary generals, such as He Yingqin, Gu Zhutong, Bai Chongxi and Liu Weizhang, wanted an open break with the CCP and the liquidation of its armed forces. A 300,000-strong army under General Hu Zongnan had taken up position on the southern border of the Special Region. This force was clearly intended to block the route south should the communists turn on the Nationalists, but it would also be ready to move against the communists if the right conditions should arise. After the southern Anhui incident the Nationalist leaders very much feared the former. The united front in fact had split apart, though this was not openly admitted.

In April the Japanese once more probed Chiang Kaishek in regard to a peace settlement. Through John Leighton Stuart, the American rector of Tsinghua University in Beijing, the Japanese transmitted a proposal for direct peace discussions. Chiang refused to entertain this message, stating that he would discuss such proposals only if they were transmitted through President Roosevelt. At this time Chiang was endeavoring to secure increased weapons supplies from the United States, the Soviet Union and, to a lesser degree, Britain. His intention was to strengthen the armies under his personal control, which he held back in the rear areas. This not only would give him greater security in the country as a whole but also would put him in a stronger position should the general situation compel him to discuss peace with the Japanese.

Chiang now began advancing the idea of a defensive alliance between the United States and China. In one of his speeches Chiang even compared the fundamental principles of the American government to Sun Yatsen's Three Principles of the People. There were many other signs as well of the growing connection between the two countries. Chinese foreign minister Guo Taiqi went to Washington for meetings with President Roosevelt and his secretary of state, Cordell Hull. In Chungking the Americans displayed particular interest in stepping up the capacity of the Burma Road, China's link to the Western world. The Americans offered to fly in a major aid shipment from Burma to Yunnan, after which the planes, some fifty to one hundred of them, would be given to China. From T. V. Soong (Song Ziwen) I learned that the American government had approved the export to China of $25 million worth of goods. Included were railway construction materials, four thousand automobiles and textiles for army needs. The arrival of an American military mission in Chungking was expected shortly.

THE LULL ON THE FRONT IN EARLY 1941

How was the military situation developing on the front at this time?

For the Japanese, the southern strategy dictated that they secure a strong position in China, which, along with French Indochina, Thailand and Hainan Island, would constitute their rear area. The Japanese high command hoped to achieve the full capitulation of Chiang Kaishek's government or, failing this, to batter the Chinese army sufficiently to knock it out of contention for a long time. Experience had shown the Japanese that without the elimination of the Chinese army, occupation of wide areas of China would not in itself bring them victory. Between January and May 1941 they launched a number of limited offensives along the front, with the intention of weakening the fighting effectiveness of the Chinese army as well as seizing valuable supplies and tightening the blockade of Free China.

In the Sixth War Zone a number of limited engagements took place. These were of a local character, and I was not inclined to assign them much importance. In Shanxi this sort of warfare had been going for the past two years with mixed results. However, Japanese moves in southern China drew my attention. On the morning of March 3, Japanese forces landed at points along some 400 kilometers of the Guangdong coastline. Guanghui, Yuanjiang, Dangbai, Shuidong and Pakhoi were occupied. After removing large stores of salt, foodstuffs and gasoline from these towns, the Japanese withdrew. These raids were intended to restock the Japanese forces. Operations of a similar nature were to be observed elsewhere on the front. They were very damaging to the Chinese, who already suffered from serious shortages of food and other provisions.

As of spring 1941 the Japanese had undertaken no major changes in their deployments in China. They had strengthened their units in the south somewhat, mainly in airpower. Troop concentrations were still heaviest in the central sector of the front, which ran from Yichang in the west through Wuhan to Nanchang in the east. Eight infantry divisions and two infantry brigades were based in this region. Some buildup was taking place in Nanchang, where the Japanese had assembled seventy tanks, twenty armored cars and two hundred trucks.

The creation of mixed army formations had become the practice by now. For example, the Japanese army based in Henan province in the north consisted of units drawn from the 3rd, 4th, 17th and 40th Infantry Divisions. The army based in Jiangsu was made up of units from the 15th and 17th Infantry Divisions and the 11th, 12th and 17th Brigades. We saw this as evidence that the Japanese suffered from a lack of reserves and that they were experiencing definite problems in holding on to so much territory.

Meanwhile, the Chinese high command gave no indication of taking the initiative. Chinese military activity remained defensive in nature.

THE NATIONALIST ROUT IN SOUTHERN SHANXI (THE ZHONGTIAOSHAN CAMPAIGN)

In May 1941 the Japanese broke the lull by launching a major offensive in southern Shanxi. They did not draw on units in Japan or Manchuria; rather, they weakened or even stripped whole sections of the front in China. They took advantage of the passivity of the Nationalist generals and the absence of cooperation between the different Chinese military regions to carry out their regrouping [See map, p. xvi.]

It soon became clear that annihilation of the 200,000 Chinese troops concentrated in southern Shanxi was the primary Japanese objective. The main thrust of the attack fell between Jiyuan and Yuanqu. Capture of the road linking these towns would bring the Japanese to the Yellow River, enabling them to completely cut off Chinese forces from their base on the southern bank. Having isolated the Chinese army north of the river, the Japanese then intended to destroy it piece by piece. Once across the Yellow River, the Japanese would sever the Longhai railway, capture the city of Luoyang, where Chinese army headquarters were located, and in effect put the whole First War Zone out of contention. The Japanese also counted on sowing panic among the Nationalist leaders and furthering the emergence of capitulationist elements in their midst.

The Japanese spent April marshaling their forces. Two columns were to carry the brunt of the attack. The eastern column consisted of two infantry divisions and a cavalry brigade; the western consisted of three infantry divisions and two infantry brigades. These formations, attacking from opposite directions, were to join up and cut off Chinese access to the Yellow River. Japanese strength totaled seven divisions and 100,000 men, with 172 planes in support. By comparison, the Chinese numbered twenty-nine divisions, one brigade and three guerrilla detachments, about 160,000 men in all, thus giving them a favorable battlefield ratio of 1.6 to 1.

Japanese battle preparations were no secret to the Chinese. They had intelligence of what was going on two weeks before the offensive began. Chiang Kaishek admitted this himself in a telegram to First War Zone commander Wei Lihuang after the battle was over. However, neither the General Staff in Chungking nor war zone headquarters in Luoyang undertook any real defensive preparations, though they could have used troops from the Second War Zone in northern Shanxi or the 34th Army Group in southern Shaanxi to cover their threatened flanks. But to do this would have meant weakening the forces concentrated against the Special Region, against the Chinese communists! The Nationalist high command preferred, at heart, to suffer defeat at the hands of the Japanese rather than lessen their containment of the communists.

The general state of Chinese defenses in southern Shanxi was also quite inadequate. There had been some haphazard strengthening of forward positions, but in the rear area no serious preparations had been undertaken. The main crossings of the Yellow River were not covered by defensive emplacements. It would not be a major effort for the Japanese to break through the Chinese lines.

On May 5 and 6, Japanese aircraft stepped up reconnaissance of the First War Zone front, particularly of embarkation points on the Yellow River. Population centers such as Luoyang, Zhengzhou and Jishui were bombed. There were five alerts on May 6 in the Luoyang vicinity alone. Through their clever selection of aerial targets, the Japanese masked the real direction of the attack. Destruction of Chinese river craft was also assigned special attention. The Japanese air force carried out this task efficiently. From the beginning, Chinese headquarters lost all possibility of moving major reinforcements to the north bank of the river.

The Japanese began their offensive on May 7 and by evening of the following day had attained initial success. The Chinese 9th Army was pushed 25 kilometers to the west under pressure of the Japanese eastern column. At the same time, the Japanese western column advanced toward the Jiangxian-Yuanqu line and in one single decisive blow broke through the 43rd Army front. Into the corridor thus created the Japanese threw their cavalry and then their infantry, which pushed forward, ignoring Chinese stragglers. On the evening of May 8 the Japanese took Yuanqu. Their cavalry did not call a halt but moved on eastward, toward the rear of the 9th Army.

In driving this wedge through the Chinese position, the Japanese severed the links between the 80th Army, the 5th Army Group and the 14th Army Group. The 80th Army withdrew into the mountains, 30 kilometers to the west of Yuanqu, where it dug in defensively, using the north bank of the Yellow River as its right flank. One of the 80th Army's infantry divisions, the 27th, was completely wiped out and its commander killed. Part of the 5th Army Group was surrounded and put into a highly dangerous situation. Panic ensued both at staff headquarters and in the field. All contact was lost with First War Zone command in Luoyang.

By May 12 the Japanese had fully completed the first stage of the offensive. The Chinese 9th Army, which had already taken heavy losses, was now threatened from the rear and withdrew its 54th Infantry Division to the south bank of the river. Two other 9th Army divisions were badly mauled and went over to guerrilla operations. Part of the 80th Army was destroyed and the remainder thrown back across the river. Units from the 15th and 98th Armies began retreating southward under enemy attack. The encircled 5th Army Group continued to fight on.

The Japanese eastern and western columns linked up halfway between Jiyuan and Yuanqu, near Shaoyuan. As they approached the north bank of the Yellow River they left small garrisons behind and threw their main force into eliminating the 5th and 14th Army

Groups. All major crossing points on the north bank of the river were now in Japanese hands. Chinese forces were completely cut off from their supply and reinforcement base south of the river. The encircled units now broke up into small detachments. Deprived of adequate supplies of food and ammunition, they were reduced to guerrilla activity. By May 20 the battle was over. The First War Zone had been cut in two. The Chinese regular army had ceased to exist in southern Shanxi.

Chinese headquarters displayed great indecisiveness and ineptitude in the initial days of the Japanese offensive. Some units only received their orders on May 9, when the battle for south Shanxi in effect had been decided. The plan I proposed as chief military adviser for coordination of forces from the First, Second and Eighth War Zones was not taken up. During the whole course of the battle Yan Xishan's Second War Zone in the north of the province remained inactive, as did the Eighth War Zone to the west. Two of Fu Zuoyi's divisions did arrive on May 25, when the campaign was already over. As for cooperation with the communist 18th Army Group, this did not happen, and it may be said with assurance that the Nationalists had no intention that it should happen. They preferred to see the Japanese grind down the communists unit by unit. Thus the First War Zone was left to its own devices, with no outside assistance. If the Second and Eighth War Zones had gone on the offensive, not only would this have eased the situation in the First Zone, but it might have altered the whole course of the campaign.

As mentioned above, First War Zone headquarters in Luoyang lost contact with the north bank of the river at the very outset of the battle. It was in complete ignorance of the situation at the front. It therefore ordered the 14th Army Group to go on the attack toward Jingshua, not realizing that this badly mauled formation had been almost completely surrounded and forced to break up into individual guerrilla detachments. Despite individual examples of heroism, Chinese forces on the north bank of the river were overwhelmed by the vigor of the Japanese offensive.

A number of factors contributed to the Japanese victory. First, the Japanese were able to supply their men with food and ammunition by air. This increased mobility in the difficult mountain terrain, as it freed their columns from cumbersome transport trains. Second, Japanese engineering battalions immediately consolidated newly won positions. For example, as soon the north bank of the Yellow River was reached, a network of defenses was constructed to cover the crossing points. Great importance was assigned to roadworks, which facilitated the troop movement and provisioning. Japanese success was also assisted by the disorganization of the Chinese rear caused by the air raids. Luoyang, headquarters of the First War Zone, was heavily bombed. On May 16, for instance, eight raids were mounted, while on May 19 enemy planes were over the city the entire day.

With the Chinese army in southern Shanxi routed and the Japanese now in position on the north bank of the Yellow River, Luoyang and Xi'an came under direct threat of attack. The fall of Luoyang would have meant the total destruction of the First War Zone. The left flank of the Fifth War Zone was also directly menaced. (A Japanese attack against the center of the Fifth Zone would have put the whole zone at risk.) Fearing these possibilities, the Chinese high command took our recommendation and hurriedly began strengthening defenses on the south bank of the Yellow River. Most importantly, the 13th Army was detached from Tang Enbo's headquarters and transferred to Luoyang. On the south bank of the river the Chinese built up sixteen infantry divisions, one independent brigade and several batteries of artillery.

The Japanese had secured total victory in Shanxi over a huge Chinese army. They were able to cut off and isolate Chinese units, which could then be destroyed piecemeal. Following the decisive breakthrough by their forward columns, the Japanese drove deep into Chinese territory and rapidly completed the encirclement. Due to the south Shanxi terrain, the Japanese could not bring armored units into the battle. Instead they relied on cavalry and light infantry, supplied by air, for the breakthrough.

The offensive severely damaged the 80th Army and the 5th and 14th Army Groups. Some formations, such as the 27th Division, were totally destroyed. Many Chinese soldiers also perished from hunger or exhaustion. But, as it turned out, the Japanese confined the battle to southern Shanxi and went no further. However, they now had a springboard from which they could keep Luoyang and Xi'an under constant threat.

THE CHINESE INQUEST INTO THE DEFEAT

After the battle was over, the General Staff operations division submitted a report to Chiang Kaishek that attempted to whitewash the high command and make it appear as if all possible measures had been taken against the enemy. The report also included some passing attacks on the CCP and made particular mention of subversive activities by a "fifth column" working behind Nationalist lines.

Nevertheless, this inquest contained a number of melancholy admissions. "Our forces employed passive tactics. . . . In several years of occupation of this region they were never moved to new areas. They never went on the offensive, nor did they learn how to camouflage their operations or mislead the enemy through deceptive troop transfers, etc. The location of our units was known to the enemy in detail. The importance of accurate intelligence was undervalued; thus mistakes were made in evaluating the enemy. Staff at First War Zone headquarters generally forwarded intelligence received [without having analyzed it] and drew mistaken conclusions about the strength, identity and intentions of enemy formations.

"Troops prepared their positions badly. Despite the fact that they had been stationed in the area for more than three years, and despite the fact that the mountainous conditions of the area offered many opportunities for constructing strong defensive positions, nothing was done. Even the roads running between our lines and those of the enemy were left intact. In the meantime, the Japanese were rapidly mobilizing the local population to build fortifications.

"Individual unit commanders displayed poor knowledge of tactics and reacted slowly to the flow of battle. The Japanese very soon detected the weak points in our defense and directed their major attacks at them.

"Supply was not properly handled. For example, essential foodstuffs were transported only as far as the Yellow River, thus forcing units on the north bank to divert up to one-third of their strength to bring the supplies across. Thus the effective complement of the forces in question was significantly reduced. Once the battle was joined, food supplies largely stopped, and many men died of hunger. When, after the loss of Yuanqu, the situation became highly critical, war zone headquarters did not take emergency measures but left the soldiers to fend for themselves. At headquarters the reports coming in were valueless. Staff officers did not go out on inspection. As a result, the actual situation at the front was not clear, battle plans were unsatisfactorily prepared, and serious mistakes were made in the direction of our forces.

"Security and intelligence were managed very badly. Petty traders were able to cross our forward lines freely, thus making it possible for fifth columnists to penetrate deep into the rear of our defensive zone. When the battle began, these agents damaged our transport trains, hospitals and depots, attacked our staff headquarters, wrecked our radio station and sabotaged our military administration. Panic set in among our troops." (These comments were blatantly designed to throw responsibility for the defeat onto the communists.)

The real reason for the defeat of the Chinese army in southern Shanxi in May 1941 was the unwillingness of the Chinese high command to weaken the forces it had concentrated on the borders of the Special Region. Troops in southern Shanxi were left to their own devices and were in fact doomed to defeat. The plan presented by the chief military adviser, which presumed collaboration of the First, Second and Eighth War Zones with units of the 18th Army Group, was not accepted. A limited offensive to be launched from the Sixth and Ninth War Zones in order to divert the Japanese attack from southern Shanxi and to direct it toward the central part of the front also fell through. In the Sixth Zone Chen Cheng refused to move. His deputy, Xue Yue, made as if to comply but in fact backed off. None of the forces in the Ninth Zone went into action either.

The Chinese high command in Chungking continued to limit itself to defensive operations as it awaited developments in Europe and the Far East. Chiang Kaishek stated: "Our principal task is to hold firm to our position and defend our present front line in order to secure the basis for the victorious offensive that will bring about the final destruction of the enemy."

A short lull now set in along the whole front. In the Fifth War Zone some intelligence-gathering efforts by the Japanese were to be observed. Units sent to Shanxi for the recent campaign now returned to their original places of deployment. An exception was made for the 21st Infantry Division. It was assigned defense of the Yuanqu-Jiyuan road and the north bank of the Yellow River.

The Shanxi campaign, combined with small-scale operations in central China, freed the Japanese from the possibility of any Chinese military initiatives. This allowed them to prepare confidently for greater aggression elsewhere.

CHAPTER 9

CHIANG AND THE PROVINCIAL MILITARISTS

In the spring of 1941 relations between Chiang Kaishek and the southwestern militarists—the Sichuan and Guangxi cliques—took a turn for the worse. As in the past, differences between the two sides arose from Chiang's efforts to reduce the power of the provinces and increase that of the central government. Inasmuch as Chiang's headquarters were now located in the southwest, in Chungking, friction with the local militarists became even more acute. The latter were behind the sudden appearance at this time of economic sabotage aimed at the central government's finances and food supplies.

CHIANG KAISHEK AND THE SICHUAN CLIQUE

The conflict between Chiang Kaishek and the Sichuan militarists dated from the late 1920s and early 1930s. The original leader of the Sichuan clique was Liu Xiang, who served as governor of the province from 1934 until his death in January 1938. Liu strove to transform Sichuan into a territory effectively independent of the central authority, with all provincial military units under his control. To this end he founded the Society for the Promotion of Morality among the Forces, to which all officers above battalion level belonged. With the help of this organization Liu succeeded in bringing the Sichuan military under a single command. Liu also gave great attention to the political and administrative unification of the province. He set up special courses for training district magistrates, through whom he endeavored to control the basic-level administration.

The remoteness of Sichuan from the political heart of the country suited the local militarists well. In the early 1930s the central government was in no position to extend its influence into the province. Here in Sichuan, perhaps more than anywhere else in China, the remains of feudalism still existed, and these served the advantage of the local military. However, the Sino-Japanese War changed the picture fundamentally. Because of the Japanese invasion, the central government had to create a new base deep in the interior. Chiang Kaishek undertook a number of measures to build up his power at the expense of the Sichuan clique, which already had been weakened by the death of Liu Xiang in 1938. Following Liu's death Chiang named Wang Zuanxu to the governorship. Wang, though a native of the province, was a follower of Chiang's. The central government now brought its troops into Sichuan. The assignment of provincial forces to the front line (six army groups totaling 400,000 to 500,000 men) further weakened the local clique. Central government appointees gradually took over the major offices in the provincial administration.

The Sichuan militarists were unhappy with the turn of events, but because they were significantly weaker than Chiang Kaishek they could take no effective measures against him. Proof of this was that during my time in Chungking the post of governor was held by Zhang Qun, a high-ranking member of the central government. When Zhang's appointment was proposed in 1939, the Sichuanese heatedly objected, with the result that Chiang briefly occupied the post himself. Zhang assumed the governorship in November 1940 and held it until the end of the war. The Sichuanese nevertheless held on to their hopes of recovering provincial autonomy. They were waiting for the right moment, which would come either with a successful Japanese advance on Chungking or with the return of the central government to Nanjing at the end of the war. Whichever happened, Sichuan units would return home from the front and the militarists would be able to reestablish themselves in the position they had enjoyed in the days of Liu Xiang.

However, the political and military influence of the central government in Sichuan was steadily increasing. A number of factors worked to bring this about. The war saw major industrial development in the province, and this gave the center economic strength against the local militarists. In addition, the central government ministries and military offices, as well as the high-ranking members of the government, party and army, had been settled in the properties and estates of the Sichuan militarists, further weakening the latter. And the state monopoly on the export of a whole range of products originating in the province (tung oil being the best example) made the Sichuan landed class economically dependent on the central government.

Chiang Kaishek worked to deprive the Sichuan leaders of their power base through bribery of individual commanders and redeployment of provincial military units. He was helped by the fact that following Liu Xiang's death, the Sichuan militarists no longer had a recognized leader. Rivalries broke out within their ranks, and their former unity was essentially lost. However, despite the fact that their power was ebbing, the Sichuan leaders, especially those who had belonged to Liu Xiang's immediate circle, still pursued their goal of a province independent of the center. They continued to seek the removal of Zhang Qun as provincial governor, though this was done covertly rather than openly. In the provincial capital of Chengdu, for example, slogans would be found stuck to the walls of homes proclaiming that if Zhang Qun were ousted and the local people took over, "rice would be a quarter the price."

LOCAL TROUBLES

In June 1941 the GMD Central Executive Committee convened a national conference in Chungking to transfer the land tax from the provinces to the central government. This measure met with strong resistance from the regional power holders. The governor of Yunnan, Long Yun, declared his opposition, as did the Sichuan and Guangxi leaders. Relations between the center and the provinces abruptly worsened. Since the provincial militarists did not have enough manpower to oppose Chiang's armies, they resorted to economic sabotage. By holding back large supplies of rice (especially rice controlled by Liu Xiang's widow and by Liu Wenhui, Liu's effective successor as clique leader), they helped bring about a food crisis in the province. The government decree limiting the price of rice to 60 dollars a picul [133 pounds] prompted landlord resistance. This gave further backing to the provincial militarists in their battle against the centralizing actions of Chiang's government.

Rice was also being hidden because the value of the central government dollar was falling by the day. Rice served as a measure of real value, as a sort of hard currency. On the black market its price reached 100 dollars a picul. Since the average monthly requirement was one picul of rice per person and the average Chinese family consisted of four or five people, the necessary minimum just to provision one family was 400 to 500 dollars. Wages of workers and low-level officials fluctuated between 75 and 200 dollars. Life was extremely hard for these people. Most of them lived in semistarvation. Efforts by the government to improve the supply of food met with no success.

Because of the shortages and high prices, discontent over the food situation became widespread. A series of spontaneous food riots broke out in Sichuan. When a rice store in Chungking was looted in April by a hungry crowd, the police opened fire, killing or wounding a number of people. In the outskirts of Chengdu a group of starving women and children attacked the experimental wheat field of the local university and pulled it up to the very last root. Near Chengdu a mob of hungry people burst into a landlord's home and tried to empty it.

Linked to the serious food situation in Sichuan was the widespread presence of banditry. This was more a political phenomenon than a criminal one. The peasants of Sichuan were making their protest felt against the harsh conditions of life. The bandit leader's appeal was simple: "Whoever wants to eat rice and escape the army, follow me!" These gangs were particularly active in the mountains near Beipai (a suburb of Chungking), in the area around Jinmuguan (an important communications and cultural center), and in the north of the province along the Guangyuan road, close to the border with Shaanxi. Behind the bandits stood the Sichuan militarists, who hoped to use the misery of the Sichuan peasants against the central government.

MILITARY STRENGTH OF THE SICHUAN CLIQUE

About forty generals belonged to the Sichuan clique. They were a variegated group, with little unity among them. Most led a dissipated life and were illiterate in military matters. Chiang, playing on the differences between them, sought, not without success, to divide them further. General Yang Sen, for example, had not supported Liu Xiang in his efforts to bring the province under his complete control. Yang, in order to preserve his own forces, went over to the central government. After the Sino-Japanese War broke out, Yang Sen went to the front as commander of the Sichuan forces, and he served in Hunan as deputy commander of the Ninth War Zone.

The Sichuan generals had seven divisions under their control. Two were placed in the northeast of the province, along the Sichuan-Hubei-Shaanxi border, under Pan Wenhu; one was in the north, near Langzhong, under Se Dekang; one was located near Chengdu, under Liu Yuantang; one was at Ya'an, to the southwest of Chengdu, under Yuan Shaixiang; one was near Luxiang, under Zhou Xiulang; and one was near Jiading, not far from Chungking, under Liu Shucheng. Liu Yuantang and Liu Shucheng were sons of Liu Xiang. Their divisions were the best armed and numbered between 20,000 and 30,000 men. Apart from the locally based divisions, six Sichuanese army groups were serving at the front: the 22nd, 23rd, 27th, 29th, 30th and 36th.

The most important members of the Sichuan clique were Liu Wenhui, Pan Wenhu, Deng Xihou and Tang Shizong. General Liu was the most ambitious of them. In January 1939 he became governor of Xikang, the province immediately west of Sichuan. He had two divisions and two independent brigades under his direct command. Realizing his comparative weakness, General Liu linked himself to Liu Xiang. After the latter's death, Liu Wenhui concluded pacts with brigade commanders Liu Shucheng and Zhou Xiulang in his bid for power. Liu's position was much shaken, however, by the December 1938 defection from the Nationalist government of Wang Jingwei, with whom he had connections. Only when Liu issued a public telegram condemning Wang did the central government indicate its continued confidence in him. Liu was unable to develop a power base in Sichuan. But he followed events closely, waiting for the right opportunity to move. Chiang Kaishek, who was aware of Liu's ambitions, continued to work on winning him over.

General Deng Xihou was pacification commander for Xikang and Sichuan provinces. He controlled two divisions and a brigade. Deng was totally a reactionary, cunning and mercenary, who used his position for personal ends. Working through his close associate Se Dekang, he sought to build a relationship with the head of Nationalist intelligence, Dai Li. General Tang Shizong was the most powerful of the Sichuan commanders in military strength. He was an outright money grabber who high-handedly oppressed and robbed his subordinates. When Liu Xiang, who had not trusted him, died, Tang tried to become governor but met with no success.

Finally, there was General Pan Wenhu, who during my time in Chungking was pacification commander for the Sichuan-Hubei-Shaanxi border area. His closeness and devotion to Liu Xiang were the source of Pan's authority among both the older Sichuan militarists and the common people. Within the province he was called the "people's father." He was head of the Society for the Promotion of Morality among the Forces, although he himself led a dissolute life, alongside which should be mentioned his utter ignorance of military matters.

Marshal Feng Yuxiang was particularly interested in the relations among the Sichuan militarists. Dissatisfied with being a "marshal without an army," Feng plainly had to look to the Sichuan clique for support if he was to rebuild his power base. (It was known that at the time of the New 4th Army incident, Feng intended to flee to the northwest and put himself at the head of a new anti-Japanese government, should there be an open break between the GMD and the CCP.) The prospects of success for Feng were very limited, however. He had neither men nor money to offer. There was little reason for the Sichuanese generals to make him their leader. In any case, it would be under only the most favorable circumstances that they would risk a move against Chiang Kaishek.

Uncertain of his position in the province, Chiang used both persuasion and force on the Sichuanese in order to bring them to heel. He named Xu Kan, a Sichuan native with links to the big landlords, as Minister of Food. At the same time, in a speech given at a party meeting in the presence of Pan Wenhu and Deng Xihou,

Chiang explicitly threatened Sichuan landlords who were holding back rice. The government convened a special conference on "pacification" in Chungking, intended ostensibly to tackle the question of banditry. Construction of concrete defensive structures around the city was accelerated. He Yingqin and Bai Chongxi went out to assess the local situation. In mid-June units of the Chungking garrison command carried out the tactical exercises described in chapter 4. Chiang ordered two of Pan Wenhu's best divisions (the 17th and 18th) to the front in eastern Sichuan. Plans were made to move three more central army divisions into the province. Nevertheless, despite these efforts, sabotage by the Sichuan militarists remained a serious problem for the central government.

CHIANG KAISHEK AND THE GUANGXI CLIQUE

No less difficult and complex were Chiang Kaishek's relations with the Guangxi military clique, at the head of which stood Li Zongren and Bai Chongxi, supported by Li Pinxian, Xia Wei and Li Jishen. Like their opposites in Sichuan, the Guangxi militarists sought to remain independent of Chiang Kaishek, and in the past they had actively opposed the central government.

Chiang Kaishek enjoyed little popularity in Guangxi. Pictures of him were to be seen only in bookstores, while those of the clique leaders, Li Zongren and Bai Chongxi, were on display in all the major towns. When Chiang appeared on the screen in movie houses, the audience usually remained seated, whereas in Sichuan and elsewhere all would have stood at once to attention. It was Li and Bai who interpreted central government administrative and political directives to the local officials. If a directive was to the advantage of the Guangxi clique, it would be followed; if not, the most effective means of sabotage was to shelve it. But as far as directives regarding the communists were concerned, the Guangxi leaders followed Chiang Kaishek faithfully.

The province retained a high degree of autonomy. Chungking's appointee as governor, Huang Xuchu, surrounded himself with a loyal staff, and Huang himself was an energetic and capable official, but he could take no decisions on his own. It was only when Li

Zongren or Bai Chongxi gave their sanction that he could begin implementing this or that measure, and then only in accord with the wishes of his "masters." This was also the case with directives coming straight from the central government. If Li and Bai had a difference of opinion, Huang would put off a decision so as not to be caught in the middle. Matters such as the provincial budget, mass political education, command of guerrilla units and even the demolition of roadworks to slow up a Japanese advance required the approval of Li and Bai. All political organizations were under their control. Dai Li's supposedly all-powerful secret police had no success in the province. Bai set up his own highly effective intelligence operation. In the first six months of 1941 it saw to the destruction of all local communist and left-wing organizations.

Guangxi was not in any way economically dependent on the central government. The province bordered on north Indochina. Trade in contraband goods went on with both the Japanese and the Vietnamese through Canton, Pakhoi, Yunzhou and other ports. Both merchants and military were involved, and government officials also did not mind "warming their hands at the fire." Even the central government resorted to this kind of trade in order to add to its revenues. From duties levied on Japanese contraband, the Guangxi generals on average collected half a million Chinese dollars per year. Chungking was powerless to interfere, as everyone responsible for controlling the trade had been bribed by the local Guangxi merchants and officials.

Two army groups from Guangxi were on the central government roster. These were the 21st Army Group, under Li Pinxian, and the 16th Army Group, under Xia Wenya. Each consisted of six divisions. A thirteenth division, the 173rd, was directly attached to Li Zongren. All told, with special auxiliary units included, they totaled 150,000 to 160,000 men. In addition, there were up to 200,000 men in local squads and guerrilla units in Guangxi and southern Anhui who reported to the Guangxi generals. Six of the thirteen divisions and most of the local units were stationed in Guangxi, while the remainder were in southern Anhui. In all, the Guangxi clique could lay claim to about 350,000 troops. From their powerful provincial base, the clique watched over their men carefully and made sure that they did not go wanting for arms and munitions.

THE CLIQUE LEADERS

The Guangxi generals did not occupy important posts in the central government. Outside their home province they were subject to Chiang's control. Thus they guarded their forces carefully and always tried to preserve unity in their ranks. They sought to keep their army in locations where the influence of the central government was weak. Chiang Kaishek worked to limit Guangxi power. After the battle for Nanjing (December 1937), during which Bai Chongxi and a number of 16th Army Group commanders had given a disgraceful account of themselves, Chiang carried out a series of organizational changes. He abolished the Southwest Command and recalled Bai to Chungking. He set up the Fourth War Zone, under Zhang Fakui, to control the two provinces of Guangdong and Guangxi, and placed loyal supporters of the center among Zhang's staff. Chiang also ordered the central government's 35th Army Group into Guangxi in order to limit the maneuverability of the Guangxi clique's 16th Army Group.

The fifty-year-old Li Zongren was commander of the Fifth War Zone. Although he had battle experience to his credit, he had little competence as a commander. He paid great attention to questions of international politics, having a keen interest in relations between the Soviet Union, the United States, Great Britain and China. He was predisposed toward the United States. On the domestic scene he stood at Chiang Kaishek's side and gave the appearance of willingly complying with Chiang's orders. Insofar as I could determine from talking with him, Li Zongren was not confident of victory over Japan. He viewed the war with a pessimism that infected his subordinates, and he held to the tactics of "drawing the enemy in" [as opposed to active resistance]. But Li enjoyed the favor of Chiang Kaishek and was firmly entrenched in his position in the government.

The other key figure in the Guangxi clique, Bai Chongxi, was deputy chief of the General Staff and chief of the Office of Military Training. Bai came from a landlord family that had gone into trade.

By 1941 he had laid up a solid fortune: he owned land and real estate worth half a million Chinese dollars, and held bank deposits totaling 200,000 Hong Kong dollars. His political outlook could be summarized as "Put your faith in money and office; and lord it over those who have neither." On the international scene, Bai leaned toward the United States and Britain and opposed strengthening ties with the Soviet Union. Outwardly, though, he showed esteem for the Soviet Union and even talked about improvement of our mutual relations—all this, of course, for the purpose of getting further assistance from us. But at the same time he was doing his best to convince his colleagues that under no circumstance should Soviet advice be followed.

The Guangxi leaders respected only Chiang Kaishek and generally held his ministers in little regard. Bai Chongxi, however, was close to He Yingqin. Telegrams from Bai and He Yingqing to Li Zongren and Li Pinxian concerning operations against the Japanese were almost identical. The difference between the two men was this: Bai Chongxi stood for continuing the war, while He Yingqin was a complete defeatist. If Bai had any inclination toward peace with Japan, it would have to be on conditions favorable to China.

Bai Chongxi was a determined foe of the CCP and a foremost partisan of covert operations against it. The measures taken to eliminate all CCP organizations in Guangxi were carried out under his instruction. He submitted the plans to Chiang Kaishek for driving the New 4th Army and 18th Army Group out of Anhui and Jiangsu. His collaboration with He Yingqin in managing the New 4th Army incident is attested to by the correspondence between them. Under the pretext of strengthening military discipline and the unity of command, Bai tried in every way to neutralize the military capacity of the CCP. He cherished the hope that the United States and Great Britain would help the Chinese government eliminate the communists. But apart from raising such matters within his own narrow circle, Bai never called openly for hostilities against the CCP.

As for lesser members of the clique, Li and Bai had in the commander of the 21st Army Group, Li Pinxian, an enthusiastic subordinate who saw to all their political and military needs. The commander of the 16th Army Group, Xia Wei, was also a devoted follower of theirs. (The 16th Army Group controlled all noncentral government units within Guangxi.) A further member of the clique was Li Jishen, a long-time former adversary of Chiang Kaishek, who was now serving the central government as inspector of the Southeast Command. Officially Li was head of guerrilla operations in that region, but in reality he had no independent administrative or military power. Actually, he was not so conservative as Li Zongren or Bai Chongxi. It would appear that he had been removed from the central government because of his relatively progressive views.

FUTURE PROSPECTS OF THE CLIQUE

By mid-1941 the 16th Army Group and the other Guangxi units had been brought up to almost full strength. But they went into action only when the province faced an immediate Japanese incursion. After the Japanese withdrew, the 16th Army Group would revert to its former defensive stance. The soldiers simply busied themselves with drill. The 21st Army Group, located in southern Anhui, also confined itself to a defensive role; if isolated clashes are discounted, more than two years passed without a major operation being undertaken by it against the Japanese. In fact, it was this force that was used to block the passage of communist troops across the Yangtze at the time of the New 4th Army incident. To this end the 16th Army Group received new supplies of equipment and ammunition, all of which ended up at the disposal of Li Zongren and Bai Chongxi.

Thus, despite four years of war, the Guangxi leaders managed to preserve their strength almost intact. Over this time there had been an improvement in the quality of their armies. The central government had been generous with equipment. Half of the men had seen some military action. Their officers had gained experience in combat. The professionalism of the command also benefited from the arrival of provincial graduates of the central army schools in Guangxi. Selection of these students lay in the hands of Bai Chongxi. However, by 1941 the clique had lost control of the main military academy in Guilin to the central government, and this gave Chiang Kaishek a base in the province.

My observation of relations between Chiang Kaishek and the Guangxi clique led me to the obvious conclusion that although the latter formally recognized Chiang's authority and were currently allied with him, their one aim was to preserve the full "independence" of their province. There was no firm basis to their alliance with Chiang. If Chiang should run into any political difficulties, one could assume that, almost without fail, they would refuse him support. But as long as Chiang held power, the Guangxi leaders did not wish to strain mutual relations. On the contrary, they sought to gain Chiang's confidence in order to enjoy suitably distinguished honors and positions.

For his part, Chiang Kaishek knew how to utilize the Guangxi generals in his battle against the CCP. Chiang was also working to appropriate the province for himself. He dispatched government forces to take over administration of the Guilin military academy. In the past the majority of the school's graduates had gone on to occupy positions as village heads. They provided the foundation of the Guangxi clique's administrative and military hold on the province. Now this source of local cadres was lost, and it could not be replaced. Chiang's move was accompanied by a reduction in the military manpower at the clique's disposal, as the province was required to provide men to the central government armies. Chiang further sought to undermine the military strength of the clique by introducing units from outside the province into the Guangxi army, but Li Zongren and Bai Chongxi were able to block this.

All in all, the Guangxi leaders realized that a bright future did not await them. They could not expect to score any major successes in their rivalry with Chiang Kaishek. The clique had too small a provincial base, and its leaders were neither popular nor widely known in the nation at large. In comparison with Chiang, who had the financial support of the "Big Four Families," the Guangxi clique was poverty-stricken. Thus their strategy was to avoid differences with Chiang as far as possible and to wait for future developments.

CHAPTER 10

PLANNING THE YICHANG CAMPAIGN

NATIONALIST DECEPTIONS

The Nationalists clung to their defensive strategy, but they needed to give the illusion of activity on the front line. Chiang Kaishek and the high command wanted to show both the domestic public and the foreign world that their three hundred divisions were vigorously resisting the Japanese and the puppets. The Chinese military did not hesitate to use deception to do this. There were reports of engagements on many sectors of the front. The Operations Section of the General Staff processed these reports and sent them on to the Military Commission. Sometimes they were published in the press, with accompanying maps. The commission looked at these reports from time to time but rarely acted on them. They were filed away under the heading of "local initiatives." When our military advisers in the field checked these claims, they found most of them to be false. It was apparent that there had been no engagements with the enemy. Although I had information to this effect in my possession, I did not wish to make an issue of it. I felt that doing so would be of no help to us. As the saying goes, the Chinese generals certainly knew how to "do themselves proud."

The following illustrates how official pronouncements served to deceive the public. In order to give the appearance of action against the Japanese, the Chinese General Staff would order a particular commander to throw half his forces into battle while keeping the other half in reserve. The commander in turn would order his generals to commit half their armies to the offensive. These generals would then send forward half their divisions. As a result, the number of troops taking part in the supposed campaign would amount to only a few companies or battalions, which, of course, were insufficient to launch an attack that seriously threatened the enemy. But the illusion had been created that the official order had been carried out. Dispatches would then be sent back to Chungking, and eventually a General Staff member would report to the Military Commission on operations that had never taken place.

A MAJOR OFFENSIVE IS PLANNED

The Soviet advisory mission tried in every way possible to induce the Nationalist government to go over to the attack. Both the Americans and British supported us. We tried to convince the Chinese that their army was becoming stronger, while the Japanese had become bogged down and could no longer undertake any major offensives. With our help, good results had been achieved in strengthening the Nationalist army defensively. Every attempt by the Japanese to make a breakthrough across the long Chinese front had met with failure. Every attack was soon repulsed.

In the spring of 1941 we began to press for a major Chinese offensive on the central sector of the front. This would fall in the vicinity of Yichang, to the west of Wuhan. The chief military adviser's headquarters already had drafted plans for such an operation. These were subsequently adopted by the Nationalist Army Operations Section, in consultation with the General Staff and the designated company commanders.

The basic objectives of the offensive were twofold: first, the destruction of the enemy army group holding the Yichang-Jingmen-Jingzhou triangle and the capture of Yichang; second, the attainment of a position on the Xiang River in northern Hunan for future operations against Wuhan. Execution of the plan was assigned to the Fifth and Sixth War Zones, with assistance from the Third and Ninth Zones. Units from the latter two zones were to cut the enemy's main communication links along the Yangtze. This would force the enemy to draw on his reserves. To carry out the whole operation a huge strike force was to be created, consisting of the 33rd Army Group (Fifth Zone) and the 26th Army Group (left flank of the Sixth Zone). The strike force would have a total strength, reserves included, of 200,000 men. It would be given major artillery support. Diversionary operations in the other war zones would complement the main offensive.

Enemy strength consisted of two Japanese divisions, the 13th and 19th, assisted by puppet units of the Wang Jingwei regime. The Nationalists saw recovery of the fertile Yichang region as a vital necessity, since it would help solve the food problem as well as ease the government's financial difficulties. We were of the opinion that Chiang Kaishek would want to demonstrate that his army could take the offensive and regain territory lost to the Japanese. The promise of American aid made it important for Chiang to acquire further prestige in the eyes of his new patrons. We knew, of course, that our Western allies would be very much interested in any offensive endeavors taken by the Chinese. And it was to our own advantage to deflect Japanese attention from further reinforcement of their army in Manchuria.

By August plans for the Yichang offensive had been completed and sent out to the regional commands for refinement. On the whole, the Third, Sixth and Ninth War Zone headquarters did their planning work correctly, with strike forces set up and tasks defined in the spirit of the General Staff directive. However, in the Fifth Zone General Li Zongren limited the strike force to only one division. He gave specific instructions to none of his armies; rather, they were left to work things out on their own. Fifth Zone headquarters had not mastered the essential task of coordinating the army group with its component armies.

In addition to this problem, we now faced a major reduction in our artillery allotment. Instead of the 287 heavy and medium guns projected for the Fifth and Sixth War Zones, we were assigned only 141 by headquarters in Chungking. Such alterations in the number of men and quantity of artillery planned for the main army groups weakened the whole operation dangerously. Even worse, the artillery was not to be moved from its original position to the designated attacking units but was to be held back well behind the front lines. The artillery commanders did not know which unit they were to support. When I reported to Chiang, I urged immediate implementation of a wide range of corrective measures.

One further point I should make. In working out the Yichang operation, I expected that the General Staff would in some way draw on communist units, either from the 18th Army Group or from local guerrilla detachments. But not a single Nationalist officer offered a suggestion to this effect, either at general headquarters in Chungking or in the various war zone commands. Some of the Nationalists feigned belief that communist guerrilla forces did not exist. Others voiced the fear that if the offensive failed, communist units would strike at the GMD rear.

I TRAVEL TO THE FRONT

Before presenting Chiang Kaishek and the General Staff with a detailed plan of the operation, I spent some time with the forces close to the front and discussed matters with General Chen Cheng, commander of the Sixth War Zone, whose troops were to play a major role in the attack on Yichang. I wanted the plan to come, as it were, from General Chen himself, while I would give him all possible support. My interpreter, Andreev, accompanied me, as did a Chinese general and colonel from the Operations Section of the General Staff. We set off in late March and were gone three weeks. The trip produced substantial results. Our discussions with General Chen and his staff resulted in a battle plan, which they sent on, with our revisions, to Chungking.

The Sixth War Zone was one of the most important in the China theater. It lay to the south of the Yangtze River, stretching almost 400 miles from Chungking in the west past Yichang almost to Wuhan in the east. (The Japanese controlled the Yangtze River upstream as far as Yichang.) The Sixth Zone had the largest number of troops assigned to it, and in Chen Cheng it had one of Chiang Kaishek's best commanders. This zone had the responsibility of maintaining the fortifications along the Upper Yangtze, which guarded the approaches to Chungking. North of the river lay the Fifth War Zone under Li Zongren.

There were few easy avenues of communication in this part of China. One was the Yangtze, which was navigable by steamer but vulnerable to Japanese air attack. The best route was to the south of the river, by land. This was the one we took to Sixth War Zone headquarters at Enshi, in the southwestern corner of Hubei province. From Chungking we set off south to Qijiang, then turned sharply eastward and traveled on through Nanchuan and Pengshui until we reached our destination. We crossed the mountains, traveling over steep rises and deep valleys that could be defended by small numbers of men. As we neared Yichang a rich fertile plain opened up. Here were grown the traditional staple crops of rice, tea, and beans.

At this time, travel in China was limited by the shortage of gasoline available at stations and rest points along the way. Fuel was enormously expensive, and any that found its way into private hands—into merchant hands—was beyond reach because of its unbelievable cost.

In Nanchuan we met the commander of the 5th Army. It was considered the best of the Nationalist armies and was held in reserve for operations in the Wuhan-Chungking and Wuhan-Guiyang sectors of the front. This army was kept up to full strength and was equipped with the best weapons in China, for the most part of Soviet make. Its soldiers were to a man literate, and chosen on a class basis—sons of the well-to-do, breathing the political spirit of China's ruling circles. The 5th Army was a pillar of the Guomindang. Chiang Kaishek kept it under his direct control.

We stayed in Nanchuan only briefly, as a long way lay ahead of us. We passed through mountainous regions, from time to time crossing narrow rivers that plunged into deep ravines. The mountains were covered with oak, pine and many other kinds of trees. Orange, tangerine and bamboo groves appeared before us. Walnuts grew in abundance, and everywhere there were tea plantations. The road we were on had been built during the war and was manned by a special military detachment. Enormous effort was needed to carve a route with hammer and chisel (there being no other means) through mountains and gorges, and along narrow ledges where boulders hung over us on one side and drops thousands of feet deep fell below us on the other. A cart, vehicle or person slipping from the road would be shattered beyond recognition.

From time to time we came across a hamlet, usually alongside a river or stream. Water was a rare commodity in the mountains, so the inhabitants had settled in the valleys. Because of the scarcity of water, no rice was grown in the mountains. String beans and soybeans were cultivated in the valleys and also on small terraces on the hillsides. Footpaths, along which one could travel only single file or on donkeys, branched off from the main road. These paths led to settlements where dwellings clung to the smallest available piece of ground. South of the Yangtze Chinese homes were usually large huts—a number of bamboo stakes driven into the ground, sides covered with matting and a roof of bamboo leaves. In each of these dwellings ten to fifteen people crowded together. The dirt and poverty leapt out at us from every doorway or opening through which we chanced to look. Yet notwithstanding their poverty, these simple people surprised us with their hospitality.

Sometimes we had to stop near one of these hamlets to rest after a long day's journey. Our vehicles were immediately surrounded by children, who asked us first of all who we were. We began by throwing out the usual reply of "foreigners" *(waiguoren)*. This did not satisfy them, and the questions continued. When they learned that we were Soviets, the children informed their parents, and the whole village set to welcoming us in whatever way possible. A metal teapot full to the top was always brought out, and sometimes dry biscuits and fruit as well. When we asked the villagers why they were receiving us so warmly, the answer was always the same: the Soviet people were helping China defeat the enemy. Such responses had been prompted, of course, by the Nationalist government. But the ordinary Chinese people understood and knew that our volunteers were doing battle with their mortal enemies, the Japanese invaders and self-serving Chinese warlords.

Yes, much has changed in China since the 1920s, I thought. But, as before, there remained the poverty, dirt, sickness, and near-universal illiteracy of these remote places through which we were traveling. The donkey and the porter with his carrying pole still served as the means of transport. Lighting came from the tung-oil lamp. The well-to-do merchants and landlords held the poor in servitude, meting out justice and punishment to them. We often encountered cripples. Doctors were almost nonexistent, and in any case the peasants could not afford treatment. In the towns itinerant dentists were to be seen at work on the street, with their stool, pliers, mug and bucket of water (and nothing else). The assistant to the "doctor," a healthy young lad, held the patient's head firmly while the dentist thrust his dirty hands into the patient's mouth in order to determine which tooth was bad, and then put the pliers into action. The experience no doubt long reverberated in the patient's memory.

The post stations where we stopped to pass the night were usually provided with restaurants or small eating places. At the entrance to such establishments we were commonly met in person by the owner, who led us to the place of honor and saw to it that we were well attended. Our companions, General Xu and Colonel Zhang, did not stint when it came to spending. According to the Chinese custom, the waiter (if he may be called that) melodiously informed the "maître d' " across the length of the restaurant of each dish ordered by us, and the latter in turn melodiously passed on our order to the kitchen, from which every imaginable aroma was emanating. In this way the waiter, the maître d'—all the service people, in fact—and the owner himself sought to make everyone present aware of the rich guests who were honoring the establishment and the dishes they were ordering.

To fall asleep on mats crawling with all kinds of vermin, surrounded by the noise of the mahjong tiles, was not easy. Our Chinese companions, the general and the colonel, carried special bedding, impregnated with some kind of substance. All insect life either hurried off or died on the spot. For learning about the country, its customs and the living conditions of the working people, our travels were indeed very valuable. This was the only way to see and feel the real China. One could live years in big cities such as Beijing, Tianjin and Shanghai, but without having traveled to the villages and hamlets and seen how the ordinary people lived and worked, one would never truly know China.

MEETINGS WITH CHEN CHENG

After a long journey we finally reached Sixth War Zone headquarters at Enshi. There we were met by General Chen Cheng, who was regarded as one of the most enlightened Nationalist commanders. Serving as adviser to General Chen was Colonel Goncharov, whom I knew as a fine officer from the Finnish War. General Chen showed us the greatest courtesy and assigned us the best quarters in town. At the same time he surrounded us with plainclothes agents, who worked in so clumsy a fashion that we spotted them at once.

My talks with General Chen were quite frank. I knew that I could not convert him to a military offensive by rhetoric alone. For a Chinese commander to lose men and matériel and attain no success meant a diminution of his personal position. I had to assure Chen Cheng that we would provide material support and obtain full backing from Chiang Kaishek. We told Chen that we would try to obtain from Chiang, at a minimum, a hundred artillery pieces and a triple complement of ammunition for the offensive. The ordnance would be obtained from Hu Zongnan, whose forces were positioned further north, guarding the southern borders of the communist Special Region. We realized, however, that it was going to prove extremely difficult to gain Chiang's agreement to such a reduction in Hu Zongnan's strength. (That such a reduction would lower tension between the GMD and the CCP was also one of our aims.)

Chen Cheng and I discussed the forthcoming campaign. The weakest part of the Japanese defense was an exposed area to the north of Yichang. It was almost completely surrounded by Chinese troops and was linked to the main Japanese force in Wuhan by only a single road. There were no strong Japanese defenses in the vicinity of Yichang, unless one counts the entrenchments and stamped earth walls of the neighboring Chinese villages. General Chen put before me a plan that he and his colleagues had worked out. (Colonel Goncharov told me that Chen Cheng had often considered such an operation to capture Yichang.) When I looked at the plan I saw that it was quite satisfactory and in almost complete form. I immediately agreed to it, making a few additions, such as the use of night operations against the enemy. I also stressed the need for General Chen to have a mobile artillery reserve at his disposal.

In the course of our discussion, we received unexpected support from the Chinese artillery commander. I wondered who this person might be, so I asked our artillery specialist to approach him personally. We soon found out that this Chinese general spoke Russian almost without accent. He had been born in Manchuria and evidently had studied with us at some time. His frank exchange with my assistant took place without an interpreter, in confidence (eye to eye, as we say in Russian). He said nothing further about himself, in fact refused to, but what he had done to help us was sufficient.

Our plan was to begin the offensive with an artillery barrage near dawn lasting ten to fifteen minutes. The first objective was to cut the road linking Yichang to Wuhan. The division assigned this task would then break into two columns, with the two cities as their targets. The column moving toward Wuhan was intended to guard against a possible counterthrust from Japanese reserve units further east. I knew from my discussions with Chen Cheng and Colonel Goncharov how keenly interested the Chinese were in recovering the Yichang region and its highly profitable two crops of rice per year. But Chen Cheng's command had to bear in mind that the Japanese would put up a hard fight for this valuable region and would be able to bring in reserves from Wuhan by either land or water. Our plan provided for our own reserve units as well as strong artillery formations to repel the likely Japanese counterattack.

Chen Cheng gave me to understand that the attack on Yichang had received Chiang Kaishek's sanction. I told General Chen he could count on the full support of his Soviet advisers. After the many customary banquets, inevitable under the circumstances, I set off with our advisers to meet one of Chen Cheng's commanders, General Wu Jiwei, whose army faced Yichang. General Wu made a good impression on me. He was lively and energetic. From talking with him and observing his character, it was plain to me that he was not the least averse to a good fight with the Japanese.

We were told by General Wu's staff that the day we arrived the Japanese had gone on the attack and captured a low rise on one section of the line but been unable to advance further. Whether this was so we had no way of knowing. It was possible that General Wu wanted to show us that his section of the front was the most active. I decided to avail myself of the opportunity at hand. When the general had us seated at the dining table, I raised my glass and offered a toast to the health of a most vigorous and enthusiastic warrior, General Wu. This pleased him very much. When the dinner ended, Colonel Goncharov suggested that our distinguished commander mount a night counterattack. To expel the Japanese from the rise they occupied should not have been that difficult, as the night was moonlit. I supported Goncharov's proposal, and again we drank to the health of our most vigorous and dedicated commander. General Wu could not refuse and at once issued the necessary orders to his chief of staff.

We never did know whether a counterattack took place, or even whether the Japanese were actually occupying the hill, but in the morning General Wu reported to me that the night attack had been successful. The hill had been retaken and major casualties inflicted on the enemy. I received the report, congratulated the general on his victory and immediately sent telegrams to Chen Cheng at war zone headquarters and to He Yingqin at the War Ministry telling them of the liquidation of a Japanese thrust against General Wu's sector of the front.

OUTCOME OF THE YICHANG PLAN

When we left to return to Chungking, we parted from the senior officers of the Sixth War Zone as friends, ready to support each other in any actions against the enemy. I also gave Colonel Goncharov some customary words of advice on how best to deal with the Chinese commanders. We then returned to Chungking by steamer, departing from a point not far west of Yichang. Mountains pressed in on the Yangtze from both sides. The voyage upstream along the deep, fast-flowing river aboard our decrepit steamer took more than three days, but it gave us good opportunity for reconnoitering, and it convinced us that no direct route lay open to the Japanese along the river. An attack on Chungking would require the use of steamers and motorized barges. The Chinese had built defensive emplacements to cover the approaches to the city. Heavy guns were mounted in well-camouflaged caves hollowed into the steep river banks. The defenders could hold the river channel under point-blank fire while being almost invisible to return fire from the river or from the air. On our way back we twice went ashore to look at these emplacements. I can honestly say that they were very good.

From our boat we could see not only the surrounding poverty but also the natural wealth of the region. Coal, copper and other raw materials for industry were being worked in various places by the most primitive means. Enjoyment of all these riches awaited a guiding hand. I do not know whether it was by accident or not, but several times Japanese aircraft appeared over the river, forcing our boat to stop and take refuge close to the shore. Waiting there with engines silenced, the boat was difficult for the planes to spot. These moments, combined with the strong adverse current of the river, slowed down our trip. Often a pilot would come on board and slowly guide us through especially dangerous rapids.

After my arrival in Chungking I reported to He Yingqin. I remarked on the dependable troops and strong fortifications that protected the Yangtze River approaches to Chungking. The Japanese would find it very difficult to overcome such defenses. I also observed that Chen Cheng's armies were capable of going on the attack and that the Japanese had lost their aggressive spirit after being passive for so long. Given their shortages of frontline troops and reserves, it was unlikely that the Japanese would be able to mount a broad offensive in the Yichang area. The general situation was now such that small Chinese forces could hold off much larger enemy ones. I also drew attention to the exposed position of isolated Japanese garrisons, which were frequently located miles from each other. Such outposts were often without tactical or even operational links with each other. They offered convenient, solitary targets that could be easily surrounded and reduced one by one. I emphasized that the Japanese 13th Division at Yichang was just such an isolated garrison.

My report was presented to Chiang Kaishek, who was pleased by it, as I later learned. I also found out that the American and British ambassadors and military attachés gained access to the report as well.

In early July Chen Cheng arrived in Chungking in order, he said, to obtain Chiang Kaishek's personal approval for the offensive. I met

General Chen shortly afterward for dinner. He informed of the state of preparations, making me hopeful that the final stage was near. Bai Chongxi was also present. As one of Chiang's close confidants, General Bai wanted to assure me that the decision already had been taken at the highest level. I had only one thing to worry about now— that Chiang Kaishek would change his mind and call off the offensive at the last moment. We knew from experience that the Chinese leadership could always find reasons to sound the retreat. However, reports from our advisers in the field seemed to confirm the movement of troops and weaponry into the war zone, if at an unhurried pace.

It was difficult for me to tell whether the Japanese knew of the preparations for the Yichang offensive. If they did, they would be of the view, to be sure, that the Chinese were incapable of undertaking any serious operations in the area. The transfer of their best units from Wuhan to the Changsha front at the end of the summer certainly indicated this attitude.

At the very end of August we received news that the Chinese had launched their attack on Yichang and that they had scored a number of successes in the opening days. We were assured that many strongholds around Yichang had been taken and that the battle for the city was under way. At a meeting of the Military Commission the war minister, He Yingqin, reported that Yichang was in Chinese hands. He repeated this at a reception held in honor of the mission led by General Magruder, which had just arrived from the United States. On this occasion fireworks were set off to signal the "victory of Yichang."

But all of this was pretense. According to information I was receiving from our advisers, the Chinese generals did not have the drive to carry the operation through to the end. Despite Chen Cheng's willingness to throw his reserves into battle in order to break the last Japanese resistance, Chiang Kaishek ordered the attack halted. There had not been a major offensive, then, in the Yichang area. Judging from appearances, a number of attacks on isolated Japanese garrisons had been staged. This could not bring about results of any substance. In my report to Moscow in mid-September

I regretfully had to confirm that "on the whole, it is unlikely that Chiang Kaishek will undertake any offensive operations in the immediate future."

As it turned out, my reading of the case was not entirely correct. Exactly two weeks later Nationalist forces went on the offensive in the Yichang region. Chiang Kaishek had been forced to this desperate move by developments on another part of the front. The Japanese had launched a full-scale attack on Changsha. This was to be the last offensive of 1941 mounted by the Japanese—and it was to end unexpectedly in defeat for them.

CHAPTER 11

THE JAPANESE DEBACLE AT CHANGSHA

The Japanese failed to take Changsha in their offensive of September 1939. In the summer of 1941 they began planning a second attack on the city. This took place as Japan found itself in an ever more complicated international situation. The occupation of southern Indochina in July of that year had abruptly worsened relations with the Western powers. On our Far Eastern borders the situation was tense because of stepped-up Japanese military activity in Manchuria and Korea. Against this background the second battle of Changsha opened on September 15.

THE JAPANESE AIM FOR A BREAKTHROUGH

Obligations to their Axis partners demanded action from the Japanese. But they were still waiting to decide when and where to make their next move. In Europe they were watching the battles on the Soviet-German front. Meanwhile, the war in China weighed on them like a heavy boulder. If the Japanese were to strengthen their global position, they would have to show the Soviet Union, Great Britain and the United States that further aid to China was futile. Those powers must be made to realize that China could not be used to check Japan. By means of a major offensive that clearly demonstrated Chinese military weakness, the Japanese high command intended to give China a "good kick." For the Chinese, who very much feared American concessions to Japan in the negotiations under way in Washington, it was essential that they prove the opposite—that the Chinese army had the capacity to continue the struggle. China wanted large-scale military aid from the United States. Chiang Kaishek therefore would have to kick back at the Japanese.

The period preceding the attack on Changsha was characterized by a relative lull at the front. Through the summer of 1941 the Japanese launched a number of limited "pacification" campaigns. In

June they targeted guerrilla areas in Shandong, in July New 4th Army bases in Jiangsu, and in August the Shanxi-Chahar-Hebei base area in the north. Use was made of Chinese puppet forces of the Wang Jingwei government. Elimination of guerrilla bases and popular resistance in occupied China was the main purpose of these campaigns, but they also had a political goal: to bring about a reconciliation between Chiang Kaishek and Wang Jingwei and thereby unite all anticommunist elements in the nation against the people's forces. If they succeeded, the Japanese would be free to use most of their China Expeditionary Army to strengthen themselves in the north against the Soviet Union and in the south against the Western powers. Although the Japanese did not have enough strength to eliminate the regular communist forces (the 18th Army Group and the New 4th Army), they were able to inflict serious losses on communist guerrilla units in these punitive campaigns.

Toward the end of August the Japanese began to regroup their forces for the drive on Changsha. The main blow was to be struck by the 11th Army, reinforced by units from the Wuhan garrison. Most of the troops to be used in the campaign were taken from the Fifth and Sixth War Zones. Chinese commanders in these zones wired reports from late August of large movements of Japanese troops between Wuhan and the Han River Valley. (Wuhan was the marshaling point for the rotation of Japanese units to and from the front.) The main staging area for the forthcoming offensive was to the east of the city of Yueyang.

The Chinese misjudged the Japanese regrouping under way at Wuhan. They thought the Japanese were reducing their forces in the region in order to build up manpower in Manchuria. The Chinese felt that the international situation was such that the Japanese would soon make a decision to move against the Soviet Union or, failing that, against the Western powers. The Chinese almost completely excluded from their considerations the possibility of Japanese action in China. Thus the attack on Changsha came as a great surprise.

The objectives of the Japanese offensive were as follows.

(1) *Destruction of the main forces of the Nationalist Ninth War Zone.* This would ensure the long-term security of Wuhan by removing the

possibility of a Chinese attack from the south and would facilitate the release of Japanese troops from central China for military operations elsewhere. (2) *Capture of Changsha.* This would give the Japanese control of the major rice-producing regions of Hunan. It would also bring them close to Hengyang, thereby threatening the Chinese communications network running through the south of the province. (3) *Positioning for a potential linkup of the Central China and South China fronts.* This could be realized by means of a two-pronged offensive south from Changsha and north from Canton, along the course of the Wuhan-Canton railway.

The principal features of the Japanese battle plan were as follows. [See map, p. xvii]. The main blow of the Japanese drive south from Yueyang would fall to the southwest of Pingjiang. The left flank of the Japanese attack would swing toward Zhuzhou (south of Changsha). Chinese defense in this area was provided by the core armies of the Ninth War Zone. The Japanese intent was to use the combined weight of their left flank and center to pin down the Chinese near Lake Dongting and destroy them there. In order to hold the Chinese in check and prevent them from moving reinforcements to the Changsha front, the Japanese would launch attacks in the north, near Zhengzhou (Henan), and in the south, near Canton. Thus the three main Chinese fronts would be active simultaneously, which was precisely what the Nationalist command hoped to avoid.

The Changsha offensive placed the Chinese in a very difficult situation. They knew that a Japanese victory would be highly damaging to the future course of the war. Three war zones would be threatened with encirclement. The whole southeastern part of the country might fall to the enemy. Chiang Kaishek did not possess sufficient backup forces to parry these Japanese blows. He also feared that some of his generals might go over to the enemy with their men. Yet to throw his last major reserves into battle—the 5th and 6th Armies—was something Chiang could scarcely contemplate doing.

THE BATTLE IS JOINED

The Japanese attack force numbered some 102,000 men. It was made up of four infantry divisions, two independent brigades, units from the 3rd Mechanized Regiment, an artillery brigade and a mountain artillery regiment. They were armed with 1,690 machine guns, 415 pieces of heavy artillery, 80 tanks and 40 armored cars. They were supported by 200 aircraft. The Chinese were able to put about 250,000 men (ten armies) into the field, but they possessed only light weaponry—4,700 machine guns. They had 19 aircraft at their disposal.

The battle can be divided into four phases. (1) The Japanese force the crossing of the Xinqiang River and regroup on its south bank. (2) The Japanese force the crossing of the Miluo River and secure a position on its south bank, on a line from Wukou through Fulingpu to Jinjing. (3) The Japanese reach the eastern approaches to Changsha along the Huanghuashi-Yonganshi line, at which point the Chinese armies from the Fifth and Sixth War Zones launch a major counterattack against the enemy's flanks and rear. (4) The Japanese disengage from battle and withdraw to their original lines in the face of continuing action by Chinese Sixth and Ninth War Zone forces.

Engagements between forward reconnoitering units preceded the main Changsha battle. These were initiated by the Japanese 6th Infantry Division in the hilly area west of Tongcheng. Chinese 58th Army units took part in these encounters, which did not result in any significant change of position for either side.

By September 12 the Japanese had finished their marshaling operations. Two strike forces were created. The larger one was made up of four infantry divisions, the 3rd, 6th, 33rd and 40th, subdivided into two columns. It was to move southward, passing to the west of Pingjiang, and make for Zhuzhou, the capture of which would result in the encirclement of the main Ninth War Zone armies. The second strike force, which was made up of the 4th Division and a brigade from the 13th Division, was to move directly on Changsha along the Hankou-Guangzhou railway line. Some marines and a cavalry regiment were included in this force, since it would be proceeding close to the shores of Lake Dongting.

On the afternoon of September 15 the Japanese crossed the Xinqiang River, encountering little resistance. By the end of the day they had ferried 10,000 troops over to the south bank; by the nineteenth all their men were across. Between the fifteenth and the nineteenth the Japanese fought Chinese 4th, 20th and 58th Army units for control of the area between the Xinqiang and Miluo Rivers. The Chinese were unable to halt the Japanese advance, but they were able to win time: it took the Japanese three days and nights to reach the Miluo (advancing an average of 15–20 kilometers per day). The Chinese withdrew to the south bank of the Miluo River, while the Japanese occupied Guiyi and moved toward Xinshi and Wukou, reaching the north bank of the Miluo on September 19.

The time gained by the Chinese defenders enabled 10th, 26th and 37th Army units to begin reaching the south bank of the river on the same day. The Chinese established a defensive line between Jinjing and Fulingpu. (Meanwhile, on September 18, the Japanese moved a force down Lake Dongting and occupied Qingshan, near the mouth of the Xiang River, downstream from Changsha.) The main battle now began.

The Japanese 6th Infantry Division immediately crossed the Miluo River on September 19 and overcame remaining resistance from the Chinese 20th and 58th Armies. After capturing Wukou, the key point on the river's south bank, the 6th Division pushed steadily on. The other Japanese column, made up of the 33rd and 40th Divisions, crossed the Miluo on September 21 and engaged units of the newly arrived 26th and 37th Armies. By September 23 the Japanese had moved all their attack force across the river. Three Chinese armies (the 4th, 20th and 58th) still remained on the north bank of the river, astride the Japanese supply and communication lines. However, they were now so wary of battle that they had no effect on events taking place south of the Miluo.

By September 25 the Chinese right flank was seriously threatened. South of the Wangjingpu-Wukou-Xinshi line the 26th and 37th Armies were in large part surrounded by the Japanese 3rd, 6th and 40th Divisions. The Chinese hurriedly sent their 72nd Army from Pingjiang in relief. Advance units of the 79th Army began at the same time to arrive in Changsha from the Sixth War Zone.

In the fighting of September 25–27 the Japanese broke the main Chinese resistance and began to close in on Changsha. On

September 29 troops of the 6th Division, after forcing the Liuyang River, occupied Zhentoushi, 40 kilometers southeast of the city. Units of the 4th and 13th Divisions were already 20 kilometers northeast of the city. Earlier, on September 27, the Japanese had made two parachute drops, 5 and 10 kilometers east of the city. This was accompanied by a diversionary raid on the city by a detachment from the 13th Division disguised in civilian clothes. The Chinese managed to ward off both forays.

During these days I was often with Chiang Kaishek, even taking my meals with him. I constantly sought to strengthen his resolve to see the battle through. On September 28 the Japanese 3rd Division captured Zhuzhou. The Japanese now held the southern approaches to the city. To the east they were grouping their main forces for the final attack. The time was now critical for Changsha.

THE COUNTERATTACK IS MADE

[Readers are directed to the Introduction, pages xxxiv–xxxvii, in regard to this section.]

On September 29 I was urgently summoned by Chiang, who asked for my confidential advice on how to counter the Japanese advance. I promised to put my ideas before him right away. My advisers and I quickly worked out a plan that was risky but decisive. It consisted basically of three stages. First, the main Chinese army group would continue its slow withdrawal from the front under strong defensive cover, thus luring the enemy into the narrow mountain defiles east and northeast of Changsha. These were well suited to mounting a strong defense. To our good fortune, a number of well-supplied batteries of Soviet manufacture were located there, and we had some of our own advisers on the spot. Second, the main battle would be joined only when the Japanese were beneath the walls of Changsha, with their supply lines overextended, and easy access to reinforcements limited by the mountainous terrain. Third, a powerful flanking attack would be unleashed against the main Japanese force as it approached Changsha. The fact was that the situation for the Chinese, while critical, was by no means hopeless. The Japanese left flank, which constituted the principal strike force, was in the process of enveloping the city, but the bulk of the Chinese Ninth War Zone armies had eluded entrapment. Only three Chinese armies (the 10th, 37th and 99th) were located within the gradually contracting semicircle. The remaining seven were holding back on the flanks of the Japanese. They posed a serious threat, which the Japanese sooner or later would have to confront.

The groundwork for moving from defense to offense already had been laid by Soviet military advisers. As mentioned in the preceding chapter, they had planned the Yichang operation. Without that experience of organizing a major offensive operation, not to mention overcoming defeatism in the Chinese high command, the Changsha counterattack would have been destined to failure.

When I showed Chiang the plan, he was not prepared to accept it in full. I had to persist in order to convince him that there was no alternative. After lengthy consideration, Chiang finally agreed to our proposal and asked me to see to its implementation. He said, "Take this plan to the General Staff and put it into operation in my name. If there are any difficulties, report to me at once." I had achieved exactly what I wanted. In addition, Chiang agreed to release, should it be necessary, the whole air force for the counterattack. From my meetings with Chiang, I knew that he needed a victory in order to show the Americans the war-worthiness of his armies.

The contents of the plan were transmitted from the General Staff to the respective war zone commanders. I conveyed the details to our advisers at the front. We gave them strict instructions to attend exactly to the plan and to let me know at once of any deviation from it. To prevent our intentions becoming public knowledge, I asked He Yingqin not to raise the matter in the Military Commission.

Our battle plan succeeded 100 percent. The Japanese, having readied their main force for the attack on Changsha, did not expect such a bold maneuver against the flanks of their 11th Army. The Chinese already had done everything to slow down the Japanese advance. For example, the Japanese could not use the rice they had seized, since the Chinese had removed all the grinding mills as they withdrew. The Japanese had to ship provisions from Wuhan along roads badly damaged by the retreating Chinese. Changsha had been further strengthened, and the roads leading to it had been mined and obstructed.

Our advisers carefully saw to the precise execution of the operation (which they spoke of as Chiang Kaishek's plan) and watched for the slightest divergence from it. When I received a report to the effect that Gu Zhutong, commander of the Third War Zone, was attempting to countermand our deployment of units from his 10th Army, I contacted Chiang Kaishek at once and told him that General Gu was presuming to ignore the letter of his orders. Chiang immediately wired Gu and told him to contact to me, where a sharp telegram of rebuke was awaiting him.

On September 27 the first units of the 79th Army reached Changsha. At the same time the 74th Army was making for Liuyang, engaging Japanese units along the way. To the north of Changsha, near Jinjing, the Chinese were preparing a major flanking attack on the main Japanese force. On the morning of the twenty-eighth the Japanese launched their attack on Changsha. But by this time they were beginning to experience shortages of munitions and provisions. Japanese radio messages to headquarters in Yueyang asking for resupply by air were intercepted by the Chinese.

As the Japanese approached the city through the surrounding mountain defiles they were almost ready to celebrate victory. However, they now encountered heavy artillery fire from the emplacements we had constructed earlier. Changsha met the attack with a stubborn defense. The Japanese took heavy losses in the battle. In the immediate vicinity of the city alone the Chinese later counted 10,000 Japanese dead.

As the battle of Changsha began, the Chinese set upon the flanks and rear of the main Japanese assault force. The 26th, 72nd and 74th Armies took part in this flanking attack, which fell just to the north of Huanghuashi. A powerful air attack was also directed at the enemy. There now appeared the real possibility that the Chinese would surround the Japanese, who were being torn to pieces outside Changsha.

By the end of September the Japanese were confronted with a very threatening situation. Chinese forces now endangered Yichang,

Jingmenzhou and other important centers in the Han River Valley. If the battle for Changsha continued, the whole Japanese front west of Wuhan might break, since it had been weakened by the transfer to Changsha of much of the 3rd, 4th, 13th and 40th Divisions. In the face of the determined Chinese counteroffensive, the Japanese began to withdraw on October 1. They did this at a forced pace. On the second they reached the south bank of the Miluo River, and on the same day they ferried most of their artillery across to the north bank of the river.

The Japanese were now back to the ground they had held prior to the Changsha offensive. In their retreat they managed to avoid battle with the pursuing Chinese, but they abandoned their baggage along the way. With more energetic action, the Chinese might have surrounded the whole of the 11th Army in the mountainous terrain north of Changsha. As for the Japanese diversionary operations in Guangdong and northern Jiangxi (Fourth and Ninth War Zones), they had little impact on the battle for Changsha. Japanese forces soon returned to their original lines in these areas.

The victory at Changsha raised the prestige of the Chinese army in the eyes of both the Chinese and the Americans and British. The Japanese had never expected such determined resistance and tactical coordination on the part of the Nationalist army. After the battle was over we of the Soviet military mission stood aside. Chiang Kaishek exultantly invited the heads of the different military missions to fly with him in his personal plane to Changsha to view the battlefield and the mounds of Japanese corpses under the city walls and in the mountain passes. He warmly invited me to be at his side, but I declined on the grounds of ill health. I directed our advisers not to be present at the parade so that the laurels of victory would belong solely to Chiang and his generals.

LESSONS OF THE BATTLE OF CHANGSHA

Thus the Changsha offensive ended in utter rout for the Japanese. It proved unrealizable because of the combined Chinese counterattack, which drew on forces from three war zones, the Third, Sixth and Ninth. The Japanese were now compelled to call off the Changsha operation in order to safeguard their front west of Wuhan. They began transferring units back to the Han River basin.

It must be said that the Chinese high command went on the attack at Changsha against its will. As soon as the situation at Changsha changed for the better, Chiang Kaishek ordered the Fifth and Sixth War Zone commanders to call a halt. Thus the counterattack was terminated, even though there was every possibility of gaining mastery of the Han River Valley and capturing Yichang before the Japanese could recover from their losses. The Changsha offensive might then have ended in a massive rout of the Japanese outside Wuhan. However, Chiang's policy was to bring about Japan's defeat at the hands of a third party (thus his hopes for war between Japan and the Soviet Union, or Japan and the Western powers). This is why the high command did not exploit to the full the favorable situation now facing them in this critical region of central China.

During the Changsha campaign another thing became clear: Chiang Kaishek was unwilling to strengthen his attack force by drawing on any of the units positioned against the communists. The Americans, by the way, were aware of this. It had become evident to them, certainly by the time of the Yichang offensive, that Chiang would not make use of his reserves or his artillery units if this weakened Hu Zongnan's blockade of the Special Region. However, the growing possibility of a Japanese move to the south prompted strong interest on the part of the Americans in unifying the Nationalist and communist armies for more active prosecution of the war. I knew that several meetings had taken place between the new American ambassador, Clarence E. Gauss, and Zhou Enlai. From the fall of 1941 the Americans were clearly beginning to show great interest in the Special Region and the communist armies. But to bring together the forces of the GMD and the CCP was no easy matter. Chiang neither wished nor would permit the Americans or anyone else to directly supply the communists with arms. And Mao had no wish to link his forces with those of the Nationalists unless he received weapons. For Chiang and Mao the primary consideration remained their own struggle for power.

The military record as it stood in the fall of 1941 showed that the Chinese were capable not only of defense but also of offense, and that the effectiveness of the latter would be increased significantly if the GMD and CCP worked in coordination. Here is an example. In the course of the battle for Changsha, the Japanese launched an offensive in north China. On September 26 three divisions crossed the Yellow River, their objective being the cities of Zhengzhou and Luoyang and the intervening stretch of the Longhai Railway. If successful, this thrust would block military transport between the First and Fifth War Zones and would create the danger of a major incursion westward into the Dongguan-Xi'an area. This in turn would open up the possibility of a combined descent on Chungking from the Xi'an region and from the east, where the 11th Army would advance up the Yangtze. The link between China and the Soviet Union would also be imperiled should the Japanese take Xi'an.

The Japanese offensive met with great success during its opening stage. The front between the First and Fifth War Zones was seriously threatened. The commander of the First War Zone, General Wei Lihuang, declared that he did not have sufficient strength to meet the Japanese advance. Our military adviser at his headquarters concurred in this. As a result, Ambassador Panyushkin and I informed Moscow of the dangerous situation now developing and asked if Mao Tsetung could be persuaded to assist Chiang by striking at the Japanese flanks and rear. I then recommended to He Yingqin that the Military Commission instruct the 18th Army Group to launch an attack. From the insistence with which I put forward this proposal He Yingqin understood that his orders would be followed. As a result of their combined operation, CCP and GMD forces halted the offensive and caused the Japanese to withdraw to their original position.

At the next meeting of the Military Commission, He Yingqin reported on how the communist attack had forced the Japanese back. Some Chinese newspapers carried stories about the assistance given by the communists to the Nationalist army. But this did not last long. The Nationalist leaders did not wish the populace to know of communist successes against the Japanese and soon stopped giving out any further information to the press. We learned, however, from Zhou Enlai and Ye Jianying that the 18th Army Group had inflicted heavy casualties on the Japanese.

The favorable outcome of this battle on the banks of the Yellow River strengthened the belief among civilians and military alike that the Japanese could be defeated. The Japanese were not all-powerful. If the Chinese fought as a united people, they were certain of success. It had been given to us Soviet advisers to show the leaders of China that, with proper coordination of Nationalist and communist forces, victory in battle with the Japanese was within reach.

CHAPTER 12

NORTH OR SOUTH?

In the spring of 1941, on the eve of the German invasion, those of us in far-off Chungking had a part in answering one of the most crucial questions facing our country: where would Japanese aggression next fall? All of us knew that we could not escape war in the west. But in the east? Would the Japanese militarists declare their solidarity with their Axis partners and stab us in the back?

Thus the two questions of the impending German attack on the Soviet Union and the Japanese response to it became fused into one. Since Ambassador Panyushkin and I were close to the situation—in the eye of the Far Eastern storm, so to speak—we were instructed by Moscow to follow events carefully and give a clear estimate of what the Japanese were likely to do. Would a second front be opened up by the Japanese within days of war in the west? Might the Japanese actually stage a simultaneous attack on our eastern regions? Many members of our staff believed that Japan would move against the Soviet Union, if not at once, then soon after the German attack.

JAPANESE HESITATIONS

The Japanese certainly had been preparing themselves for war with the Soviet Union. Following their seizure of Manchuria in 1931–32 they built up the region, along with Korea, as a potential springboard against us. By 1941 thirteen special fortification zones faced the Soviet border. The preceding year saw the Kwantung Army increased from nine to twelve divisions. Its complement now stood at 350,000 men. The General Staff in Tokyo was projecting further increases in men and weapons for this army. The Manchurian and Inner Mongolian puppet forces were also enlarged during 1940–41.

Nevertheless, after studying the situation in the Far East from intelligence at my disposal, I was more and more inclined to the conclusion that Japan was more likely to move to the south, against the Americans and British, not to the north, against us. This conviction was based on a number of factors, both general and specific. No evidence was needed of the fact that Japan was deficient in strategic resources—in raw materials such as iron, coal, oil and tin. Without these the Japanese could not see themselves taking on the world's leading industrial powers. Before becoming involved in a conflict of such dimensions, Japan had to find the right moment when the Western powers were tied down elsewhere to seize their resource-rich but poorly defended colonies. This would allow Japan to wage war alongside its German and Italian allies against the United States and Britain—and the Soviet Union.

At the outset of 1941 Japan possessed the strongest air force and navy in the Far East. These had not been committed to battle to any significant degree. Despite the Anti-Comintern and Tripartite Pacts, which called for close military cooperation with Germany and Italy, it was apparent that Japan would follow its own agenda of conquest. There was no coordination of any kind between Japan and its Axis partners. Japan was waiting for the right moment to launch a lightning attack on its next victim, preferably a weak one, so that there would be no risk of its becoming bogged down, as had happened in China. On the Chinese front the Japanese were moving carefully, sparing their forces, and attacking only vulnerable, weakly defended points.

In September 1940 Japan exploited the defeat of France and the weakness of the French overseas to effortlessly occupy the northern part of Indochina. This further solidified the base Japan was building for further expansion of its air and sea power in the south. From intelligence at my disposal it was clear that Canton and Hainan Island, both of which had been occupied in late 1938, and Haiphong, in northern Indochina, were being transformed into forward military positions by the Japanese. The necessary preparations for an advance to the south were being carried out with the greatest speed.

This was corroborated by an unexpected source. In March 1941 a plane carrying a Japanese admiral to Haiphong experienced difficulties and was forced to land in Guangdong. The admiral, with all his documents and baggage, fell into the hands of Chinese guerrillas. I soon learned of this from contacts at General Staff headquarters. It appeared that these materials were of great value. I therefore decided to approach Chiang Kaishek personally for access to them. I knew that without his agreement I would receive nothing from his staff. I told Chiang that, as adviser, I wished to familiarize myself with the documents so that I could work out plans for countering a possible new enemy offensive in the south. Chiang replied that they had not yet reached him, that they were still on the way and he did not know when they would arrive. This was true.

A major new development increased pressure on me to gain access to these materials. Matsuoka Yosuke, the Japanese foreign minister, was at this moment passing through Manchuria en route to Germany. From newspaper reports it was known that he would be stopping in Moscow for important talks with the Soviet leaders. I informed Moscow of the capture of the Japanese documents. A reply came shortly. I was to try to obtain these documents and send them at once to Moscow. A plane would be sent to Lanzhou to fly them back. Such urgent instructions were prompted by the fact that Matsuoka was now on his way to Moscow.

At last the documents arrived. As soon as they were passed on to me I had them photographed and sent on to Lanzhou, where a plane was waiting for them. They reached Moscow a few days prior to Matsuoka's arrival. From our hurried reading of the documents, Andreev, Roshchin and I saw that they were extremely valuable. The Japanese admiral had been carrying highly detailed plans for the development of military bases in Hainan and Haiphong. Enclosed were diagrams of aerodromes, dockyards and disembarkation facilities for land forces. In our view, these materials were genuine. (Later events confirmed this.) Comparing them with intelligence I had received from the French military attaché, Colonel Yvon, and with information received from other channels, I had no doubt that the Japanese were readying themselves for an offensive against the Anglo-American colonies in Southeast Asia.

I was inclined to believe that for the present Japan would not move against the Soviet Union. I will not conceal the fact that at the time I was very much worried. I often thought, what if I am wrong?

But I had to hold my position. I shared the opinion of all my colleagues that we could not weaken our European defenses. If my reading of the situation was correct, we would be able to transfer some of our forces in the Far East to the west if Hitler attacked.

The Japanese militarists did not attack the Soviet Union in 1941. History offers many objective reasons for this. In the first instance, our party and government accurately read the complicated Far Eastern situation and took the right decisions. The Japanese needed to reach an understanding with us in order to prepare their offensive against the Western powers. Our leaders had in their possession reliable information about Japan's wish for an agreement with us. The conclusion of the neutrality pact with Japan in April 1941, when Hitler was readying himself to attack us, was a great triumph for our diplomacy. Yet the Japanese must have known that Germany would attack the Soviet Union sooner or later. That they signed the pact once again underlines the fact that coordination of military operations between the Axis powers was not a reality.

For Chiang Kaishek the arrival of the Japanese foreign minister in Moscow could not but seriously affect his interests. Chiang would have realized that Matsuoka's final Berlin destination was only a cover for more important matters. But neither Chiang nor his Western patrons could do much to influence or frustrate the impending agreement. The conclusion of a neutrality pact meant that the chances of a military confrontation between the Soviet Union and Japan were significantly reduced. Chiang had no alternative but to keep presenting himself as a close friend of the Soviet Union. He and his wife, Soong Meiling, held a picnic for Ambassador Panyushkin and the Soviet embassy staff, to which members of my office and long-serving military advisers were also invited. The Chinese press portrayed this gathering as evidence of the close connection between the Soviet Union and China. The intent was to suggest to the Japanese that they could not rely on the Soviets, let alone enter into any vital agreements with them. These efforts by Chiang and his circle proved to be of no avail, however.

On a different matter, I should mention that we made use of the above social engagement to persuade Chiang and Soong Meiling (who was formally head of the air services) to replace the commander of the air force, General Zhou Zhirou. This man had been carrying out an overtly obstructionist policy in using our war aid. His efforts to discredit the quality of our aircraft appeared highly suspect to us. In order to prove General Zhou's unfitness as air force commander, we presented Chiang with a carefully prepared statement offering many suggestions for improvement of the Chinese air force. Chiang listened to our proposals. Subsequently he summoned He Yingqin, Bai Chongxi and the leading members of the General Staff and reviewed in detail the inadequacies of the air force, as indicated in our report. He even threatened to have General Zhou shot. Chiang emphasized his agreement with the Soviet advisers' analysis. Soon afterward General Mao Bangchu, whom we had recommended, was named air force commander.

SCHEMES AND RUMORS IN CHUNGKING

It was not just Chiang Kaishek but the American and British diplomats in Chungking as well who sought to draw the Soviet Union into conflict with Japan. They tried in every way to make the Japanese aware that, despite the neutrality pact, the Soviet Union was still providing aid to China and was thus violating the agreement. They tried to create suspicion in our ranks by saying that, according to their intelligence, the Japanese were systematically building up their forces in Manchuria. The Americans and British also kept pressure on Chiang Kaishek, informing him that the Japanese were constructing bases in south China and Indochina for a Pacific offensive. And both Western powers continued to make concessions to Japan, but it was obvious that any concessions only further encouraged the aggressor.

Intrigues designed to strain our relations with the Japanese were stepped up at this time. I recall one widely reported gathering in Chungking, which had been arranged on Chiang's personal instruction. It was held in a leading restaurant in the city. This event was paid for by Chen Lifu and Chen Guofu, the wealthy brothers who were Chiang's closest political allies. The Soviet, American and British ambassadors were invited. In their opening remarks the Chen brothers passionately called on us all to unite in the common struggle against Japan. The Chinese speakers stressed time after time that there was already in existence an anti-Japanese great-power bloc, consisting of China, the United States, Great Britain and the Soviet Union. The following suggestion was actually made: if bombing raids on Japan could not be staged from China, then some other nation should offer its territory (in other words, we should offer our maritime province), from which aircraft (presumably Soviet) would carry out attacks on the Japanese islands. The organizers of the banquet employed every device to get the ambassadors present, ours in particular, to give a speech, and in so doing confirm, even if indirectly, the existence of an anti-Japanese alliance. But Ambassador Panyushkin understood the intentions of our hosts, and to their disappointment he addressed his remarks to matters that had no bearing on our relations with Japan. The Chinese tried to get me to speak in my capacity as chief military adviser, but I flatly refused. The Americans and British, seeing they could not draw us into such a discussion, were also forced to confine themselves to generalities.

The Nationalist politicians would not leave off, however. The Chinese press, as if on command, began to write a great deal about the Soviet Union's "generous and selfless aid to China." Only the Soviet Union "was helping and was prepared to offer more help." Without such "magnanimous assistance" from the Soviet Union, China would have found it difficult to wage its war of resistance. Of course, what they were saying was true, but its public advertisement in the press at this particular time had only one goal—the provocation of a conflict between the Soviet Union and Japan. After the Germans attacked us, this strategy became all the more pronounced. Soong Meiling took an active part in troublemaking. The GMD disseminated a story to the effect that in a press interview the Soviet military attaché, V. I. Chuikov, had spoken of increased Soviet aid to China. Needless to say, there had been no interview. This idle invention was the work of political schemers.

Beginning in the spring of 1941 rumors that the Germans were about to attack the Soviet Union gathered momentum. General Zhang Chong, who was head of the GMD Central Executive

Committee International Relations Bureau, told me his sources indicated a German offensive in June, or July at the latest. Zhang informed me in confidence, and with complete assurance, that Hitler and his foreign minister, Ribbentrop, were putting strong pressure on Matsuoka through their ambassador in Tokyo, Eugen Ott, for a Japanese attack on the British possessions in Southeast Asia. Singapore was first on the list, as Hitler believed that its capture would break British resistance and that this in turn would isolate the United States and prevent its entry into the European war. We were given similar information by the head of Nationalist government military intelligence, Admiral Yang Xuancheng.

Reports of an impending German attack increased especially after the flight to Britain in May of Hitler's longtime comrade in arms, Rudolf Hess. In Chungking the prevailing view was that Hitler wanted a compromise peace with the British in order to attack the Soviet Union. The Hess mission removed this from the realm of speculation. We knew then that war with Germany was only a matter of time—very near, in fact. Since we realized how tense our western border had become, we now had to obtain the most accurate information possible about developments in the Far East. Which way would the Japanese turn? We did not linger over any intelligence that came our way but sent it at once to Moscow. The task of evaluating and interpreting it belonged to the center. Still, the reports coming to me in ever larger number indicated that the Japanese military buildup was taking place in south China and around Haiphong.

About a month before the German attack General Zhang fell seriously ill. As head of GMD intelligence, he had seen it his duty to keep me, as chief military adviser, informed of the situation not only in China but also in those countries in which Chinese military attachés were posted, Germany among them. As events were to show, General Zhang accurately identified the time of the German offensive. General Zhang's illness worsened, and severe complications soon led to his death.

THE GROWING AMERICAN AND BRITISH PRESENCE

The Western powers, in order to prevent further aggravation of tensions with Japan, continued to offer the latter concessions in their hope of finding some common ground. The agreement by which Britain was to provide Thailand with petroleum products testified explicitly to this approach. Thailand by this time was already on its way to becoming a Japanese "south seas" base. Further evidence of the Western attitude was provided by President Roosevelt, who spoke of the stable nature of Japanese-American relations, and by Secretary of State Hull, who declared that the United States would continue supplying oil to Japan.

However, the situation in the Pacific continued to deteriorate. The breakdown of talks in March 1941 between Japan and the Dutch East Indies over oil illustrated this clearly. At a meeting of Chinese business leaders in Hong Kong, the British ambassador to China, Archibald Clark Kerr, declared that it was China's fundamental duty to fight on, and that so long as Chiang Kaishek resisted Japan, Britain would help. For the present, though, these were only words. It is true that Britain had been forced to take some recent military steps, but these were for defense of its Southeast Asian possessions, not in aid of China. Reports began to appear in the press of the steady buildup of British and Indian forces in Malaya and Singapore and of the arrival in Singapore of a detachment of American fighter planes. Both Japan and the Western powers were ready to use military and economic pressure to advance their position. The Japanese concentrated a number of units, including the 18th Infantry Division, in the immediate vicinity of Hong Kong and increased their naval strength in nearby waters prior to the British agreement to provide oil to Thailand. American economic pressure on the Japanese could be seen in the Dutch agreement to terminate oil negotiations with them.

Now that the Americans and British realized the possibility of a confrontation with Japan, they increased their verbal support of the Chinese and even began to speak of joint military operations. It was in connection with the latter that General Shang Zhen undertook a trip to Burma, arranged by the British military command in Hong Kong. At the meeting mentioned above, Ambassador Clark Kerr went so far as to speak of de facto Anglo-American-Chinese military cooperation and to state that such cooperation would become closer if Japan launched a southern offensive. I also learned that the Nationalist Army Operations Section had been working on plans for using Chinese forces in the defense of Burma. However, an agreement on Anglo-Chinese cooperation had not been signed, due to the unwillingness of the British to allow Chinese troops onto their territory.

In late spring 1941 the Americans sent an air force party to Chungking under Major-General H.B. Clagett. He was to continue the work begun by Laughlin Currie. But whereas Currie's task was to determine how much support China might provide in the event of war between America and Japan, Clagett's mission was more technical in nature. Clagett was to assess the Chinese air force and its facilities, since American military aid would take the form of aircraft, pilots and ground personnel. He was also to attempt an evaluation of the combat value of the Chinese air force to the Americans. Clagett's party spent its time largely in Chengdu and Kunming.

The Americans were to send China one hundred planes, along with pilots and technical personnel. We learned of this from air force commander Mao Bangchu. Through the commander I personally got to know some of the American instructors, who told me frankly why they were there. Chinese pilots now began to study American methods of aerial warfare, which on the whole differed little from Soviet flying tactics. The Americans did not make use of the air bases we had set up in Chengdu, Lanzhou and other points north. They were interested, rather, in the region south of the Yangtze, where they established bases in such centers as Kunming and Guiyang. In our view, these were intended to facilitate joint operations with Chinese ground forces against Japanese staging points further south. This reconfirmed our view that the Japanese were preparing for a move into Southeast Asia and beyond.

On June 14 Commander Mao flew to Singapore for official delivery of a squadron of American fighters, which Chinese pilots took over in Rangoon. The planes were to be combat-ready by the fall, though this would be too late to counter the summer bombing raids. On the whole, American military assistance at this time did not go far beyond good intentions. China received little of substance. In an expansive gesture, the United States government declared that at the end of the Sino-Japanese War it would give up extraterritorial jurisdiction. But this offer carried no value at present. It was intended rather to symbolize American good relations with China

THE WAR BEGINS AT HOME

On June 22, 1941, Nazi Germany attacked the Soviet Union. The Great Patriotic War had begun.

Those were difficult days for me. My heart was back at home with my comrades, but my task in China was still unfinished. The news of the German attack did not come as a surprise, as we had been sending reports from Chungking to Moscow about this possibility. But once the war broke out, it had a serious effect on us. Our working conditions became much less comfortable. The first defeats suffered by our armies brought joy to those in China who had always viewed our presence there unfavorably. Despite sympathetic statements from government figures and the press, many Chinese officials privately took great delight in our misfortunes.

All of us in Chungking now felt even greater responsibility for the information we were sending to Moscow. In these early critical moments of the war, when our armies were in retreat and taking heavy losses, a second front might suddenly be opened in the east. Today, with so many of the documents public, we know that on June 24 Ribbentrop asked Oshima, the Japanese ambassador in Berlin, "to keep the Russian question in mind" and advised "combined operations" with the Japanese "to put the enemy completely out of the war by the end of the year." Earlier that spring Hitler and Ribbentrop had been pressing Japan to move against Britain by occupying Singapore. But Hitler had not revealed to the Japanese his plans for the Soviet Union. One of his directives stated that the "Japanese must not be given any knowledge of Operation Barbarossa." Now Hitler abruptly abandoned his interest in Singapore and sought Japan's immediate entry into the war against us.

(For their part, the Japanese were equally secretive in keeping their plans from the Germans).

On July 10 Ribbentrop wired the German ambassador in Tokyo, Eugen Ott: "I ask you to continue working to secure the earliest participation of Japan in the war against Russia, which I have already addressed in my telegram to Matsuoka. Use every means at your disposal, since the earlier the Japanese enter the war the better. As before, our goal is that by winter Germany and Japan shall meet along the Trans-Siberian Railway. With the collapse of Russia, the position of the Axis powers in the international arena will be so advantageous that the question of England's defeat, that is, the total annihilation of the British Isles, will be only a matter of time." In reply, Ott wrote: "I am trying by every means to bring about Japan's entry into the war against Russia in the immediate future. . . . [I am working on] Matsuoka personally, as well as the Foreign Ministry, military circles, nationalists and other well-disposed people. . . . Judging by the state of preparedness here, I am certain that Japanese entry into the war is imminent."

During the summer months the Japanese press gave great play to some boats supposedly sunk by our warships in the Sea of Japan. This, however, was merely to distract attention from the ongoing Japanese preparations for a move to the south. Meanwhile, the war between the Soviet Union and Germany had become central to Chinese foreign policy calculations. The great mass of the Chinese people showed their deep sympathy for the Soviet Union. But Chiang Kaishek and the GMD leaders were pursuing their own self-serving schemes, all the while stressing their friendship with us.

Chiang believed that war was now inevitable between the Soviet Union and Japan. This would lead to a rapprochement between the Soviet Union, Great Britain and the United States and a Far Eastern military alliance, of which China would be a member. On July 2 Chiang's government announced the severance of diplomatic relations with Germany and Italy following their recognition of the Wang Jingwei puppet regime in Nanjing. This was more than a formal gesture on Chungking's part. It marked Nationalist China's accession to the international alliance of nations opposing fascist aggression. China's rulers wanted more aid from the United States, Britain and the Soviet Union, and now they hoped to bring our country, and then the other two, into open conflict with Japan. In the eyes of the Chinese, war between the Soviet Union and Japan would fundamentally alter the Far Eastern situation in their favor. The Nationalists, therefore, still hoped for a military alliance with the Soviet Union. Chiang Kaishek made definite approaches to us about this. The Americans and British evidently did not disagree, since any such understanding would ease their position in Southeast Asia.

Could we be certain of the sincerity of the Chinese government? Did there not exist the danger that Chiang would take advantage of the German attack on the Soviet Union to make a compromise peace with Japan and then attempt to eliminate the CCP? Such a possibility could not be ruled out. I had received information that this was being discussed in government circles, especially by Chiang and Bai Chongxi. I nevertheless concluded that Chungking would take this course only if the United States and Great Britain came to terms with Germany, thus allowing the latter free rein in its war with the Soviet Union. The Chinese would then make a deal with the Japanese and try to persuade them to attack us. But there was little likelihood of this at present. One other factor I should mention kept Chiang Kaishek from coming to terms with Japan. This was his fear that such a move would lead to widespread popular revolt. The sympathy of the Chinese people was with the Soviet Union. These conclusions I reported to Moscow.

From the Nationalists came official assurance that the Soviet Union should not fear Chinese capitulation and that in the case of a Japanese attack on Soviet territory we could count fully on Chinese military power. Transparent demagoguery! At such a tense and difficult time for us Chiang Kaishek continued to complicate our relations with the Japanese and more than ever hoped to provoke us into war. Ambassador Panyushkin had to be ever on the alert in order to inform our government of Chiang's schemes. A heavy burden of responsibility also lay on my office and on our whole advisory complement.

THE CHINESE COMMUNISTS FAIL TO SUPPORT US

After Hitler's treacherous attack, both the Nationalist and communist armies (especially the latter) looked as if they might take the offensive against Japan, either singly or together. However, instead of actively assisting the Soviet Union at this most urgent moment, Chiang decided to adhere to his policy of delay and provocation. He personally proposed to me that the Soviet Union should attack Japan and eliminate it first. Here Chiang showed his true face as a political provocateur. This proposal was so far-fetched and inappropriate that no one close to Chiang mentioned it again.

What position did Mao Tsetung and the CCP leaders take at this time? Moving ahead somewhat, I can say that in the fall of 1941, when the Germans were approaching Moscow and the Kwantung Army stood in full battle readiness on the Manchurian border, Mao Tsetung, instead of pinning down the Japanese in north China through military action, spread comments suggesting inevitable Soviet defeat. Mao had already launched his nationalistic *zhengfeng* [rectification] campaign, which was to reform the party's "work style." In reality it served as camouflage for the promotion of an anti-Soviet political line. It also undermined the united front of the Chinese people against Japan. The principal objective of the campaign was the establishment of Mao's dictatorship over both party and army.

The best evidence of the foregoing is Mao's speech of November 1941 to the party school in Yenan. Mao allocated his forces thus: "10 percent to the struggle against the Japanese, 20 percent to the struggle with the GMD, and 70 percent to the growth of our own power." In keeping with this, the CCP did not undertake active operations in the latter part of 1941 against the Japanese. As Hitler's armies approached Moscow, Mao Tsetung offered his opinion that the Red Army should withdraw to the east, beyond the Urals. From there it could conduct guerrilla war against the Germans, based on the Chinese example, while awaiting an Anglo-American offensive in Western Europe. The Maoists emphasized that the main task of humanity was the defense of China. In October 1941 the CCP army newspaper *Jiefang Ribao* [*Liberation Daily*] claimed that the "principal role in leading the oppressed nations of the world belongs to the Chinese nation."

Chiang Kaishek and Mao Tsetung each in his own way pursued self-serving and self-centered political goals while disregarding the higher interests of the Chinese people in their struggle for national liberation.

CHAPTER 13

RETURN TO THE MOTHERLAND

The Japanese did not come to an immediate decision on where to strike. They were carefully following the outcome of events in Europe. Despite our recent neutrality pact with Japan, the threat of attack hung menacingly over our Far Eastern region. As we now know, on July 5 the Japanese war minister, Tojo Hideki, approved Operation Kantokuen (special maneuvers for the Kwantung Army), the plan for war against the Soviet Union.

The Japanese remained at a crossroads until September. The initial success of the German blitzkrieg appeared to have given them the opportunity to act. But Operation Barbarossa failed to break the Red Army. The Japanese general staff now had to take into account our stiffening resistance. Calculations that the Soviet Union would transfer much of its Far Eastern reserve to the western front were proven wrong. This came as an unwelcome surprise to the Japanese, since they did not want to find themselves in a protracted war with us. Now they feared they would lose the opportune moment for seizing the British, Dutch and American colonies. The Western powers had begun to strengthen their defenses and troop complements in these territories. And in the United States the war industry was now producing a whole new range of weapons.

We now know that on August 9 Operation Kantokuen was shelved, one month after it was approved. Since Barbarossa had failed to bring about a Soviet collapse, the Japanese general staff turned to the southern strategy. This decision was taken at the imperial conference of September 5. Thus the labors of Hitler and his diplomats to open up a second front in the Far East came to naught. The principal reason for this was the heroic resistance of the Red Army, which had stymied German hopes for a lightning victory over the Soviet Union.

GROWING COMPLEXITIES AND SOME CURIOUS INCIDENTS

Following the Clagett mission, American fighter planes and volunteer pilots began to arrive. In October the United States extended China $50 million, which was to be used in part to build the necessary aerodromes, roads and storage depots. Chinese pilots were now working on flying in the "American style." Chiang Kaishek and the General Staff began to attune themselves to the American way of doing things—they could not ignore the well-filled American pockets. With war production on the rise, the Americans had made lend-lease available to China as of May 1941. We saw American influence in Chinese government and military circles steadily growing, and we could only welcome such help to China's war of resistance. We sought only to ensure that this aid would be used not to intensify internal political divisions but rather to assist the struggle against the national enemy.

From August onward I bore a particularly heavy responsibility as military attaché. I had to be on guard not to be taken in by provocative "intelligence" coming from many directions to the effect that a Japanese attack on us was imminent. This stream of disinformation came not only in the guise of rumors but also in the shape of countless documents, including military reports from the Chinese General Staff. I will not attempt to estimate how much spurious material reached my office from the American and British missions. The most zealous providers of such "intelligence" were the Chinese, who kept impressing on our military advisers in Chungking and in the field that Japanese forces in Manchuria and Korea were preparing to move. In the Military Commission even the head of the Operations Section repeated these fabrications. This man went to great lengths to prove that the Kwantung Army was being brought to full battle readiness. He emphasized the return to Japan of officers' wives and the cancellation of leave for all ranks.

Under these circumstances a discussion I had at the time with the head of intelligence of the Military Commission, Admiral Yang, was of great value. Admiral Yang was quite progressive in his views and was well disposed toward the Soviet people, and to me personally. Andreev and I often dropped in on him at his office, where we talked of our travels about the country and shared general impressions. Admiral Yang told me in very careful language that any suggestion of Kwantung Army preparations for an attack on us was completely groundless. He said that the Japanese, having reached an impasse in China, were behind schedule in their strategic buildup in the south. Japan was not ready for war against a more powerful opponent. He did not deny the possibility of an attack on the Soviet Far East, but only if the Germans occupied Moscow and major industrial regions such as the Urals. The Japanese would attack only if the Soviet Union was so weakened that a war would demand little in manpower and resources from them.

A matter of grave concern at this time both to Chiang Kaishek and the General Staff was the weak state of defenses on China's southern border. Chiang instructed He Yingqin to bring this issue before the Military Commission. A review of the army engineering units was ordered, to test their ability for the required work. He Yingqin took personal charge and invited the Soviet advisers in Chungking to attend.

Cadets from the military academy spent a week constructing a defensive perimeter around a battalion. Our advisory group went several times to the site, where strenuous trenching work was going on. We noted numerous mistakes and deficiencies. In particular we were struck by tactical ignorance in the placement of defensive fortifications. For the moment we kept our observations to ourselves. The official review was attended by many high-ranking officers of the General Staff. He Yingqin awarded high marks to the exercise in general and to the engineers in particular. My opinion was then requested. I did not want to direct my criticism at the organizers themselves, so I cautiously touched on certain inadequacies in the work of the cadets. I made three specific points. First, defenses were ineffectively positioned on rises and hilltops. They did not give the defenders a clear field of fire into the valleys and gullies below; instead, the enemy could advance without hindrance to within a short distance of the defenders' positions. Second, within the defensive area there were many "dead angles," where the enemy could safely marshal their forces prior to attack. Third, no provision was made for flanking fire or crossfire to cover the approaches to the defensive position, which meant the defenders could only fire directly ahead at the enemy.

Nothing could be said to refute my remarks. He Yingqin asked me if I would arrange a special training exercise, which he and officers of the General Staff would attend. I agreed to this request. But for me the main item of the day was not this but, rather, what I heard He Yingqin say in his own words. He indicated that plans were in progress for a line of defenses along the border with Indochina. (Japanese forces had entered northern Indochina in September 1940.) I saw from this that the Chinese knew of the Japanese buildup in the south. What the Chinese expected was an offensive into Yunnan, aimed at Kunming, the terminus of the Burma Road, over which China's aid from the Western powers came.

We held our training exercise south of Chungking. We demonstrated how to use the local topography to build fortifications not only to create a strong defensive position but also to ensure fewer casualties among the defenders. Everyone was pleased with our efforts. The lessons learned would be applied by Chinese forces stationed along the Indochina border. He Yingqin then invited us back to the military compound to dine at the officers' club. As we entered the compound, my attention was immediately drawn to the rifles of the honor guard. All were up-to-date models of Soviet manufacture. The principal of the academy told us our rifles were regarded as the best in the world. I then entered the banquet hall with He Yingqin. From the ceiling were hanging the flags of the major nations of the globe. There were only two exceptions—Japan and the Soviet Union! I decided that I could not let this go without protest. When He Yingqin finished thanking the Soviet advisers and the Soviet nation for their help in the war and invited us to join him at the table, I replied in exactly the following words: "I am very flattered by your praise, Mr War Minister, and I thank you for the invitation to this abundant and splendid banquet, but as a Soviet general, it is uncomfortable for me to sit in a hall under the flags of every nation but my own."

My words were as if a bomb had gone off. He Yingqin shot fire and lightning out of his eyes at the principal of the academy, who rushed off in search of a Soviet flag. He had to report back that none could be found. He Yingqin, seeing that we were making ready to leave, ordered all the flags removed from the hall.

This incident indicated once again what was going on inside the Chinese leaders' minds. We had to make them understand that we knew how they regarded the Soviet Union, which nevertheless was giving their country such selfless aid. For the war minister to remove the flags of all the capitalist states from the hall must have been as welcome to him as forcing a dog to eat mustard. Chiang Kaishek learned of the incident, as did the Americans and the British. A few days later my senior colleagues and I were invited to take tea at Chiang's out-of-town residence. He Yingqin, Bai Chongxi and several other generals were also present. The Nationalist leaders clearly wanted to attribute the incident to misunderstanding or accident and to put it behind them. We, for our part, let it be seen that we were no longer troubled by what had happened.

There is another incident I should relate. Chiang Kaishek personally arranged that summer residences in the picturesque mountains south of Chungking be made available to Ambassador Panyushkin and myself. I often spent the night at mine in order to escape the 40-to-42-degree heat in the city. Panyushkin did not go as often. On one of our free days we were at our dachas when a colleague invited us to dinner. During the meal the air raid warning sounded. Japanese planes were nearby. Fortunately, all the buildings in the vicinity escaped damage. But when Panyushkin and I returned to our summer homes, we saw only devastation.

It was hard to explain how this could have happened. Without detailed directions the Japanese could not have hit our residences. We knew there was already someone helping guide Japanese planes toward the Soviet embassy. But it was equipped with a strong bomb shelter. (I never used it, though, preferring instead to leave the city during a raid.) For Japanese planes to find the dachas occupied by the Soviet ambassador and myself was possible only if some person or organization intent on embroiling the Soviet Union and Japan in difficulties was at work. It would appear that only Dai Li could have been behind this.

In the early fall of 1941 a massive transfer of Japanese aircraft from northern China and Manchuria to the south began. Our advisers in the outlying military districts repeatedly confirmed this. But both the Chinese and the Americans saw this as a Japanese countermeasure prompted by the arrival in Kunming and Guilin of the American volunteer air force group under General Claire Chenneault. For the Americans, it may have been a case of wishful thinking that the Japanese buildup was directed against China and not intended for a move to the south. Just the same, they felt a certain unease with the way events were moving. American aid to Chiang was now more forthcoming.

The Japanese also began moving land forces by sea to the south. We learned of this from sources in the ports of embarkation. We knew almost nothing about the Japanese navy. The Japanese were able to maintain the highest security around this service. But after receiving confirmation of the transfer to the south of a thousand aircraft I was finally convinced that Japanese preparations for a Pacific war were genuine. I was certain that Chiang had similar information and that he had passed this on to He Yingqin when the latter was in Yunnan in October. He Yingqin was accompanied on his inspection tour by two of our military specialists (in artillery and engineering), who were to help in detailed planning of defenses along the southern border. Upon his return, He Yingqin came to see me at my office. He arrived equipped with maps and—rarity of rarities—personally briefed me on the local situation. In his words, the defenses, including those covering the Burma Road, were completely unsatisfactory. This was a judgment with which my colleagues concurred.

I believed the Americans and British were in possession of similar intelligence about the state of China's southern defenses. However, there was nothing they could do to substantially strengthen them. They lacked the capacity to do so. As for the Chinese, He Yingqin's trip itself told me that Chiang Kaishek and the General

Staff were deeply perturbed by developments in the south and that they were awaiting events of the greatest magnitude there.

THE PACIFIC WAR BEGINS

At the beginning of December I left Chungking for Chengdu, the capital of Sichuan and the site of one of our air bases, for treatment of an old wound that was causing me trouble. This was a critical time for my country, with the battle for Moscow at its height. The Germans had crossed the Moscow-Volga canal to the north of the city and were moving up toward it from the south.

When I arrived in Chengdu on Saturday, December 6 I learned that the American ambassador, along with his military attaché and a few airmen, had arrived at the same hotel where I was staying. (One of the American squadrons that had come to China under General Chenneault was to be stationed in Chengdu.) Several British officers were with them. In the dining room we introduced ourselves and exchanged views on the Far Eastern situation. The Americans and British spoke with one voice in saying there was no reason to fear any major developments. The Chinese victory at Changsha, along with the Red Army victory at Rostov and the stubborn defense of Moscow, meant that the Japanese would scarcely risk a war with the Western powers, especially as they were already tied down in China. Since there was no present cause for concern, my dinner companions had decided to come to Chengdu for a rest, away from the discomforts and aggravations of Chungking. In actual fact, and of this I had no doubt, they had come to Chengdu to look into conditions for their planned air deployments. They too may have believed that the heavy fighting around Moscow would tempt the Japanese into launching an attack on our Far Eastern territory.

What amazes me is this: how could American and British intelligence organs, which had long operated a wide network of agents in both China and Japan, been so deeply mistaken in their assessments? How could they not have noticed the moves the Japanese were making toward the south? In this regard, I have also thought that Chiang Kaishek and Dai Li were intentionally withholding intelligence in their possession from the Western powers, so as not to put any impediments in the way of the expected Japanese strike, whether against the Soviet Union in the north or against Britain and the United States in the south.

In the early autumn I had occasion to send my colleague N. V. Roshchin to Hong Kong on business. Now that our countries were allies, Roshchin paid a visit to British intelligence headquarters. The British were disposed of a highly active and clandestine network, which we felt could not be mistaken in its prognoses. The commanding officers received my colleague warmly and offered him their opinion on how the situation in the Far East was developing. When he returned, Roshchin told me that the British were fully convinced that there was no way they could miss any moves made by the Japanese. The British shared much valuable information with Roshchin—intelligence gathered, no doubt, in concert with the Americans.

I had been certain of my judgments, but now I suddenly asked myself if I had been mistaken. Would the information I had been sending to Moscow, that the Japanese were about to move south at any moment, now be proven wrong? Had I been the victim of disinformation from my sources?

On the night of December 7–8 I fell asleep only toward dawn. After rising, I had just made myself ready to go down to breakfast when my air force assistant, Colonel Rybakov, suddenly appeared and told me that the British and Americans had left hurriedly for Chungking. This at once put me on the alert. The easy spirits they had displayed the night before could not have disappeared so quickly. Without some compelling reason they would not have left for Chungking with such alacrity.

In the breakfast room I heard many anxious conversations going on. Andreev, my interpreter, quickly got hold of some local newspapers. Special editions had been printed with the news that the Japanese air force and navy had attacked the American naval base at Pearl Harbor without warning and had inflicted heavy losses on the Pacific Fleet.

The next Japanese blow fell on the British in the waters of the South China Sea, and it too met with success. The battleship *Prince of*

Wales and the battle cruiser *Repulse,* which had arrived in Singapore shortly before, were both sunk. With the great damage inflicted on the American and British fleets in the first days of the Pacific war, the Japanese gained mastery of the seas. This enabled them to mount wide-ranging offensive operations in the Philippines, Malaya and the Dutch East Indies without fear of countermoves by the Western powers.

First Days of the War

I was ordered by wire from Moscow to return at once to Chungking. It was now approaching the middle of the month. I was struck by the open joy with which the Nationalist political and military leaders received the news of the outbreak of the Pacific war. Everyone was happy, beginning with Chiang Kaishek, who together with his colleagues had long been awaiting this moment. This was not the least surprising. For more than four years China alone had carried on the struggle against Japan. Now the rich and powerful nations of the West—the United States, Great Britain and many smaller powers as well—stood at China's side in the war.

The Nationalists counted on obtaining major credits and arms deliveries from their Western allies. (It is known that Mao Tsetung also expected to receive some of this aid.). Much of the Nationalist leadership, beginning with Chiang Kaishek himself, thought that from this point on the burden of the war would fall on other shoulders and that China would enjoy something of a respite.

The Western powers had a different outlook. In exchange for credits and supplies, they expected Chinese forces to become actively involved in the war. This would ease their own position in Southeast Asia and the Pacific. Consequently the two sides clashed again in Chungking in December 1941, though now as allies. The basis of disagreement remained the same. The Nationalists wanted to receive as much aid as possible and to use it for their own purposes, while their new allies were prepared to give them help but demanded the sacrifice of Chinese blood in payment.

During these weeks American and British military envoys flooded into China. Every form of cajolery was used on the Chinese military leaders. Western diplomats gave Chinese politicians every assurance of their sincere friendship. I recall one meeting with the Chinese in December 1941. The American, British and Soviet ambassadors were present. (I was there as Soviet military representative in China.) The British ambassador, Archibald Clark Kerr, spoke first. He humbled himself before the Chinese, assuring them of Britain's peace-loving and well-disposed intentions. He said that his aspiration—his dream—of becoming an ally of the Chinese in this struggle against the common enemy had been realized. Britain and China were full-fledged comrades in war.

We knew how the British colonialists, together with other nations, had divided up China into spheres of influence, seized Hong Kong and Kowloon, dictated the unequal treaties, helped extinguish the Taipings and quite recently taken part in furthering the politics of a "Far Eastern Munich" at China's expense. It was interesting to observe the British ambassador twist and turn, trying to prove the unprovable to the Chinese government and people.

The Americans promised a substantial loan and large quantities of aircraft and war supplies. We learned of this from the commander of the Chinese air force, General Mao, who happily shared the news with us. The Americans now became interested, as never before, in activating an anti-Japanese united front, in which the communist 18th Army Group would play a definite role. In effect, the Americans wanted to draw on all sources of military strength for prosecution of the war, not only within China but also beyond its borders. Both the Americans and the Chinese saw it as vital to hold on to the Burma Road, against which a Japanese attack through that country was spearheaded.

Chiang Kaishek believed that the time had now come for creation of a military council to coordinate efforts against Japan. This body would be made up of the four powers in the region: China, the United States, Britain, and the Soviet Union. Chiang apparently saw the situation as follows. Since the United States had declared war not only on Japan but also on Germany, and since the Soviet Union and the Americans were now allies against Germany, the Soviet Union was therefore obligated to declare war on Japan. Chiang already had made the ostentatious gesture of declaring war on Japan's Axis partners, Germany and Italy, which, to all appearances, was intended to pressure us into a reciprocal move against Japan. It was quite obvious that this diplomatic move had been taken with specific political goals in mind.

In late December Chiang made the proposal of a Far Eastern Council at a meeting with the American, British and Soviet military attachés. It was clear that he had not put aside his hopes of drawing us into the war. His aim was to turn the main thrust of the anti-Hitlerite coalition against Japan. When I asked who would be the head of this new council, Chiang replied that it would be the Americans. His answer indicated the direction in which he was moving. In early 1942 General Joseph Stilwell arrived in Chungking to become Chiang's adviser. Stilwell was to go on to command the Chinese Expeditionary Force in Burma and then serve as chief of staff of the Nationalist Army.

I noticed in meetings of the Military Commission that the Chinese could not hide their optimistic expectations about the outcome of the war. But for the moment there was nothing to take delight in. The Japanese were pressing the Allies on three different fronts: China, Southeast Asia, and the Pacific. The Americans and British understood very well that Germany, not Japan, was their immediate enemy. Not until they had brought Hitler to his knees would they put their full effort into the war against Japan. Chiang's efforts to forge a Far Eastern Council thus met with failure.

The Allied defeats in Southeast Asia and the Pacific during the first months of the war were a disappointment to the Nationalists. Foreseeing the likely occupation of Burma by the Japanese, Chiang Kaishek, speaking mainly through Commander Mao, sounded me out as to how the Soviet Union would regard the movement of American war aid from the Persian Gulf to Xinjiang via our Central Asian republics. I dodged the question, since it fell outside my competence as chief military adviser to the Chinese armed forces.

The Allied defeats and the threat of the loss of Burma compelled Chiang Kaishek formally to remain on good terms with our representatives in China, especially our military mission, even though he was clearly leaning toward the Americans by this time. Chiang and Soong Meiling invited the chief military adviser's staff to their 1942 New Year's Day reception. At such a gathering major business matters were not discussed. However, once it was over, members of Chiang's entourage immediately began to press us on a whole range of issues. How would the Soviet government receive Chiang's proposal of a Far Eastern Council? Would the Soviet Union permit the shipment of American war aid through its Central Asian territories? Would the Soviet Union be sending more volunteer pilots to China?

The Americans and the British both sought to convince the Chinese to go on the offensive and pin down as many Japanese troops as possible, thereby relieving the pressure they were facing. It was the Americans who were most concerned about the Chinese war effort. They saw no reason why contact with the communist forces should not be made. The Nationalists, however, were not at this moment interested in taking the initiative in the field. The severing of the Burma Road by the Japanese had reduced allied military supplies to China to a minimum. This made the situation for the Chinese forces difficult. Chiang continued to champion the war of resistance, but in reality he was waiting. Rather than fight the Japanese in China, he had sent some of his best divisions to the defense of Burma, where the British had met with defeat.

In China the initiative remained, as before, in the hands of the Japanese, who saw preservation of their pre–Pearl Harbor front line as their first task. However, in order to tie down Nationalist armies in the south and push Chiang further toward capitulation, the Japanese high command launched an offensive in Hubei and Hunan. On December 24 the 11th Army launched the third attack of the war on Changsha. The Japanese deployed 100,000 men, while the Chinese replied with 250,000. After a battle under the walls of Changsha the Japanese succeeded in forcing their way into the city. On January 5, 1942, the Chinese counterattacked. In mid-January the Japanese were forced out of the city and the front returned to its former state.

I RETURN TO FIGHT FOR THE MOTHERLAND

I was coming to the conclusion that I had fulfilled my principal tasks as chief military adviser. We had kept our Defense Ministry accurately informed of the situation in China, and our advisers had assisted the Chinese armies in fighting off Japanese attacks on all fronts during 1941. But with the outbreak of the Pacific war, the Americans began to supply Chiang Kaishek with military aid. As noted above, the orientation of Chiang's government toward the United States was becoming ever more apparent. I felt that under the circumstances the position of chief military adviser no longer carried its former weight with the Nationalist high command. For us to compete with General Stilwell would be inadvisable and even harmful. To intrude with advice to Chiang and the Chinese General Staff on how to help the Americans and British in their war with the Japanese was something I could not do, nor wished to, especially as the Chinese would now be treating any advice with heightened suspicion. And I did not wish to answer before Chinese public opinion for defeats suffered in Burma by the best Chinese troops, fighting under American and British command. I wanted to return to my homeland and throw myself into my people's struggle against the German invader.

In my dispatches to Moscow I indicated that our military advisers could no longer play a leading role in China. Finally I received a short telegram summoning me back to Moscow to give a report. I knew this meant I would not be returning to China. There were many farewell banquets for me. I was overwhelmed with attention, compliments, wishes for a speedy return, and a general's decoration, second rank. At last my plane arrived, and I set off by way of Lanzhou and Urumqi. In both places I was met with an honor guard. Evidently the local governors were following instructions from Chiang Kaishek to demonstrate Chinese friendship toward the Soviet people, now victorious in the battle for Moscow.

In late February 1942 I landed in Alma Ata, the capital of Kazakhstan, where I was met by a representative of the Defense Ministry and by the head of the Alma Ata academy, Colonel Filatov, an old friend from the Civil War. In 1919 I had commanded the 43rd Red Flag Rifle Regiment of the 5th Division while Colonel Filatov had commanded the 44th Regiment. Although our meeting was brief, he was able to tell me something of events at the front. From Alma Ata I went by rail to Kuibyshev. At every station I saw the preoccupied looks on people's faces, but I also observed the comradeship and determination so evident in those days of peril. The trains were running exactly on schedule. The railway staff had aged, as the younger members had been called into the army, but work went on efficiently. Where men had toiled recently there now stood women in padded jackets, with hard, weather-beaten faces.

I was anxious to go to the front so that I could do battle at once with the German enemy. Soon after my return I was named commander of the First Reserve Army, which was in training near Moscow. In early July 1942 we were sent to the front, where I found myself at once in the cauldron of war. I am proud that soon thereafter, at Stalingrad, I was able to play a part in one of the epic battles of the century.

APPENDIX

CONFLICT ON THE CHINESE EASTERN RAILWAY

EDITOR'S INTRODUCTION

The confrontation in 1929 between Chinese and Soviet forces on the Manchurian border resulted from the unilateral abrogation by local Chinese authorities, supported by the central government in Nanjing, of the 1924 Sino-Soviet agreement on joint management of the Chinese Eastern Railway (CER). The armed takeover of the railway and the dismissal of all Soviet administrative staff, which took place on July 10, was accompanied by the closure of Soviet diplomatic and commercial offices in Harbin. On July 14 Moscow sent Nanjing an ultimatum demanding restoration of the status quo ante. Four days later Moscow broke off diplomatic relations and began deployment of major military formations at selected points on the frontier. The westernmost of these was just to the north of the Chinese border town of Manzhouli, the last station prior to the egress of the CER onto Soviet soil. General Chuikov's narrative concerns his experience of operations carried out by Soviet forces between November 17 and 20, which resulted in the capture of Manzhouli and the elimination of Manchurian forces in the vicinity. Nanjing was forced to open negotiations and on December 22 signed the Khabarovsk Protocol, restoring the pre-July joint management of the CER. Apart from providing a detailed account of the mechanics of the operation, Chuikov characteristically brings out the human dimension of this short but harshly fought campaign. Chuikov's high regard for Vasilii Blyukher, the commander in chief, reflects similar appraisals of the man not only by his colleagues but also by Chiang Kaishek, whom he had formerly served as military adviser.

CONFLICT ON THE CHINESE EASTERN RAILWAY

In August 1929 I arrived in Vladivostok. I was ordered to Khabarovsk, where our Far Eastern army had set up a special headquarters to deal with the disturbing situation that had arisen on our border with China. An armed conflict was threatening, provoked by the Guomindang militarists. The commander of the Special Far Eastern Army was General Vasilii Konstantinovich Blyukher. His chief of staff was Albert Yanovich Lapin. Both knew me from the Civil War. As I was familiar with the Chinese language and with conditions in China, I was attached to general staff headquarters.

With each passing day the atmosphere became more tense. Instead of random, banditlike provocations along the border, we might expect at any moment a full-scale offensive by the Chinese. From early November our headquarters had been receiving reports about a three-division-strong central government army that was on the move from Harbin to Hailar. Other large military formations were also identified, some of them heading toward our maritime region. We could hesitate no longer.

On November 15 the special headquarters was moved under Blyukher's command from Khabarovsk to the Danuli station, close to the Chinese border town of Manzhouli. I was deputed to headquarters for special assignments. It turned out that I was to be at the center of events.

We were by this time sufficiently well informed about the Chinese forces concentrated along the frontier. Their main strength was an army corps under the direct control of the Nanjing government. It was at full roster and equipped with the latest weaponry. Each of its two brigades included three infantry regiments, a sappers' battalion, an artillery battalion, and a signals company. These brigades were maintained by the central government and were completely loyal to Chiang Kaishek. They could be considered regular army units. They exhibited good military discipline and had officers who were graduates of the military academies, such as Whampoa. Each brigade was commanded, according to practice, by a general. The total complement of a brigade was upward of 12,000 men.

There were also forces of the Manchurian warlord Zhang Xueliang on the scene. These provincial detachments ordinarily were used to conduct punitive missions against peasants and communists or to shoot down striking workers; they also guarded warehouses and did garrison duty. They had no experience of major battles. They were armed in the most motley way and supplied most haphazardly. It is revealing that during the height of the CER crisis Chiang Kaishek categorically refused to strengthen Zhang's forces.

The Chinese units were deployed as follows. The 9th Brigade, under General Liang Zhongjia, was stationed in Manzhouli, which had been turned into a major stronghold. The 17th Brigade occupied Zhalainur. Along the Argun (Ergun) River the regular border forces were strengthened by provincial troops. A provincial brigade was spread out eastward from Zhalainur to Hailar to guard the stations along the railway line. The strongest enemy concentration was toward Hailar. A corps consisting of three brigades under General Hu Yukun was making its way toward that town. [See map, p. xviii.]

From the above it is apparent that Chinese forces were stretched out like a wire along the railway, which put them in a highly vulnerable position. Soviet headquarters at first leaned toward an "attack in depth." This would be directed at the rear of the Chinese position. Through one forceful blow the defenses around Hailar would be breached and the main enemy concentration destroyed. With Chinese forces to the west now outflanked, we could fall upon their strong points one by one, with Zhalainur and Manzhouli the main targets. There was the promise of a quick and decisive victory. However, we had to reject this plan, as we did not have available the required strength to ensure its success.

Our battle order consisted of the following units: three rifle divisions, a Kuban cavalry brigade, and a Buryat-Mongol cavalry division. With such forces it was risky to penetrate far behind Chinese lines. We might well encounter serious problems. North of Harbin were a number of Cossack settlements. Many of their inhabitants had been White Guards, guilty of heinous crimes against the Soviet government. The arrival of Soviet troops would be a death sentence for them. It was very possible they would join up with the Chinese and threaten our battle lines and communications from the rear.

Our headquarters decided to reduce the depth of our penetration into enemy territory. Our plan was to encircle Zhalainur by thrusts from the north and east, destroy the garrison there, and then turn west to encircle Manzhouli. This would eliminate the major enemy formations. To put it simply, we would reduce the enemy unit by unit through bringing numerical superiority to bear on each in turn. Prior to our offensive, we were strengthened by the arrival of a company of MC-1 tanks. Ahead of us lay the first battle to be fought in the Far East featuring a coordinated tank and infantry attack.

The final battle plan was as follows. The 21st Division (under P. I. Ashakhanov) and the Buryat-Mongol cavalry division were to surround the Manzhouli garrison from the north, south and west. The 36th Division (under E. V. Baranovich) and the tank company were to strike southward between Manzhouli and Zhalainur in order to sever the link between the Chinese 9th and 17th Brigades. This move would also block the sole avenue of retreat eastward for the Manzhouli garrison.

The 35th Division (under P. S. Ivanov) was to launch a major offensive southward toward Zhalainur. One of its battalions was detailed to capture Hill 101, which stood 3–5 kilometers east of Zhalainur. The autumn floods of the Hailar River and its tributaries had left the whole area around Hill 101 covered with ice. Hill 101 rose out of the plain as a small flat island. The 5th Kuban Cavalry Brigade (under K. K. Rokossovski) was to sweep past Hill 101 to the southern outskirts of Zhalainur, from which it would launch its attack on the town and the railway station. With Hill 101 taken, we could impede the Chinese retreat eastward to Hailar. But Hill 101 could hold a detachment no larger than a battalion. This was too small a force to completely block the withdrawal of the enemy. We had no alternative, however. Further support for our ground operations was provided by an air squadron and an air reconnaissance unit.

There was one weak point in our plan. If the southern approaches of Manzhouli were not secured by our troops, the enemy garrison might try to escape by going around Lake Hulun, which lay to the south. But this route would have taken the Chinese through desolate, uninhabited wasteland. It would be a long and risky retreat. Our assumption was that General Liang would not choose to do so.

On November 15 our forces, under the field command of General Stepan Vostretsov, began to move up to the attack positions. A piercing wind blew across the steppes, and a bitter frost lay on the snowless ground. Our men were fitted out in warm fur jackets and felt boots. The heavy winter clothing slowed down their advance. So as not to be observed by the Chinese, we located our headquarters in the village of Abagaitui, 1 kilometer from the boundary. According to plan, all troop movements took place under cover of darkness.

On November 16 our headquarters carried out a detailed reconnaissance of the local area, noting all Chinese positions in view. Our troop deployments were carefully reviewed, and approval was given to the operational plans of the divisional commanders. The attack began the following morning. At daybreak on the seventeenth we opened with an artillery barrage supported by air strikes. This lasted an hour. I cannot say our actions were unexpected by the Chinese. They clearly had learned of our troop movements. Their men were awaiting our attack in well-fortified positions.

Our offensive proceeded most successfully. The sector between Manzhouli and Zhalainur assigned to the 36th Division and the tank company proved of great interest, as this was the first time we had witnessed a combined tank and infantry attack. There were ten tanks in the company. When the artillery barrage ended, they began moving forward from our lines. Our use of tanks was a long way from what it would be in the Second World War. We did not use them to break through the enemy lines; rather, they were to cover our advancing infantry. The attack came as a complete surprise to the Chinese. Even our own Red Army men were no less startled. I was standing at the observation post with General Blyukher. Through our field glasses we watched the Chinese soldiers lean almost halfway out of their trenches when they caught sight of the tanks. We thought they were about to flee in panic, but their amazement was so great that not only their will but even their fear seemed to be paralyzed.

Our own men also reacted most strangely. They could not keep up with the tanks. Some of them, as if spellbound, stood staring as the fire-breathing steel tortoises advanced. We must remember that this was 1929. Our peasant lads knew only by hearsay of tanks, and tractors for that matter. The tanks reached the enemy lines without hindrance and opened fire along the trenches. Our machine guns awakened the Chinese from their trance. They fled in panic. Our tanks had broken through the enemy lines without a single loss.

If we had better coordinated our tanks and infantry, we might have scored a lightning victory. However, our men had not anticipated such immediate success. They stormed into the enemy trenches, but instead of quickly pressing on, they delayed there for some time. Meanwhile, our tanks had pushed 5 kilometers toward Zhalainur before halting lest they find themselves too far ahead without infantry support. Nevertheless, they had severed the railway link between Manzhouli and Zhalainur. Our rifle units finally caught up with them after eliminating scattered pockets of Chinese defenders, who were for the most still numbed by the tank attack. To sum up, despite delays in our advance, we had gained our objective of cutting off communication between the two Chinese garrisons.

To the east, Rokossovski's cavalry brigade, supported by a battalion from the 35th Division, launched a night attack across the ice fields on Hill 101 and soon captured it. As this was happening, a Chinese army train passed by en route from Manzhouli to Zhalainur and Harbin. Rokossovski at once opened fire with his artillery, and several shots hit the engine. After seizing the train, the cavalry brigade again went on the offensive and reached the southern outskirts of Zhalainur. The rifle battalion and artillery battery now dug in on Hill 101. The 35th Division was unable to break through the enemy's defenses, however. An exchange of fire ensued for some time.

As a result of the day's operations, two Chinese brigades, numbering approximately 20,000 men, had been completely encircled. The second stage of the battle now began—the reduction of the garrisons in Manzhouli and Zhalainur. Throughout the day Blyukher had been in contact with Moscow. Several times he was called to report on the progress of the battle. Defense Minister Kliment Voroshilov spoke with him directly. In the evening

Voroshilov called to express his doubts about whether we could press our encirclement of the enemy to a successful conclusion. He went on to suggest that we might limit ourselves to the action already taken, and withdraw to our own territory.

There were grounds for Voroshilov's concern. The Special Far Eastern Army did not at that time possess the means to completely overwhelm the enemy. We were particularly short of artillery. I should note here that we never dreamt of the density of artillery fire that we would employ in the Second World War to accompany our infantry offensives. The theoretical formulation of this had not even begun. Several heavy artillery divisions would have eased our task, but we would have needed time to transport them to the site and put them in place. We were limited, therefore, to quick maneuvers, sudden forward thrusts and the concentration of great superiority of numbers against selected sectors of the front.

Blyukher understood Moscow's concern and gave it consideration. Before the onset of darkness that day he time and again reviewed our battle forces. He remained firm in his resolution to push ahead. At five in the afternoon he summoned his most trusted commanders and told them he had decided to launch a major offensive at dawn. The plan remained the same. Artillery and tanks were to breach the enemy's defenses at a number of points, like puncturing an air bubble. Elsewhere along the line, the enemy's defenses would totter under the impact of these breakthroughs. Having outlined his plan, Blyukher handed over responsibility to the divisional commanders to decide which specific points of the Chinese defense they would launch their assault against.

We set off in the darkness to inform each unit of the battle plan. I was sent to Rokossovski's Kuban cavalry brigade, just south of Zhalainur. I completed my task, but because it was so late I had to stay overnight with the brigade. Thus I was able to observe in person the offensive launched the next morning. Rokossovski and his officers must be commended on their late-night planning of the coordinated infantry-cavalry attack and artillery barrage. The cavalry charged the exposed Chinese positions at a quick gallop, while the artillery cleared a path ahead of them. The cavalrymen hacked their way through the defenders' stronghold. A hundred enemy soldiers fell to their sabers on the frozen Manchurian steppes.

Returning later that day to our command post, I stopped at Hill 101, from where I caught sight of a huge gathering of Chinese troops outside Zhalainur. In all likelihood they were preparing to attempt a breakout eastward to Hailar. They were under attack from our air force, which was flying over them in bombing formations of five or six planes. When I reached headquarters I reported to Blyukher on the Kuban cavalry operation earlier in the day. By this time the whole Zhalainur picture had turned in our favor. Our forces were closing in on the town. Everywhere our attack had met with success. Reconnaissance reported that the commander of the Chinese 17th Brigade had been killed.

From our command point we watched as thousands of Chinese troops poured out of Zhalainur, making their way in great disorder eastward across the ice-covered steppes. Their escape route took them past Hill 101. Some of our artillery had been moved into the open so that direct aim could be taken at the fleeing army. Blyukher, seeing the shells spewing forth into the retreating throng, gave the order to hold fire. "Enough blood," he said. "Let them escape and tell the others that Soviet territory is not to be violated."

By the night of November 18 we had taken Zhalainur and knocked out the 17th Brigade. We stationed our 35th Division in the town. Now we turned toward Manzhouli and the Chinese 9th Brigade under General Liang. From the east we struck with our 36th Division and from the south with the Kuban cavalry. The 21st Division and the Buryat-Mongol cavalry blocked the town on the north and west. Manzhouli was now caught completely in our ring. We either had to destroy the garrison or force its surrender.

General Liang, who clearly saw that his position was desperate, decided to attempt a breakout toward Zhalainur and on to Hailar. In the early morning a fierce battle took place between our forces, advancing to the west, and the Chinese, trying to break through to the east. A whole regiment of enemy troops, more than 2,000 men, was advancing toward us along the railway line. Our forward unit, the Buryat-Mongol cavalry division, was outnumbered by eight or ten to one. It had to withdraw eastward to link up with our main force, which was coming from Zhalainur in full battle order. Having completed their withdrawal, the cavalry then executed a successful flanking maneuver and attacked the Chinese regiment from the south.

As this was taking place, a number of us from the command post hurried on to the battle zone ahead of the main body of troops. We watched our cavalry charge into the enemy's flank and with masterful swordsmanship spread terror and panic everywhere. And now, coming from the south of Zhalainur, appeared the Kuban cavalry brigade, to help press the enemy back toward Manzhouli. Our planes began to bomb the enemy. Several bombs landed not far from our vehicles. We had to add insignia to identify them to the airmen as our own.

The battle continued over the whole expanse around Manzhouli. Every attempt by the Chinese commanders to find a weak point for a breakthrough was repelled by our men. It was then that our signals chief reported to Blyukher that a group of Chinese officers had arrived at the Otpor (now Zabaykal'sk) station, together with some officials from the Japanese consulate in Manzhouli, to discuss surrender of the garrison. They wanted to speak to a representative of the Soviet command. This came as a surprise to us all, Blyukher included. He decided to send me to handle the negotiations, or rather present our ultimatum for capitulation of the garrison. By car I quickly covered the 25 kilometers of difficult road from our position just outside Manzhouli to the Otpor station, where in a small cottage I met the Chinese military representatives and the Japanese consular officers. I immediately informed the Chinese of our demands: that they lay down their arms on the spot, terminate all looting and acts of violence, and collect all their men and officers at two separate camps outside Manzhouli for the surrender.

The Chinese representatives accepted our terms unconditionally. I asked about Commander Liang's present whereabouts. The Japanese said he was at their consulate. Both parties then requested that I go with them to meet General Liang. I first contacted Blyukher to report on the meeting. He ordered me to go to Manzhouli, where I was to keep a careful eye on the activities of the Chinese and a particularly close watch over General Liang. A car flying the Japanese flag drove ahead, bearing the Chinese and Japanese. I followed behind with an interpreter and two Red Army men.

When we arrived in Manzhouli we could see Chinese troops crowding into the town from every direction as our forces moved forward in battle order but holding fire. Reaching the center of the town, we saw before us a terrible scene of wholesale looting. Shop doors and windows had been smashed in by rifle butts, and hordes of marauders were forcing their way inside, while other were pouring out, loaded down with everything they could put their hands on. Many of the soldiers were wearing civilian clothes over their uniforms, while others were in the midst of changing from one set of clothes to the other. It is difficult to convey a picture of what was happening on that twentieth day of November, 1929, in Manzhouli. There are times when conquered cities are looted by the victors, but we had never before seen a city being looted by its defenders.

Our vehicles stopped short of the consulate, as the way was blocked by abandoned rifles, grenades and shells. It was dangerous to drive on. We got out and went by foot. Just before reaching the consulate we saw a car approaching, bringing Corps Commander Vostretsov. Our forces had now entered the town. Seeing me, he stopped the car and asked where General Liang was. I explained that I was expecting to find him at the Japanese consulate. "Do you know him by sight?" I replied that I did. Vostretsov got out of his car and asked me to accompany him to the consulate. General Liang and his senior officers met us in the reception room. I at once recognized him and pointed him out to Vostretsov, who informed the Chinese that as of that moment they were prisoners of war of the Red Army. General Liang and his men surrendered their personal arms. They raised no objection to the terms of surrender. This brought to a close the military operation that has gone down in history as the Chinese Eastern Railway conflict.

In the battles of November 17–20, 1929, our forces routed two reinforced brigades, 20,000 strong, taking half their men prisoner. The Chinese also took heavy casualties in dead and wounded. Our headquarters did not attempt to cut off and destroy the whole Chinese army. A few units made their escape from Manzhouli and Zhalainur. Their retreat brought them face-to-face with the relief force advancing under General Hu Yukun. The linkup took place not far from Zhalainur. This produced the most surprising result. The sight of the garrison forces retreating in disarray caused the relief army itself to turn and flee. The Red Army moved up to the Xing'an Mountain Range and then stopped.

The tone of Chinese officialdom now suddenly changed. On the twenty-third we received the first telegram indicating official Chinese readiness to meet us and accept our demands. But before this took place, a solemn ceremony was held at the end of the month at the Dawuli station to honor the officers and men of the Far Eastern Army who had fallen in defense of our Soviet land. To the flag flying over the gravesite General Blyukher attached the heroes' medal of the Red Banner. Then, on December 22, Soviet and Chinese representatives signed the Khabarovsk Protocol, which settled the dispute over the Chinese Eastern Railway and the Soviet-Chinese border.

This should be the end of the chapter. But I have to recall an incident so characteristic of the Japanese official mentality of the time. During the battle for Manzhouli a stray shell killed a Japanese woman who worked in one of the Japanese brothels there. The day after the Chinese surrender, the Japanese consulate presented the Soviet command with a claim for 22,500 yen. The bill specified how many years the deceased would have lived, how many clients she would have served, and how much income she would have made for the brothel and, for that matter, probably for Japan itself. The demand was presented to us without any embarrassment. Needless to say, Soviet headquarters turned it down.

* * *

In 1929 Chiang Kaishek received a lesson from the Red Army not to be forgotten. We had shown the whole capitalist world that the borders of the Soviet Union were inviolable and that the Red Army knew how to deal with those who infringed upon it. Unfortunately, not every aggressor nation understood this. One of those was to be Japan.

Attached to Japanese consulates in China, including the one in Manzhouli, were high-ranking military officers. The moment our forces entered Manzhouli we at once became aware of the unsubtle operating methods of the Japanese military and their fellow espionage agents. They used a variety of pretexts to insinuate themselves into our headquarters, where they "talked over" military matters and even tried to gain access to our confidential documents. Our staff headquarters train in Manzhouli was kept under constant surveillance by them. Blyukher told us not to interfere.

Our intelligence managed to intercept a number of Japanese dispatches, among them a report to Tokyo from the senior military representative in Manzhouli. It referred in complimentary terms to our troops. Special note was taken of our high level of discipline, maneuverability in combat, orderly battle lines, high-quality equipment and battle dress and correct attitude toward civilians and prisoners of war. The execution of our battle plan was rated as excellent.

Unfortunately the example we had given was soon to be forgotten by the Japanese, and we would have to remind them of it a decade later on our eastern border in the battles of Changgufeng and Nomonhan.

Glossary

Chinese personal names are given in pinyin transcription, with the former Wade-Giles version given in square brackets.

The following abbreviations are used in the glossary:

AG: Army Group.

EA: "Encirclement and annihilation" campaigns waged by the National Government against communist base areas, 1930–35, primarily in southern Jiangxi, but with the Hubei-Henan-Anhui (Eyuwan) provincial border region as an important secondary area.

GMD: Guomindang (Nationalist Party; also written as Kuomintang, or KMT).

MAC: Military Affairs Commission (the effective highest-ranking organ of the Nationalist government).

NG: National Government of the Republic of China, headed by Chiang Kaishek either in his capacity as president of the Executive Yuan or as chairman of the Military Affairs Commission.

Baoding and **Whampoa** refer respectively to the principal military academies of the pre-Nationalist government and early Nationalist government eras.

Principal biographical sources:

RLPC (1943): the report held in the Public Record Office, London, entitled "Record of Leading Personalities in China," which was forwarded from the British embassy in Chungking to the Foreign Office in April 1943 (FO371: 35844). An update, **RLPC (1944)**, containing a small amount of supplementary information, was sent the following year (FO676: 459). The two documents were declassified in 1994.

Reference works: Howard Boorman and Richard C. Howard, eds., *Biographical Dictionary of Republican China* (BDRC), 4 vols. (New York: Columbia University Press, 1967–71); Chen Xulu and Li Huaxing, eds., *Zhonghua Minguoshi Cidian* (Shanghai: Shanghai Renmin Chubanshe, 1991); He Benfang, ed., *Zhonghua Minguo Zhishi Cidian* (Beijing: Zhongguo Guoji Guangbo Chubanshe, 1992); Huang Meizhen and Hao Shengchao, eds., *Zhonghua Minguoshi Shijian Renwulu* (Shanghai: Shanghai Renmin Chubanshe, 1987); *Great Soviet Encyclopedia* (New York: Macmillan, 1973–83).

Major Figures and Events:

Bai Chongxi (1893–1966) [Pai Ch'ung-hsi], b. Guangxi, d. Taiwan. Baoding graduate, 1916. Organized military government in Guangxi with Li Zongren, 1936, recognizing authority of NG. Named deputy commander of Guangxi army, redesignated 5th Route Army. Upon outbreak of war, committed himself to NG, becoming deputy chief of staff of MAC in July 1937, a position he held until end of war. Also director of Military Training Board of MAC. Held high military positions in Taiwan after 1949. A Chinese Muslim, he served as wartime president of Chinese Islamic National Salvation Federation. RLPC (1943) called him Chiang's "right-hand man" as deputy chief of staff and stated that he was "considered one of China's best strategists."

Barrett, David D. (1892–1977). Entered U.S. Army, 1917. Assistant military attaché, Beijing, 1924–28; assigned to U.S. Army Intelligence, Tianjin, 1931–34; assistant military attaché under Stilwell (q.v.) in Beijing, 1936–39; sent to Chungking to represent Beijing-based military attaché's office, 1939; de facto military attaché in Chungking, 1939–42; military attaché, Chungking, 1942–43. Led U.S. observer group to Yenan, July 1944, recounted later in his book, *Dixie Mission* (Berkeley, 1970). Returned to USA, 1950. Known for his forthrightness of manner and mastery of Chinese.

Blyukher, Vasilii Konstantinovich (1889–1938). Distinguished veteran of Russian Civil War, Blyukher (under the alias Galen) was sent by the Soviet government to Canton in 1923 as head of the Soviet military mission to Sun Yatsen. Blyukher served as chief military adviser to Chiang Kaishek and played a major role in planning the 1926–27 Northern Expedition. Following the GMD break with the CCP in 1927, Blyukher was recalled, and subsequently appointed to a number of high commands in the Soviet Far East. In 1938 he fell victim to Stalin's purge of the army. Chiang Kaishek held Blyukher in the highest esteem.

Changgufeng. Also known as Khasangol, from the lake nearby Changgufeng Ridge on the border between the Soviet Union and Korea, and close to the border of Japanese-occupied Manchukuo (Manchuria), this area witnessed heavy fighting between Soviet and Japanese divisional-strength forces during the summer of 1938. The Soviets prevailed decisively in capturing the disputed ridge, after which they agreed to negotiate a final settlement of the border with Japan.

Chen Cheng (1898–1965) [Ch'en Ch'eng], b. Zhejiang, d. Taiwan. Baoding graduate, 1922; Whampoa instructor, 1924; participant in Northern Expedition. Held high military appointments under NG after 1928, including command of 18th Army, 1930. Commander of Sixth War Zone, 1939 (headquarters at Enshi from late 1941). To support NG defense of Changsha, September 1941, launched Yichang offensive, temporarily capturing city. (See chapters 10 and 11.) While remaining Sixth War Zone commander, took effective charge of NG forces in Yunnan, 1943. Transferred to command of First War Zone, May 1944. After 1949 held high military and political positions on Taiwan, including vice presidency. RLPC (1943) speculates on his failure to fully realize his considerable potential: "Regarded as one of China's best strategists and a student of economics and political science, his name has been often canvassed as that of a possible successor to Chiang Kai-shek."

Chenneault, Claire Lee (1893–1958). Upon retirement from U.S. Air Force was invited by Soong Meiling (q.v.) in 1937 to serve as adviser to Aeronautical Affairs Commission of MAC. Returned to USA in 1940 to raise a volunteer fighter squadron to serve in China, and received approval from U.S. government in August 1941 to establish the American Volunteer Group under his command. This force went into battle in December 1941, becoming known famously as the "Flying Tigers." In 1943 it was redesignated the 14th Air Force. Chenneault was close to Chiang, who shared his belief in the superior effectiveness of air war, though it was the need to conserve his land forces rather than strategic thinking that determined Chiang's position. Chenneault retired from the military in 1945 but returned to serve Chiang in developing air transport in China and, after 1949, in Taiwan.

Clark Kerr, Archibald (Lord Inverchapel) (1882–1951). British ambassador to China, 1938–42; ambassador to the Soviet Union, 1942–46; ambassador to USA, 1946–48. A man of liberal leanings, he was a strong supporter of Chinese resistance to Japan and a proponent of a cooperative, non-imperialistic policy toward China.

Deng Xihou (1889–1964) [Teng Hsi-hou], b. Sichuan, d. China. Baoding graduate, 1912. Protégé of Liu Xiang (q.v.). Supported Liu's campaign to force Liu Wenhui (q.v.) from Sichuan governorship, 1932–33. After outbreak of war in 1937, moved his forces successively to Shanghai and Xuzhou fronts, in response to NG directives. Pacification commissioner for Sichuan-Xikang and commander of 22nd AG from March 1938 until end of war. In December 1949 joined Liu Wenhui in declaring allegiance to People's Republic of China; held honorific posts in PRC government after 1949.

Gu Zhutong (1891–1987) [Ku Chu-t'ung], b. Jiangsu, d. Taiwan. Baoding graduate, 1919; Whampoa instructor, 1924. Held NG military appointments, 1926–31; governor of Jiangsu, 1931–33;

Guizhou, 1935–36; EA campaign, 1933–34. Governor of Jiangsu and deputy commander of Third War Zone, August 1937; commander of Third War Zone from late 1937 to 1945. In January 1941 his forces eliminated communist troops south of the Yangtze in the New 4th Army incident. (See chapter 5.) Commander in chief of NG Army, 1946–48, 1949–50. Held high military and political offices in Taiwan. RLPC (1943) called him "one of the most trusted lieutenants of Chiang Kai-shek."

Feng Yuxiang (1882–1948) [Feng Yü-hsiang], b. Hebei, d. Soviet Union. Rose from humble origins, largely self-educated, achieving brigade command in 1914. Participant in the 1911 revolution, a convert to Christianity, and a commander whose army maintained a degree of discipline and respect for the civilian population unusual for the time. By 1920 a major player in the warlord politics of north China. Joined GMD in 1926, subordinating himself to Chiang. Following establishment of NG, opposed efforts by Chiang to extend his authority into the north, resulting in civil war in 1930 that saw Feng's forces decisively defeated. Subsequently reconciled with Chiang, holding a succession of high honorific posts. A strong advocate of resistance to Japan, before and after the outbreak of war in 1937. Because of past reputation, his voice carried weight, though he had lost his military base. Died returning from trip to Soviet Union.

He Yingqin (1890–1987) [Ho Ying-ch'in], b. Guizhou, d. Taiwan. Graduate of Officers Military Academy, Tokyo, 1914. Whampoa instructor, 1924; participant in Northern Expedition. Minister of war in NG, 1930–44; and chief of staff, MAC, 1938–44. Commander in chief of Chinese Army, December 1944 to May 1946. Held high political and military positions on Taiwan after 1949. The leading member of the Whampoa Clique of commanders loyal to Chiang Kaishek. Regarded as pessimistic about China's capacity to resist Japan. U.S. Army chief of staff George Marshall told President Roosevelt in March 1943 that He Yingqin represented a "school of thought now existing in the

Chinese Army that a military 'watch and wait' policy should be followed" (BDRC: 2, p. 83).

Hu Zongnan (1896–1962) [Hu Tsung-nan], b. Zhejiang, d. Taiwan. Whampoa cadet, 1924. Held NG military commands, 1926–37; EA campaign, Eyuwan. Organizer of officers' societies loyal to Chiang Kaishek (e.g., Lixingshe: Moral Endeavor Society). From 1938 to 1945 commander of 34th AG and head of Xi'an Office of the Supreme National Defense Council, with supervision of First, Second and Eighth War Zones. Held high NG military commands in Civil War, 1946–50. Held senior military positions in Taiwan. RLPC (1943) states: "His present command is in effect that of the cordon sanitaire around the Communists in the northwest. He has not, as yet, been used in any important active command against the Japanese."

Kung, H. H. (Kong Xiangxi) (1889–1967) [K'ung Hsiang-hsi], b. Shanxi, d. USA. Born into Shanxi native (traditional) banking family. Studied in USA, 1901–07, graduating from Yale with MA in economics. Minister of finance in NG, 1933–44. As president, vice president, and later acting president of Executive Yuan, 1938–45, served as de facto premier of the NG. Retired from political life, 1945; lived in USA after 1948. Brother-in-law of Chiang Kaishek through marriage to sister of Soong Meiling (q.v.); highly trusted by Chiang.

Li Pinxian (1892–1987) [Li P'in-hsien], b. Guangxi, d. Taiwan. Baoding graduate, participant in Northern Expedition. Border defense commissioner for Guangxi, 1931–35; chief of staff, Guangxi army, 1936. Followed NG directive to move forces to front, 1937; took part in battle of Xuzhou, 1938. Commander of 11th AG, 1940; governor of Anhui, 1943. Member of Guangxi clique.

Li Zongren (1890–1966) [Li Tsung-jen], b. Guangxi, d. China. Graduate of Guangxi Military Academy (Guilin), 1913. Leading member Guangxi military clique, which, while nominally subordinate to NG, exercised autonomous power in that province, 1924–36. Named pacification commissioner for Guangxi and commander of 9th Route Army, 1932. Came to terms with NG in 1936 following expansion of NG military power into the province. Upon outbreak of war, strong supporter of NG. Commander of Fifth War Zone, 1937 to early 1945. Involved in GMD politics after war: vice president of NG, 1948, and acting president, 1949, following Chiang Kaishek's resignation. Retired from politics and left for USA, December 1949; returned to China, 1965.

Liu Wenhui (1895–1976) [Liu Wen-hui], b. Sichuan, d. China. Commander of 24th Army (based at Yaan), 1927–45, and commander of Sichuan-Xikang Border Defense, 1928–45. Governor of Sichuan, 1929–33, forced out of province by Liu Xiang (q.v.), returned to Xikang base. Deputy director of Chiang Kaishek's Chungking office, 1938; appointed governor of Xikang, January 1939, upon creation of the province. Relieved of 24th Army command, 1945. Declared allegiance to People's Republic of China, December 1949; served in honorific posts in PRC government after 1949.

Liu Xiang (1888–1938) [Liu Hsiang], b. Sichuan, d. China. Military academy graduate, Sichuan, 1910. Rose in Sichuan provincial army ranks, becoming commander of 2nd Army. Chosen by Sichuan generals as commander in chief, 1920; dominant figure in province until 1937, maintaining local autonomy despite nominal integration into NG. Eliminated rival forces under provincial governor Liu Wenhui (q.v.), 1932–33; named governor of province, 1934. By 1937 local autonomy challenged by NG financial and military power. Upon outbreak of war led Sichuan forces in defense of Nanjing. After his death in early 1938 NG further strengthened its hold over Sichuan.

Liu Zhi (1892–1971) [Liu Chih], b. Jiangxi, d. Taiwan. Baoding graduate, 1916; Whampoa instructor, 1924–26. Held high military commands, 1926–37; EA campaign, Eyuwan. Commander of 2nd AG and deputy commander, First War Zone, 1937. From 1939 to 1945 head of Chungking Garrison Command and Chungking Air Defense Command. Held high NG Civil War commands, 1945–49. After 1949 held advisory positions in Taiwan.

Long Yun (1887–1962) [Lung Yün], b. Yunnan, d. China. Graduate of Yunnan Military Academy, 1912. Held provincial military positions, 1912–27. Took power in Yunnan, 1927; declared support for NG, 1927; recognized by NG as governor of Yunnan, 1928, a position he held until 1945. Upon outbreak of war, supported NG. Director of Chiang Kaishek's Kunming headquarters, 1941. Sought to maintain provincial autonomy, but with arrival of NG forces in Yunnan, 1943, lost his maneuverability. Removed from office, 1945, and assigned nominal NG positions. Retired to Hong Kong, 1948; returned to China, 1950, serving in honorific posts in PRC government.

Mao Bangchu (1904–?) [Mao Pang-ch'u], b. Zhejiang, d. Mexico (?). Studied in Soviet Union. Sent to USA and Europe to study aviation, 1934. Head of Air Defense Academy, 1937. Chief of operations of Aeronautical Affairs Commission during Chuikov's tenure in Chungking. In 1941 effectively in command of Chinese air force (cf. Zhou Zhirou). Transferred to Air Staff College as commandant, 1943. Deputy commander, Air Force headquarters, 1946–50. Head of NG Military Commission at the United Nations, 1950; relieved of position, 1951, on grounds of financial irregularities. Left public life, went abroad. Date of death, likely in Mexico, unknown. RLPC (1944) states that he spoke English and Russian well.

Nomonhan. Skirmishes between Soviet and Japanese forces broke out in early 1939 in the Nomonhan region (also known as Khalkhingol, from the nearby lake), where the borders of Chinese Inner Mongolia, Japanese-occupied Manchukuo (Manchuria) and the Soviet satellite state of Mongolia converged. In late May clashes escalated to the regimental level, and on July 1 the Japanese attacked in divisional strength. This thrust was overwhelmed by a Soviet counterattack, following which a massive Soviet force pushed the Japanese back to the border line. The victor at Nomonhan was General Georgii Zhukov, later to become the Soviet Union's most illustrious commander in World War II.

Northern Expedition (1926–28). Launched from Canton in July 1926 by the National Revolutionary Army under Chiang Kaishek, with aim of unifying China under the NG of the Guomindang. First stage, 1926–27, saw the elimination of warlord power between Canton and the lower to mid-Yangtze Valley, with Changsha, Wuhan, Nanjing and the Chinese suburbs of Shanghai secured. Purge of the communist allies of the GMD, beginning in April 1927, brought end to first stage of expedition. A second stage was launched in early 1928 to bring China north of Yangtze under NG control, but due to local regional militarist strength and Japanese interference, only a nominal integration of the north was attained.

Panyushkin, Aleksandr Semyonovich (1905–1974). Sent to China as head of special economic mission, July 1939. Named ambassador in August 1939, following death of serving occupant, and held position until 1944. Ambassador to the People's Republic of China, 1952–53. Regarded as a highly competent professional diplomat. Author of a limited-circulation memoir of his appointment to the National Government, *Zapiski Posla: Kitai, 1939–44* (Notes of an ambassador: China, 1939–44).

Second United Front (1937–45). Officially established between the NG under Chiang Kaishek and the Chinese Communist Party in September 1937, in order to coordinate armed resistance to Japan. Its way had been prepared by Chiang's suspension of the campaign against the communist base area in northern Shaanxi, following the Xi'an incident, December 1936, when Chiang's generals refused to prosecute the campaign further. The Second United Front was riven by suspicions between the two partners from the beginning but did not break down until the New 4th Army incident, January 1941, after which it survived in name only until the end of the war.

Shang Zhen (1884–1978) [Shang Chen], b. Hebei, d. Japan. Attended military school in Baoding, then studied in Japan. Served under Yan Xishan in Shanxi, 1916–27. Supported Chiang Kaishek in 1930 civil war against Yan Xishan and Feng Yuxiang.

Held NG military commands in north China, 1931–40; EA. campaign, 1931–32. From November 1940 to March 1944, head of Foreign Affairs Bureau of MAC and head of MAC executive office. Led a Chinese military delegation to India, Burma and Malaya, July 1941. Head of NG military delegation in Japan, 1947–49. Remained in Japan after 1949. Spoke English.

Soong Meiling (Mme. Chiang Kaishek) (1897–2003) [Song Meiling], b. Shanghai. Educated in USA. Married Chiang in 1927. Sister-in-law of H. H. Kung (q.v.) and Sun Yatsen. Her brother, T. V. Soong (Song Ziwen), served as NG finance minister, foreign minister and special foreign envoy. Mme. Chiang was her husband's "English voice" to the Western world. During Chuikov's tenure in Chungking, she served as secretary general of the Aeronautical Affairs Commission of the MAC. Actively involved in high politics. After Chiang Kaishek's death in 1975 left Taiwan to live in USA.

Stilwell, Joseph (1883–1946). Sent to China in 1919 as army language student, later U.S. Army battalion commander in Tianjin, 1926–28, and U.S. military attaché in Beijing, 1935–39. In January 1942 Chiang Kaishek accepted President Roosevelt's recommendation that Stilwell be named chief of the Chinese General Staff, as well as U.S. military representative to Chiang, in the latter capacity succeeding Chuikov as chief military adviser. From 1942 to 1944 Stilwell built up Chinese forces for the Burma campaign. Following serious reverses suffered by Chiang's armies in China in 1944, Stilwell asked Roosevelt to pressure Chiang to name him commander in chief of the Chinese army, to which Chiang objected and secured Stilwell's recall. Apart from being at odds with Chiang and the Chinese military establishment, Stilwell, a proponent of the land war, also clashed with General Chenneault (q.v.) and the air war proponents.

Voroshilov, Kliment Yefremovich (1881–1969). Soviet minister of defense, 1934–40; deputy chairman, Council of Ministers, 1940. Became associated with Stalin in the southern front battles during the Russian civil war and assumed high government positions following Stalin's rise to power. Held a number of army commands subsequent to the German invasion in 1941. An astute military politician, trusted by Stalin for his political and personal loyalty, but of limited competence as a strategist or field commander.

Wang Jingwei (1883–1944) [Wang Ching-wei], b. Guangdong, d. Japan. Joined Sun Yatsen's Tongmenghui (Alliance Society) upon its formation in Tokyo in 1905. As one of Sun's closest disciples and colleagues, Wang saw himself as Sun's successor upon the latter's death in 1925 but was soon outmaneuvered by Chiang Kaishek. From 1932 to 1935 served as premier in the NG. In December 1938, despairing of China's hope of survival in the war against Japan, Wang launched his "peace movement," aimed at an honorable settlement of the war. Japanese negotiators struck a hard bargain, which Wang, for reasons not fully explained, accepted. Wang's regime, styled the NG, was set up in Nanjing in March 1940 but never escaped client status. Wang is seen in China as the preeminent twentieth-century embodiment of treason, though he is credited with a patriotic early career.

Wei Lihuang (1896–1960) [Wei Li-huang], b. Anhui, d. China. Rose through ranks of NG army. Later graduated from National Military Academy, Nanjing. Held high NG commands, 1930–37; EA campaign, Eyuwan, 1935. Commander of 14th AG and deputy commander of Second War Zone, 1937; commander of First War Zone and governor of Henan, 1939. NG forces under his command were routed by Japanese in May 1941 at battle of Zhongtiaoshan. (See chapter 8.) Supporter of GMD-CCP cooperation; maintained good relations with communist 8th Route Army. Transferred to Xi'an office of MAC, late 1941. Commander of Chinese Expeditionary Army in Burma, 1943. Relieved of NG Civil War command in Manchuria, 1948; left for Hong Kong. Returned to China, 1955, and held a number of nominal positions in PRC government.

Whampoa Academy/Whampoa Clique. Established in 1924 on Whampoa Island near Canton, with Chiang Kaishek as commandant, the academy aimed to create an elite GMD military force modeled on the party-controlled and ideologically indoctrinated Soviet example. Soviet military advisers and CCP political workers played major roles in training cadets prior to the GMD purge of the CCP in 1927. Whampoa cadets served as officers in the Northern Expedition (q.v.). The Whampoa Clique was made up of officers who trained under Chiang and remained steadfastly loyal to him through the 1930s and 1940s. He Yingqin (q.v.) was its most prominent member.

Xia Wei (1893–1973) [Hsia Wei], b. Guangxi, d. Hong Kong. Attended military schools, including Baoding. Held commands in Guangxi provincial army, 1916–26. Took part in Northern Expedition, 1926–28. Joined opposition to Chiang Kaishek in 1930 civil war; upon defeat retired to Hong Kong; resumed military office in Guangxi, 1931, and took part in anticommunist operations. After outbreak of war appointed by NG to high military positions in Guangxi, including command of 16th AG. Governor of Anhui, 1948. Retired to Hong Kong after 1949.

Xu Kan (1888–1969) [Hsü K'an], b. Sichuan, d. Taiwan. Held high posts in Ministry of Finance, 1928–41, including vice minister, 1935–41. Minister of food upon creation of ministry in 1941. RLPC (1943) states that he was regarded "as one of H. H. Kung's men" and that as a Sichuanese, he was "careful of the vested interests of the province."

Yang Sen (1884–1977) [Yang Sen], b. Sichuan, d. Taiwan. Graduate of Sichuan Army Primary School, 1906. Protégé of Liu Xiang (q.v.) through 1920s until outbreak of war, 1937, when he followed NG directive to move his forces, designated as 6th AG, to Shanghai front. Deputy commander, Ninth War Zone, 1938–44, and commander of 27th AG from 1938 until its destruction by Japanese in Operation Ichigo, 1944. Took part in battle of Changsha, September 1941. Governor of Guizhou, 1945–48, mayor of Chungking, 1948–49. In Taiwan after 1949.

Yang Xuancheng (1890–1962) [Yang Hsüan-ch'eng], b. Hunan, d. Taiwan. Graduate of Military Cadet Academy, Tokyo, 1910, and of artillery and naval schools at Yokosuka, 1912. Sent to USA by

Hunan provincial government to study business, 1913. Held Hunan government positions and taught Japanese, 1915–27. Subsequently held NG offices; NG military attaché in Tokyo, 1933. In 1941, vice admiral and director of military intelligence (Second Department of Military Operations Bureau of MAC). Succeeded Shang Zhen (q.v.) in March 1944 as head of MAC Foreign Affairs Bureau. Held high positions in government and business in Taiwan after 1948. RLPC (1944) concurs with Chuikov's assessment: "Admiral Yang was invariably friendly and courteous to foreign military attaches. His long tenure of office [in military intelligence], and intimate knowledge of Japanese personalities and affairs enabled him to make appreciations of the military situation which were both shrewd and appropriate. Above all, he was for a Chinese government official, extremely frank in his comments on almost all topics."

Zhang Qun (1889–1990) [Chang Ch'ün], b. Sichuan, d. Taiwan. Entered Military Officers' College, Tokyo, 1907, with Chiang Kai-shek. Held high civil offices in NG after 1928, including mayor of Shanghai, 1929–31, governor of Hubei, 1933–35, minister of foreign affairs, 1935–37. Named governor of Sichuan, January 1938, but resigned in August due to opposition from Sichuan militarists. Secretary-general of Supreme National Defense Council, 1939-42. Reappointed governor of Sichuan, November 1940, and held position until end of war. After 1949 held a number of high offices in Taiwan. RLPC (1943) remarks: "He is very close in the councils of the Generalissimo [Chiang], but lacks the courage to press views which he knows to be distasteful to his Chief."

Zhou Enlai (1898–1976) [Chou En-lai], b. Hebei, d. China. RLPC (1943) notes that he had been unable to improve relations between the GMD and the CCP, which "still remain bad." The following observations are of interest in light of Zhou's career after 1949: "Less radical than many of the younger generation of Chinese Communists . . . his comparative moderation makes him a more suitable representative with the Central Government than an out-and-out 'Red,' who would only precipitate a crisis. … A 'cool, logical and empirical' mind."

Zhou Zhirou (1899–1986) [Chou Chih-jou], b. Zhejiang, d. Taiwan. Baoding graduate, 1925; Whampoa instructor, 1925. Held NG military appointments, 1925–33; EA campaign, 1931–33. Sent to USA, 1933, to study aviation. Commander of Central Aviation Academy (Hangzhou), 1934; head of Aeronautical Affairs Commission of MAC, 1936–38 and 1941–45 (i.e., head of air force). After 1949, held high military office in Taiwan; Taiwan provincial governor, 1957–62. RLPC (1943) states: "The defeats suffered by the air force in the spring of 1941 brought him considerable censure, and he was for at time under a cloud, Mao Pang-chu [Bangchu] taking over all operational control," but adds that by 1943 Zhou had fully recovered his position and influence.

Zhu Shaoliang (1891–1963) [Chu Shao-liang], b. Fujian, d. Taiwan. Graduate of Military Officers' College, Tokyo, 1911. Held NG military and political appointments after 1927. Governor of Gansu, 1933–35 and 1947–40. Commander of Eighth War Zone, 1937–45, with principal task of blockading communist Special Region from the west. Governor of Xinjiang, 1944; deputy head of MAC, 1945–47; pacification commissioner for southwest China, 1948, and for Fujian, 1948–49. After 1949 held advisory positions on Taiwan.

FURTHER READING

In addition to materials cited in the introduction, the following works provide background to the China that General Chuikov describes.

The Nationalist wartime government is vividly if unsympathetically portrayed in Theodore H. White and Annalee Jacoby, *Thunder out of China* (New York: Da Capo Press, 1975; reprint of first edition, 1946). Theodore H. White's edition of *The Stilwell Papers* (New York: Schocken Books, 1972; reprint of first edition, 1948), also offers harsh judgments of Chiang Kaishek by Chuikov's successor as chief military adviser. Graham Peck, in *Two Kinds of Time* (Boston: Houghton Mifflin, 1950), provides a memorable anecdotal account of the war years. Two very fine studies of the period, both more pessimistic than Chuikov in their estimates of Nationalist China's military potential, are Ch'i Hsi-sheng, *Nationalist China at War: Military Defeats and Political Collapse, 1937–1945* (Ann Arbor: University of Michigan Press, 1982), and Lloyd Eastman, *Seeds of Destruction: Nationalist China in War and Revolution, 1937–1949* (Stanford: Stanford University Press, 1984). Joseph W. Esherick has edited *Lost Chance in China: The World War II Dispatches of John Service* (New York: Random House, 1974), which offers informed contemporary comment on wartime China by a noted American diplomat. Important topics pertaining to the Nationalist government are treated in *China's Bitter Victory: The War with Japan, 1937–1945* (Armonk, N.Y.: M. E. Sharpe, 1992), edited by James C. Hsiung and Steven I. Levine.

The tours of duty in Chungking served by Ambassador Clark Kerr and Attaché David Barrett are summarized respectively in Donald Gillies, *Radical Diplomat: The Life of Archibald Clark Kerr, Lord Inverchapel, 1882–1951* (London: I. B. Tauris, 1999) and in John N. Hart, *The Making of an Army "Old China Hand": A Memoir of Colonel David D. Barrett* (Berkeley: Institute of East Asian Studies, University of California, 1985). Colonel Barrett wrote of his famous later assignment to the communist Special Region in *Dixie Mission: The United States Army Observer Group in Yenan, 1944* (Berkeley: Institute of East Asian Studies, University of California, 1970). General

Chenneault recounts his China years in Claire L. Chenneault, *Way of a Fighter: The Memoirs of Claire Lee Chenneault* (New York: Putnam, 1949).

Soviet memoirs in English of nationals who served in China immediately prior to Chuikov's arrival are Alexander Kalyagin, *Along Alien Roads,* translated with an introduction by Steven I. Levine (New York: East Asian Institute, Columbia University, 1983); and, for the Soviet air volunteers, S. V. Slysarev, "Protecting China's Airspace," in *Soviet Volunteers in China, 1925–1945: Articles and Reminiscences,* translated by David Fidlon (Moscow: Progress Publishers, 1980), 247–84. Biographies of the Soviet military figures mentioned by General Chuikov are to be found in Harold Shukman, ed., *Stalin's Generals* (London: Weidenfeld and Nicolson, 1993).

For a compact survey of the Sino-Japanese War years, see Jonathan Spence, *The Search for Modern China* (New York: W. W. Norton and Co., 1990), chapter 17, "World War II," 443–83. Spence's book is also helpful for coverage of the political and social conditions prevailing in China during the years treated in General Chuikov's memoir.

INDEX

Andreev, Stepan P., 24, 63ff, 114, 138, 151, 157

Bai Chongxi, xxxi, 39, 55, 88, 105-10 passim, 122, 140, 147, 154

Barrett, David D., 72, 74-77, 81, 82-83

Beevor, Antony, xxiii-xxiv

Blyukher, Vasilii K., xxviii, 165f, 169-76 passim

Changgufeng (Khasangol), Battle of, 86, 176

Changsha, Second Battle of, xxxiv-xxxvii, xlii, 123, 125-33

Changsha, Third Battle of, 161

Chen Cheng, xli, 84, 97, 114, 117-19, 120ff

Chen Guofu, 140

Chen Lifu, 140

Chenneault, Claire L., 155f

Chiang Kaishek (Jiang Jieshi): xix, xxv-xxxvii passim, 13-18 passim, 29, 31, 33f, 39, 64f, 71, 83, 96, 109, 118f, 126, 138, 155f, 158, 165; character, xxvii, 18, 25-26, 36, 61ff; as Nationalist China's war leader, xxvii-xxviii, 86f, 89, 99-110 passim, 111, 121ff, 129-33 passim, 152; and Chinese Communist Party, xxi, xxvi, xxx-xxxii, 21, 36-37, 47-50, 52f, 57ff, 75-76, 87; and blockade of communist Special Region, 22, 34f, 47, 58, 88-89, 118, 133; relations with the Americans and British, xxxiii, 70-71, 88-89, 140, 143-44, 151, 159-62; relations with the Soviets, xxviii-xxix, xxxiii-xxxiv, 24, 56, 59, 71, 80, 82f, 139, 146-47, 154, 159ff, 162

Chiang Kaishek, Mme. See Soong Meiling.

Chinese Eastern Railway, xxii, 4, 7f, 81, 165, 175

Chuikov, Vasilii I.: military career, xix-xxv, 3, 23, 162-63, 165-74; contacts with Chiang Kaishek, xxvii-xxix, xxxi-xxxii, xxxiv, 24-26, 61ff, 113, 129-31, 138ff, 154, 161; contacts with He Yingqin, xxxi, 39ff, 53-55, 64-65, 71, 121, 134, 152-54, 155; contacts with Zhou Enlai, xxxi, 47, 65, 67, 135; on the Nationalist Chinese Army, xxviii, xxxvi-xxxvii, xxxix-xliii, 33-35, 37-46, 97, 111-12, 120-23, 152-53; on the Chinese Communist Party's role in the war,

MISSION TO CHINA
Memoirs of a Soviet Military Adviser to Chiang Kaishek
Vasilii I. Chuikov

Vasilii I. Chuikov served as chief military adviser to Chiang Kaishek in 1941–42. Born into a peasant family, Chuikov joined the Bolshevik cause in the Russian Civil War. Following Chinese-language study, he was twice posted to China as a young officer. In late 1940 General Chuikov was appointed head of the Soviet military mission in Nationalist China. Upon his return to the Soviet Union in 1942, he was assigned to the Stalingrad front, where he commanded the successful defense of that city. After 1945 Chuikov held a succession of high-ranking military offices and, in recognition of his illustrious wartime service, was named a Marshal of the Soviet Union. In later life, he wrote a number of memoirs, including the one published here. Marshal Chuikov died in 1982.

David P. Barrett is Associate Professor of History, McMaster University, Hamilton, Ontario. He has written on the political history of Republican China (1912–1949), with particular emphasis on the Sino-Japanese War (1937–45) and the wartime collaborationist regime under Wang Jingwei.

Signature Books
Doug Merwin, Imprint Editor

The **Signature Books** imprint of EastBridge is dedicated to presenting a wide range of exceptional books in the field of Asian and related studies. The principal concentrations are texts and supplementary materials for academic courses, literature-in-translation, and the writings of Westerners who experienced Asia as journalists, scholars, diplomats, and travelers.

Doug Merwin, publisher and editor-in-chief of EastBridge, has more than thirty years' experience as an editor of books and journals on Asia and is the founding editor of the East Gate Books imprint.

CPSIA information can be obtained
at www.ICGtesting.com
Printed in the USA
LVHW081052160122
708702LV00021B/486